Edexcel GCSE

Poetry Anthology

Student Book

Caroline Bentley-Davies
David Grant
Pam Taylor

A PEARSON COMPANY

Contents

Collection D *Taking a Stand* — 108

Unseen Poetry — 142

Sample examination papers and mark schemes — 162

Sample controlled assessment task and mark scheme — 172

Glossary — 174

Introduction

This book is designed to support you in studying for **Edexcel GCSE English Literature Unit 2: Understanding Poetry** and the **Poetry Reading task in Edexcel GCSE English Unit 3: Creative English**.

Here is an overview of how you will be assessed in each unit.

The Edexcel GCSE English Literature and English specifications

Edexcel GCSE English Literature Unit 2: Understanding Poetry
How is this unit assessed? An exam
What is this unit worth? 25% of the total GCSE
How long does the exam last? 1 hour and 45 minutes
What is Section A? You will have to answer one question about an unseen poem printed in the exam paper. This section is worth 20 marks.
What is Section B? You will have to answer one two-part question on the collection of poems you have studied from the Edexcel Poetry Anthology. This section is worth 30 marks.
Can I choose which poems to write about? In Section B you can choose to answer on two named poems or on one named poem and a poem of your choice from the Anthology collection you have studied.

Edexcel GCSE English Unit 3: Creative English – Poetry Reading Task
How is this task assessed? Controlled assessment
What is the Poetry Reading Task worth? 10% of the total GCSE
How long do I have to complete the Poetry Reading Task? 2 hours
What is the task? You will have to answer one question about a literary heritage poem set by Edexcel and two poems from the collection you have studied from the Edexcel Poetry Anthology.
What form can my response take? You can respond to the task in one of three ways: written, digital media or multimodal

How is this book structured?

This book is divided into three sections.

Section 1: Exploring the poems

This section looks in turn at all the poems in the Edexcel Poetry Anthology. For each poem you will work through the following stages:

- **First thoughts** After reading the poem for the first time you will think about your initial reactions. What is the poem about? How does it make you feel? What questions does the poem raise?

- **Looking more closely** You will begin to focus on the language of the poem. You will annotate the poem, highlight key parts and make notes to help you understand the poem in greater depth.

- **Developing your ideas** For each poem you will develop an understanding of:
  - theme (the ideas at the heart of the poem)
  - content (what happens in the poem)
  - viewpoint (the point of view or opinions of the speaker/poet)
  - mood (the atmosphere/tone of the poem and how the poet wants you to feel when you read it)
  - style (techniques used by the poet and their effects).

- **Developing your response** You will consider how the poem makes you feel and practise writing a response.

- **Self/Peer assessment** This section will help you to reflect on your own work, to identify its strengths and weaknesses, and to redraft it to move towards your target grade.

At the end of each collection there is a **Build better answers** spread which gives extracts from sample student answers with examiner comments to help you prepare for the assessment. There is also a spread on comparing the poems in the collection.

Section 2: Unseen Poetry

This section is relevant for students taking Edexcel GCSE English Literature only. It aims to give you the skills and confidence to answer an exam question about an unseen poem. These lessons focus on some of the poems in the Anthology (some of those marked with an asterisk* on the Anthology contents page). None of these poems will be the unseen poem in your exam, but learning how to approach them will give you the skills to use when approaching any unseen poem. You will learn to:

- read a poem carefully

- work out **what** the poet is saying (the main ideas and themes)

- understand **how** the poet presents these ideas (through choice of language, structure and form)

- answer the question effectively.

The final lesson focuses on two unseen poems (which are not in the Anthology) to give you the opportunity to practise all the skills you have learned.

Section 3: Assessment practice

This section contains sample exam papers and mark schemes with tips written by an examiner to help you understand exactly what will be involved in your assessment and what you need to do in order to perform well. You will also find guidance on the Controlled Assessment relevant to the Poetry Reading Task, together with a sample task and mark scheme.

Relationships

My learning objectives

- to explore and develop my response to 'Valentine' by Carol Ann Duffy
- to understand how Duffy uses imagery and language to portray her understanding of love.

Comparing Poems

To prepare for your English Literature exam:

- explore specific comparisons and links between Duffy's 'Valentine' and other poems in the collection, for example the writer's view of relationships in 'Our Love Now', or the view of romance in 'Sonnet 116'
- practise comparing in detail and evaluating the ways in which two poets express their ideas and achieve effects.

Valentine by Carol Ann Duffy

First thoughts

Activity 1

1. Make a list of the traditional 'valentine' images used in the poem. Why do you think the poet includes them?

2. How does the poet refer to these images? Why do you think she treats them in this way?

Looking more closely

Activity 2

1. Look at the following lines of the poem:

   'I give you an onion.
   It is a moon wrapped in brown paper.'

   Write down three questions you would like to ask the poet about these lines. Explain why you want to ask these questions.

2. Look at the grid below. Match up each comment about the poem with the most suitable quotation and the effect that this has on the reader.

Comment about the poem	Quotation	Effect of language on the reader
The image of the onion suggests love can be harsh and painful:	'Its platinum loops shrink to a wedding-ring,'	This image is menacing because it suggests that it lingers desperately. The last word is sinister as it appears to threaten violence.
Love is described as intense, jealous and impossible to escape:	'It is a moon wrapped in brown paper.'	Here the onion is almost described like a lover. The love sounds quite violent and controlling.
Duffy makes the onion sound beautiful and special, like her view of love:	'It will blind you with tears'	The image is a romantic one because 'moonlight' suggests magic and the idea of wrapping suggests a gift.
Loyalty is suggested by the image of an onion:	'Its scent will cling to your fingers, cling to your knife.'	Here the image suggests pain and hurt. The distress is so intense that the person cannot see.
Marriage and commitment is suggested by the image:	'Its fierce kiss will stay on your lips,'	The smallest part of an onion ring is described as looking like a wedding ring.

Developing your ideas

1. The poet has used a particular structure. For example, three of the *stanzas* only have one line. What effect do these lines have?

2. **a.** The poem appears to follow the development of a relationship from start to end. Do you agree?

   b. How does the narrator first express his/her love?

   c. What evidence is there of a serious commitment to each other?

   d. Is there any suggestion of an end to the relationship?

3. Think about the poem as a whole. Students have made the following comments. Decide whether you disagree or agree with each, and find evidence to support your opinion.

Glossary

platinum: a valuable metal, sometimes used for wedding rings

Student A

This poem is very romantic. The narrator shows real love by refusing to use *clichéd* images like cards and hearts. The image of the onion is unusual and therefore shows her love is original and special.

Student B

This poem is rather sinister and threatening. The image of an onion is too everyday to be really romantic. The lines at the end of the poem show the onion being sliced up and the poet suggests that love can become a dangerous obsession.

Student C

This poem shows a realistic depiction of love. Onions are everyday objects, but this poem shows that an ordinary person can be transformed by love. The poem uses romantic images such as the 'moon' and the idea of gifts to show how precious and special love is. The poem is also realistic by showing that love can cause pain and tears as well as happiness.

Developing your response

1. Duffy surprises the reader with the ending of the poem.

   a. What happens at the end of the poem?

   b. Many people find the last two lines disturbing. What is your reaction to them?

2. Look at this example of an examination-style question:

   Explain how Duffy conveys the complexity of relationships in 'Valentine'. Use examples from the poem to support your answer.

   Write one section on language and imagery that could be included in your answer.

ResultsPlus
Self/Peer assessment

1. Read this paragraph written in response to the task above.

2. Annotate your paragraphs using similar notes to those given on the right. If you have forgotten to include anything in your paragraphs, add it in.

3. Using the mark schemes on pages 166 and 171, decide which band your paragraphs would fall into.

— A clear point   Evidence to support it —

Duffy presents relationships as both everyday and romantic. She refuses to use clichés to represent her love, this shows how love can be complex: 'Not a red rose or a satin heart.' The poem is unusual because it appears to start negatively explaining what the narrator will not do. She appears to reject traditional images of love, perhaps because they are stereotypes and are used without much thought. Instead she offers an unconventional image of love, by giving her lover an onion. This can appear more romantic. It is described as being a gift that 'promises light.' This appears a thoughtful and original image and it develops throughout the poem to show her developing feelings.

An explanation of the effect of the quotation

How it reflects the poet's point of view

Close focus on language choice

My learning objectives

- to explore and develop my response to 'Rubbish at Adultery' by Sophie Hannah
- to understand how Hannah uses structure, tone and language to paint a humorous picture of an unfaithful relationship.

Comparing Poems

To prepare for your English Literature exam:

- explore specific comparisons and links between Hannah's 'Rubbish at Adultery' and other poems in the collection, for example the writer's view of relationships in 'Our Love Now', the view of marriage expressed in 'One Flesh' and the use of a narrator in 'My Last Duchess'
- practise comparing in detail and evaluating the ways in which two poets express their ideas and achieve effects.

Rubbish at Adultery
by Sophie Hannah

First thoughts

Activity 1

1. Read the poem. Note down your first impressions about:
   - the relationship between the narrator of the poem and the man
   - the man's life
   - why the narrator is annoyed with the man
   - whether you think the relationship has any future.

Looking more closely

Activity 2

1. The poet uses *rhyme* throughout the poem. Look at the words that rhyme. Can you identify a rhyme pattern?

2. The poem has a distinct **rhythm**. Read the poem aloud and see if you can detect the number of beats per line. What effect does this have?

3. What do you think the rhyme and rhythm suggest about the narrator's mood and tone?

4. Copy and complete the grid below. It will help you to explore the woman's viewpoint through the language she uses.

Quotation showing what she wants in an ideal world	Meaning	Comment on language
'I'd settle for a kiss.' 'I'm after passion, thrills and fun.'	She wants romance and a demonstration of his feelings for her.	'settle for,' suggests that really she wants much more romance than this, but she would be prepared to accept this as a minimum.
'Couldn't you, for an hour or so, / Just leave them out of *this*?'	She wants him to stop talking about his family all of the time.	
'Must I give up another night / To hear you whinge and whine'	She is bored of all their time together being wasted while he complains about feeling guilty for cheating on his wife.	'Must I,' this sounds angry and accusatory. The words 'whinge' and 'whine' also ridicule the man making him sound pathetic and annoying.
'You say fun takes its toll, / So what are we doing here?'		
'ten minutes off from guilty / Diatribes – what bliss.'		

Developing your ideas Activity 3

1. The poem is a form of *dramatic monologue* – we only hear the opinions of a woman who is angry with her lover. Why do you think the poet wrote the poem in this form?

2. Look at the first lines of the poem:

   'Must I give up another night

   To hear you whinge and whine'

   It is as if the narrator has suddenly burst out with her angry feelings at her lover. Why do you think the poet started the poem in this way?

3. Each *stanza* tackles a different complaint she has about her lover. Write a sentence for each stanza explaining her feelings. For example, in stanza 1 'She is angry about wasting another night hearing him moan.'

4. The narrator offers her lover some harsh advice in the final lines. How effective do you find this as an ending to the poem? Explain your answer.

Developing your response Activity 4

1. Students have made the following comments about the poem. Decide whether you agree or disagree with each point, finding evidence from the poem to support your ideas.

   Student A
   I find the narrator of the poem hypocritical. She complains that the man is a cheat and hopeless at relationships, but she does not feel any guilt about taking somebody else's husband herself.

   Student B
   The poem is meant to be a humorous look at the depressing reality of extra-marital affairs. They are thought to be exciting and romantic, but this poem shows that they are often depressing and disappointing. It shows that the person who cheats is a poor husband and a hopeless lover.

   Student C
   I notice the anger in this poem most. The narrator can barely contain herself and her final repeated words: 'You stupid, stupid git', shows her extreme frustration at the man. All her high hopes of romance have turned to hatred and contempt.

   Student D
   This poem is quite a moral poem. It shows that if a relationship starts off being secret and underhand it will eventually sour and ruin itself.

2. How successful do you think Hannah is at capturing the feelings of a person whose relationship is breaking down? Give reasons for your answers.

3. Look at this example of an examination-style question:

   Explore how Hannah presents her ideas about an unfaithful relationship in 'Rubbish at Adultery'.
   Use examples from the poem to support your answer.

   Write one section on tone and humour that could be included in your answer.

Glossary

diatribes: strong verbal attacks

fidelity: faithfulness

ResultsPlus
Self/Peer assessment

1. Answer true or false to the statements below.
   I can find evidence for and comment on:
   a. Hannah's presentation of the man
   b. Hannah's presentation of the narrator's wishes
   c. the narrator's use of strong vocabulary to show anger
   d. Hannah's presentation of the reality of a secret relationship
   e. Hannah's use of *irony* and humour to mock the man
   f. how the writer uses structure and form to present her ideas.

2. If you answered 'false' to any statements, compare your ideas with a partner's. Look again at the poem and your answers to the questions on these pages to help you.

3. What else can you say about this poem? Write five more true or false statements to assess a partner's understanding of 'Rubbish at Adultery.'

4. Look again at the paragraphs you wrote in Activity 4, question 3. What could you change or add to improve your answer? Use the mark schemes on pages 166 and 171 to identify the two things most likely to improve your mark.

My learning objectives

- to explore and develop my response to 'Sonnet 116' by William Shakespeare
- to understand how Shakespeare uses form, structure, language and imagery to explore the nature of love.

Comparing Poems

To prepare for your English Literature exam:

- explore specific comparisons and links between Shakespeare's 'Sonnet 116' and other poems in the collection, for example the writer's expression of feelings in 'Our Love Now', or the way writers present their ideas in 'My Last Duchess' or 'Even Tho'
- practise comparing in detail and evaluating the ways in which two poets express their ideas and achieve effects.

Sonnet 116
by William Shakespeare

First thoughts

Activity 1

1. This *sonnet* is a defence of the power of true love. Read through the poem and pick out positive language or imagery about love.

2. Look at these two lines:

    'love is not love
    Which alters when it alteration finds,'

    Discuss what you think the poet means in these lines.

Looking more closely

Activity 2

Shakespeare uses a range of images and ideas to highlight that perfect love lasts and endures. He shows that real love is not just about the good times, but about how lovers weather the trials and difficulties of life together.

1. Think about the language Shakespeare uses and how he crafts each line. Copy and complete the following grid, making notes on:
    - what is interesting about each image
    - what the language suggests to you.

Image	What is interesting about it	What the language suggests
'it is an ever-fixèd mark/That looks on tempests'	It is an image of a permanent beacon or signal like a lighthouse for ships. It guides them through and keeps them safe in the stormy seas.	The 'ever-fixèd' suggests it is permanent and everlasting. This is a romantic notion for true love is thought to be endless. The stormy seas are a good image to suggest life's hardships and difficulties.
'It is the star to every wandering bark'		
'though rosy lips and cheeks Within his bending sickle's compass come;'		
'But bears it out even to the edge of doom:'		
'Love alters not with his brief hours and weeks'		

2. The poem is a sonnet and has several interesting aspects to its structure. Look at:
    - the *rhyme* pattern of the sonnet. What do you notice?
    - the final *couplet*. Why do you think it has been written like this?

Developing your ideas

Activity 3

1. **a.** This sonnet focuses on love's steadiness in a time of change. There are lots of references to time and time passing. Re-read the sonnet and pick out references to time that are:
   - related to ageing
   - related to the end of time itself
   - related to movement or travel.

   b. Why has Shakespeare used these images to show that true love is unchanging? Consider how he uses *personification* to make his point.

Developing your response

Activity 4

1. Look at the couplet at the end of the poem:

   'If this be error and upon me proved,
   I never writ, nor no man ever loved.'

   a. How do the two lines relate to the rest of the poem?

   b. How does Shakespeare make the message of his poem persuasive in these two lines?'

2. Look at this example of an examination-style question:

   Explore how Shakespeare shares his thoughts and feelings about the nature of love.
   Use examples from the poem to support your answer.

   Write one section on language, structure and *form* that could be included in your answer.

Glossary

impediments: objections

alteration: change or conflict

ever-fixèd mark: permanent beacon or signal for shipping

tempests: storms (often at sea)

wandering bark: lost ship

sickle: an implement with a sharp blade for cutting crops

compass: reach; instrument showing due north used as a navigation aid on ships

edge of doom: first onset of Doomsday (the end of time)

writ: wrote

ResultsPlus
Self/Peer assessment

1. Read this paragraph written in response to the task above.

2. Annotate the paragraphs you wrote in Activity 4, question 2 using similar notes to those given on the right. If you have forgotten to include anything in your paragraphs, add it in.

3. Using the mark schemes on pages 166 and 171, decide which band your paragraphs would fall into.

— A clear point   Evidence to support it —

The sonnet suggests that true love is constant and unchanging: *'Love's not Time's fool, though rosy lips and cheeks / Within his bending sickle's compass come;'*

These lines show that time does have an effect – it can destroy the freshness of beauty. This is shown by the image of 'rosy cheeks' being harvested by the sickle. This is an emblem of time passing and youth ending – however the point he is making is that even though lovers will age their love will remain firm and true.

— An explanation of the effect of the quotation   How it reflects the poet's view   Close focus on the writer's choice of language —

My learning objectives

- to explore and develop my response to 'Our Love Now,' by Martyn Lowery
- to understand how Lowery uses structure and imagery to explore different perspectives on changes within a relationship.

Comparing Poems

To prepare for your English Literature exam:

- explore specific comparisons and links between Lowery's 'Our Love Now,' and other poems in the collection, for example the writer's reflections on love in 'Sonnet 116' and the view of relationships in 'My Last Duchess' and 'Song for Last Year's Wife'

- practise comparing in detail and evaluating the ways in which two poets express their ideas and achieve effects.

Our Love Now
by Martyn Lowery

First thoughts

Activity 1

1. This poem can be read either from left to right, or reading all the left-hand side first, then the right. It is unclear how the poet intended the poem to be read. Try reading the poem in both ways.

   a. Why might Lowery have written the poem in this way?

   b. Which reading do you prefer? How does your choice affect the impression that the poem makes?

Looking more closely

Activity 2

1. This poem is a *dialogue* between two narrators. Experiment with different ways of reading each person's voice.

   a. What *tone* works best?

   b. Do you think that particular words should be emphasised? If so, which ones and why?

2. Think about the poem and its title. Why do you think this poem is called 'Your Love Now'? What idea do you get about the state of their love and what it might have been like before the conflict?

3. The male narrator uses particular images to express his feelings about the relationship. Copy and complete the grid below to explore what some of the images suggest and their effect on the reader.

Key image	What it suggests	Effect on the reader
'wound' or 'cut'	Pain and physical hurt. It sounds unpleasant, however the first narrator suggests it will eventually 'heal' and get better.	The image intrigues the reader. We wonder what has happened to hurt the relationship. Is it a literal wound or does it suggest an emotional hurt?
'the scab of the scald, / the red burnt flesh is ugly,'		
'when you cut your hair, / you feel different,'		
'the raging storm / damages the trees outside.'		

Developing your ideas

Activity 3

1. The female narrator gives a different perspective to the male narrator's images. Plot her feelings in each *stanza* on a mood graph like the one on the right. Select a quotation to support your choices for each stanza.

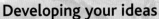

8–12   20–24   32–36   45–50

2. It is unclear why the couple have come into conflict with each other. What reasons might there be for this conflict? Find ideas from the poem to support your ideas. For example, a wound suggests hurt; how can people be hurt in a relationship?

3. The last two lines of the poem are very important. Below is an ideas map with one student's thoughts about these lines. Discuss the student's findings and pick two further lines of the poem which you feel make a crucial point about their love. Create your own ideas map with them.

Why tree? This could be a symbol of their love. Usually trees are living and growing, but here it is dead.

These words are very final. There is absolutely no hope of bringing it back to life.

'The tree is forever dead. Such is our love.'

Full stops make the lines seem abrupt and final. The last full stop signals the end of all possible discussion.

The word 'love' contrasts with the image of death. This suggests finality.

4. Do you think the female narrator should give the male narrator another chance? Do you think the relationship can be repaired? Use examples from the poem to support your ideas.

Developing your response

Activity 4

1. The poet chose to write one side of the poem in the *first person* 'I said,' rather than the *third person* 'he said,'. Why do you think Lowery has used the first person?

2. Look at this example of an examination-style question:

   How does Lowery present the two sides of a changing relationship in 'Our Love Now'?
   Use examples from the poem to support your answer.

   Write one section on *metaphor* and structure that could be included in your answer.

Results Plus
Self/Peer assessment

1. Read this paragraph, written in response to the task above.

2. Annotate your paragraphs using similar notes to those given on the right. If you have forgotten to include anything in your paragraphs, add it in.

3. Using the mark schemes on pages 166 and 171, decide which band your paragraphs would fall into.

— A clear point   Evidence to support it —

This poem shows the end of a relationship through the use of metaphor and structure. The male narrator is desperately trying to convince the second narrator that their relationship can be mended. This is shown by the words: 'Our beauty together is such.' This suggests that there is hope and positivity in the relationship, despite the conflict that has happened. The poet uses violent images and metaphors such as 'wounds,' and 'storms' to illustrate how painful conflict can be. The male narrator uses images to suggest re-growth and improvement, however the female narrator sees the damage as permanent and because of this the relationship is ruined.

Explanation of the effect of the quotation   How it reflects the poet's point of view   Focus on writer's choice of words

My learning objectives

- to explore and develop my response to 'Even Tho' by Grace Nichols
- to understand how Nichols uses imagery and language to portray relationships.

Comparing Poems

To prepare for your English Literature exam:

- explore specific comparisons and links between Nichols' 'Even Tho' and other poems in the collection, for example the way the writer expresses feeling in 'Our Love Now', or the way writers present their ideas in 'Sonnet 116' and 'Rubbish at Adultery'
- practise comparing in detail and evaluating the ways in which two poets express their ideas and achieve effects.

Even Tho

by Grace Nichols

First thoughts

Activity 1

1. **a.** There are several clues that this poem is written from a female perspective. Find as many as you can.

   b. Why do you think Nichols has chosen to write her poem in the *first person*, from a women's viewpoint?

Looking more closely

Activity 2

1. Nichols uses Caribbean *dialect* in the poem. Some readers think that this gives the poem more energy and truth. Find some examples of how she uses dialect. What effect do you think it has on the reader?

2. In the second *stanza* the poet uses exotic fruit imagery to describe the woman's reaction to the man. Why do you think the poet uses these fruits?

3. Discuss the following line with a partner:

   'even tho I'm all seamoss and jellyfishand tongue'

   Write down two things that you find effective about this description.

4. The fourth stanza voices the woman's comments to her man. She encourages him to go with her to the carnival, but ends the poem stating:

   'But then leh we break free yes,
   leh we break free And keep to de
   motion of we own person/ality'

   a. How do you think the woman feels here?

   b. Choose one word that shows her emotions. Explain in a sentence why you think it has been used.

Developing your ideas

Activity 3

1. Look carefully at the poem's structure and language techniques. The following features have been used:

- exotic fruit imagery to depict the woman's feelings
- repetition of the phrase 'even tho'
- first person narrator
- Caribbean dialect
- *rhyme* and *rhythm*.

2. For each feature, think about why the poet has used it and find an example to demonstrate this. Here is a sample answer for the first point:

> 'I'm all watermelon /and starapple and plum / when you touch me', these images are very soft and suggestive, they appear very sweet and yielding. They suggest that the woman feels as if she has become a slice of exotic fruit, something that is delicious to eat. It suggests that she is excited and full of 'butterflies' when she is close to the man.

Glossary

devour: completely and quickly consume

starapple: exotic, sweet fruit

seamoss: soft seaweed

brace-up: press against to support

Developing your response

Activity 4

1. How would you describe the overall mood or atmosphere of the poem? Select two *adjectives* from the list below. For each, explain your reasons in a sentence and find at least one quotation to support your idea.

happy	jubilant	romantic	oppressive	strained	excited
mysterious	loving	exotic	joyful	hopeful	euphoric
relaxed	secretive	cheerful	magical	sensual	passionate
dull	nostalgic	thoughtful	hurtful	celebratory	serious

2. Imagine you could ask Grace Nichols three questions about this poem to help you develop your ideas further. What would you ask her?

3. One view is that this poem is more about the need for a couple to keep their own individuality, rather than being just a poem about being in love. Do you agree? Explain your answer by using quotations to support your ideas.

4. Look at this example of an examination-style question:

Explain how Nichols presents her thoughts and feelings about the nature of the relationship in 'Even Tho'.
Use evidence from the poem to support your answer.

Write one section on language and structure that could be included in your answer.

ResultsPlus
Self/Peer assessment

1. Answer true or false to the statements below. **I can find evidence for and comment on:**

  a. the way the poet makes love sound exciting and passionate
  b. how the woman wants to keep her own identity
  c. the way the poet uses senses to make the poem vivid
  d. how the poet structures the poem to create an effect on the reader
  e. how the poet shows that love is fun and exciting
  f. how the poet uses dialect to present her ideas about relationships
  g. my own response to the poem.

2. If you answered 'false' to any statements, compare your ideas with a partner's. Look again at the poem and your answers to the questions on these pages to help you.

3. Look again at the paragraphs you wrote in Activity 4, question 4. What could you change or add to improve your answer? Use the mark schemes on pages 166 and 171 to identify the two things most likely to improve your mark.

My learning objectives

- to explore and develop my response to 'Kissing' by Fleur Adcock
- to explain how Adcock uses structure and the concept of kissing to explore the nature of relationships at different ages.

Comparing Poems

To prepare for your English Literature exam:

- explore specific comparisons and links between Adcock's 'Kissing' and other poems in this collection, for example how the writer presents thoughts and feelings on relationships in 'Even Tho', or the way in which writers present pictures of love in 'Sonnet 116', or 'Valentine'

- practise comparing in detail and evaluating the ways in which two poets express their ideas and achieve effects.

Kissing
by Fleur Adcock

First thoughts
Activity 1

1. The poem is called 'Kissing' and deals with the idea of passion and love.

   a. What is your first impression of this as a title?

   b. If you were asked to pick a photograph of a couple to illustrate this title, what sort of couple would you choose? What would they look like? How old would they be?

Looking more closely
Activity 2

1. Re-read *stanza* 1, describing young lovers by the riverside.

   a. How does the poet describe the lovers? Find a couple of words from the verse that you think are interesting and explain them. For example:

   > The poet writes that they are: 'clamped together'. This shows that they have physically attached themselves to each other. This suggests how close and passionate they feel.

   b. The poem starts with a long opening sentence, followed by two shorter sentences. Why do you think the poet decided to write this stanza in this way? What effect does it have on you as a reader?

2. Look at this extract from the second stanza:

   'Seeing's not everything. At this very
   moment the middle-aged are kissing
   in the back of taxis, on the way
   to airports and stations.'

   Discuss why the poet may have wanted to show older people in this poem. Why do you think she chose to put them in a different setting?

3. The older couples act differently from the teenager lovers. Look carefully at their description:

   'Their hands are not inside each other's clothes
   (because of the driver) but locked so tightly
   together that it hurts: it may leave marks
   on their not of course youthful skin, which they won't
   notice. They too may have futures.'

   a. Why do you think the poet includes so much detail about the couple, for example, describing their skin as 'not of course youthful'?

   b. Choose one word in the quotation above and explain why you think it has been used? For example:

   > The poet uses the word 'tightly' to describe how the lovers' hands are held together. The fact that they are 'tight' describes the passion and depth of feeling they have for each other.

Developing your ideas

1. Look carefully at the end of the poem. Compare it to the last line of the first stanza. Do you think that this is a positive ending to the poem? Give reasons for your answer.

2. Look at the punctuation of the poem. Many ideas run on to the next line. Read the poem aloud. What effect does the poet's use of punctuation have?

Developing your response

> **Glossary**
>
> **clamped:** held tightly together
>
> **courteous:** polite
>
> **detour:** a round about route instead of a direct one

1. Students have made the following comments about the poem. Decide whether you agree or disagree with each point, finding evidence from the poem to support your ideas.

Student A

The most interesting thing about the poem is the depiction of the older couple. It is a very positive poem because it shows that even when couples are older, love and passion are still important and exciting.

Student B

The poet's use of setting is the most striking thing about the poem. The riverside description really captures how couples in love use the surroundings as an excuse to be together, the word 'pretending' shows that the waterlilies are just an excuse to go on the riverbank. The taxi description is a good contrast to this and shows how your everyday life changes when you get older.

Student C

I find the last lines disturbing. The poet says that the older couple 'may too have futures,' the word 'may' makes it sound very uncertain, it suggests that for some couples the excitement and passion will not last.

Student D

The poem is very visual and descriptive. It is almost like the poet is looking through a camera lens, describing what they are seeing. The fine detail, such as: 'their mouths are soft and powerful' and the marks on the couple's skin is really realistic and makes the reader feel that they are seeing through the window of the taxi.

2. How successful do you think Adcock is at capturing the passion between couples in a relationship? Give reasons with evidence from the poem for your answers.

3. Look at this example of an examination-style question:

   Explain how Adcock uses the idea of kissing to explore the nature of relationships at different ages.
   Use evidence from the poem to support your answer.

   Write one paragraph that could be included in your answer.

ResultsPlus
Self/Peer assessment

1. Look at the paragraphs you wrote in Activity 4 and at the mark schemes on pages 166 and 171. Which band would your answer fall into?

2. What could you change or add to improve your answer? Use the mark scheme to identify the two things most likely to improve your mark.

3. Redraft your answer, making these changes.

4. Look again at the mark scheme. Check that your work has moved into a higher band.

My learning objectives

- to explore and develop my response to 'One Flesh' by Elizabeth Jennings
- to explore how Jennings uses structure and linguistic features to describe the autumn years of a relationship.

Comparing Poems

To prepare for your English Literature exam:

- explore specific comparisons and links between Jennings' 'One Flesh' and other poems in the collection, for example the writers' views of marriage in 'Rubbish at Adultery' and 'My Last Duchess', or the ways in which the writer conveys feelings in 'Kissing'
- practise comparing in detail and evaluating the ways in which two poets express their ideas and achieve effects.

One Flesh
by Elizabeth Jennings

First thoughts   Activity 1

1. **a.** What are your first impressions of the couple's relationship?
   b. How similar are they to your own thoughts about couples in long relationships?

2. Look again at the poem. How would you explain the couple's relationship to someone who had not read the poem?

Looking more closely   Activity 2

1. Re-read the first *stanza*, which describes the couple lying in bed.
   a. How does the poet describe their actions? For example, why do you think he is described as reading a book late at night?
   b. How does the poet make the setting appear depressing? For example, look at the use of light used in the poem.

2. In the second stanza the poem explains the lack of passion and emotion in their marriage. Find two words that show this.

3. **a.** Discuss the following lines:

   'Strangely apart, yet strangely close together,
   Silence between them like a thread to hold
   And not wind in.'

   b. What poetic techniques has the writer used and how effective are they?

4. Look at the final three lines of the poem.
   a. Why do you think the poet chose to write the poem from this viewpoint? What effect does it have on the reader?
   b. Why do you think the narrator's identity is only revealed at the end of the poem?

Developing your ideas   Activity 3

1. Think about the poem as a whole. Decide whether you agree or disagree with the following student comments and find evidence to support your opinion.

Student A
This poem shows a huge amount of pain and unhappiness. Both people are clearly miserable in their marriage, and even the narrator of the poem (their child) seems depressed by their current situation.

Student B
This poem is really realistic. Jennings shows that many relationships start with passion and excitement, but marriage inevitably ends up as tired, dull and loveless.

Student C
Jennings may show that marriage lacks passion and excitement, but the poem shows that long term relationships do offer stability and companionship. This makes it a realistic depiction of marriage.

Student D
The imagery in the poem is so depressing. The reader can really imagine a tired couple, barely speaking, sleeping apart in a dingy bedroom. The image of their marriage being like 'flotsam' some sort of wreckage really highlights the depressing nature of their love.

2. The poet has used a particular structure and included various poetic devices. In pairs, discuss the choices Jennings has made, and think about why she has written the poem in this way. Copy and complete the grid below. One example has been done for you.

Feature of the poem	Its effect	Why it has been chosen
Words connected with darkness and light: 'Her eyes fixed on the shadows overhead.'	It creates a depressing effect, the word 'shadows' suggest her worries or concerns. It also indicates something threatening in the background.	It creates a barrier between the couple. He is choosing to read, and his light has left her in shadow. This choice of words starts the poem off in a negative way, setting the mood for the rest of it.
Narrator is the adult child: 'Do they know...'		
Images connected with heat and cold: 'Whose fire from which I came, has now grown cold?'		
Description using clear visual detail: 'He with a book, keeping the light on late'		

Glossary

flotsam: wreckage or cargo found floating after a shipwreck

former: of an earlier time

confession: admission of wrong doing

chastity: choosing not to have sexual intercourse

Developing your response

Activity 4

1. Jennings paints a pessimistic picture of the reality of a long-term marriage. Do you think this is realistic or just a viewpoint?

2 **a.** If the couple were questioned about their marriage, what aspects of each other's behaviour might they comment on? Find evidence from the poem.

   b. Write a few lines showing how either the man or the woman feels about their marriage now and how they felt about it a few months into marriage.

3. The poem hints that there is not much for the couple to look forward to except death. Find evidence that hints at the destructive nature of time on the couple's relationship.

4. Look at this example of an examination-style question:

   Explore how Jennings presents her thoughts and ideas about the relationship in 'One Flesh'.
   Use evidence from the poem to support your answer.

   Write one section that could be included in your answer.

ResultsPlus
Self/Peer assessment

1. Look at the paragraphs you wrote in Activity 4 and at the mark schemes on pages 166 and 171. Which band would your answer fall into?

2. What could you change or add to improve your answer? Use the mark scheme to identify the two things most likely to improve your mark.

3. Redraft your answer, making these changes.

4. Look again at the mark scheme. Check that your work has moved into a higher band.

Comparing Poems

To prepare for your English Literature exam:

- explore specific comparisons and links between Patten's 'Song for Last Year's Wife' and other poems in the collection, for example the way writers present pictures of marriage in 'Rubbish at Adultery' and 'My Last Duchess', or the way in which the writer conveys thoughts and feelings in 'One Flesh'
- practise comparing in detail and evaluating the ways in which two poets express their ideas and achieve effects.

Song for Last Year's Wife
by Brian Patten

First thoughts

Activity 1

1. Look at the first two lines of the poem. What do you expect the poem to be about from these lines?

Looking more closely

Activity 2

1. The husband is the only narrator, which makes this a *dramatic monologue*.
   a. Find examples from the poem that show that it is all from one person's point of view. What effect does this single point of view have?
   b. What information is given about the narrator's relationship with his wife?

2. It is possible to feel sympathy for the narrator of the poem. There are also lines that present a less pleasant impression of him. Match up the words that describe his attitude with the appropriate quotation and meaning in the grid below.

Husband's attitude	Quotation	Meaning
Thoughtful	'Alice, this is my first winter / of waking without you,'	He is very aware of his stark surroundings. They appear to reflect his depressed and unhappy mood.
Observant	'So ordinary / a thing as loss comes now and touches me'	Spying sounds sneaky and underhand. Suggests he is in control: he 'sends' them out to report back.
Sly and manipulative	'The earth's still as hard, / the same empty gardens exist;'	He is perhaps considering the significance of their parting, reinforced by the fact that he addresses her, even though she cannot hear him.
Nostalgic	'I send out my spies / to discover what you are doing.'	He is imagining that she might look the same, but she will be in a strange place.
Melancholy	'of knowing / that you, dressed in familiar clothes / are elsewhere,'	The word 'loss' makes it sound like he is grieving for the end of the relationship.

3. Look at the description of the surroundings. Why do you think the poet has used a winter setting?

4. The structure of the poem is interesting. What references can you find to time?

5. Why do you think the narrator is addressing the absent wife? Which of these possibilities can you find evidence for in the poem?

- She lives in the same city as her husband
- She looks very different now they are not together
- She has a new lover
- It is exactly a year since they parted
- She is an attractive, good looking woman
- She was badly treated by her husband
- She is forgetful of important dates.

Developing your ideas

1. The poem builds up a picture of a man who misses his wife. Why do you think the marriage has broken down? Find evidence from the poem to support your answers.

2. Some lines are *ambiguous*. Look at the following lines. What do you think might have happened?

   'I wake with another mouth feeding
   from me, yet still feel as if
   Love had not the right
   to walk out of me.'

Developing your response

1. From the student responses below, select two points that you agree with and two you disagree with. Find evidence to support your view.

> **Student A**
> The reader initially thinks his wife is dead, and he appears to be mourning her loss. It is a shock when we hear she is alive, living in another city.

> **Student B**
> The narrator can't get over the end of his marriage. His harsh description of the winter highlights his unhappiness. He appears almost obsessed with her.

> **Student C**
> We feel sorry for the narrator. He is mourning the end of his marriage and misses his wife. He is desperate to hear what she is doing even though he cannot see her.

> **Student D**
> There are lots of mysteries in this poem. It is unclear why the marriage ended and whether it was the narrator's fault. This is suggested by the title; perhaps he has replaced her with a 'new' wife?

2. Look at this example of an examination-style question:

   Explore how Patten conveys his thoughts and feelings about loss and relationships in 'Song for Last Year's Wife'.
   Use evidence from the poem in your answer.

   Write one section on language, viewpoint or comparison that could be included in your answer.

Results Plus
Self/Peer assessment

1. Read this paragraph written in response to the task above.

2. Annotate the paragraphs you wrote in Activity 4, question 2, using similar notes to those given on the right. If you have forgotten to include anything in your paragraphs, add it in.

3. Using the mark schemes on pages 166 and 171, decide which band your paragraphs would fall into.

┌─ A clear point   Evidence to support the point ─┐
The narrator appears depressed by the end of his marriage: 'Have / you noticed? The earth's still as hard, the same empty gardens exist.' The language here portrays the lack of love and sense of loss the narrator is experiencing. Throughout the poem he uses harsh, cold language such as 'empty' and 'hard' to show the lack of warmth and love. The way he addresses the poem to his absent wife suggests he really misses her.
└─ Explanation of the effect of the quotation   How it reflects the poet's point of view   Focus on the writer's use of language ─┘

My learning objectives

- to explore and develop my response to 'My Last Duchess' by Robert Browning
- to understand how Browning uses language and structure to portray the Duke's character in relation to the Duchess.

Comparing Poems

To prepare for your English Literature exam:

- explore specific comparisons and links between Browning's 'My Last Duchess' and other poems in the collection, for example the way the writer presents love in 'Valentine', or the ways in which the writers convey their thoughts and feelings in 'Rubbish at Adultery' or in 'Song for Last Year's Wife'
- practise comparing in detail and evaluating the ways in which two poets express their ideas and achieve effects.

My Last Duchess
by Robert Browning

First thoughts
Activity 1

This poem is based loosely on historical events. The narrator is Alfonso II, Duke of Ferrara who married Lucrezia de Medici when she was 14 years old. She died three years later, perhaps as a result of poisoning. In this poem the Duke, who is due to be married again, describes a painting of his dead wife to a messenger.

1. Look at these first two lines of the poem and try to work out three things that might have happened concerning the Duchess:

    'That's my last duchess painted on the wall,
    Looking as if she were alive.'

2. What two questions would you like to ask the Duke?

Looking more closely
Activity 2

1. The Duke is the only narrator, which makes this a *dramatic monologue*. He speaks in a careful and even graceful way, but the things he suggests are quite startling. What is the effect of this?

2. Look at the description of the Duchess. Which of the following statements can you find evidence for in the poem?

    - She blushed easily.
    - She was a flirt.
    - She loved her husband.
    - She was polite.
    - She treated all people equally.
    - She was ungrateful to the Duke.

3. The Duke gives away his attitude towards his wife with each comment he makes. Match up the words that describe his attitude with the appropriate quotation and meaning in the grid below.

Duke's attitude	Quotation	Meaning
Proud	'since none puts by / The curtain I have drawn for you, but I'	I have supreme control and my orders are carried out. I do not need to undertake any unpleasant task – I have servants to do that for me.
Controlling	'That's my last duchess painted on the wall.'	It is beneath me to explain myself or ask others to change their ways. They should already know how to behave.
Disdainful	'I gave commands; / Then all smiles stopped together.'	I am the owner of the portrait and the person who controls when it is viewed.
Refuses to explain himself or compromise	'She thanked men– good!'	It is appropriate to be polite, but certainly not to treat all people equally.
Authoritarian and rather frightening	'E'en then would be some stooping; and I choose / Never to stoop.'	She belongs to me, and her fate could be considered a warning to other women who don't give me total respect.

4. Look at how the writer uses the following techniques in the poem and consider what effect they have on the reader. Why do you think the poet chose these particular techniques?

   a. *rhyming couplets*   b. *enjambement*   c. *parentheses*

Developing your ideas

1. The poem builds up a picture of the Duchess's life with the Duke. What information is there about what her life was like?

2. What do we learn about the Duke and his current situation? Think about who is visiting him and why.

Developing your response

1. Students have written the following notes on their responses to the poem. Select two points that you agree with and two you disagree with. For each, find evidence from the poem to support your view.

   Student A *The Duke is presented as an unsympathetic tyrant.*

   Student B *The Duke's story is really a warning and a message to his next Duchess.*

   Student C *Browning appears to see the Duke as an obsessive and irrational character.*

   Student D *We feel sorry for the Duke.*

   Student E *We feel that the Duchess was probably a flirt.*

   Student F *The Duchess is presented as an innocent victim of a jealous man.*

2. Look at this example of an examination-style question:

   Explore how Browning presents the relationship in 'My Last Duchess'. Use evidence from the poem to support your answer.

   Write one section on Browning's use of language or structure to portray the Duke's personality that could be included in your answer.

Results Plus
Self/Peer assessment

1. Read the paragraph below, written in response to the task above.

2. Annotate the paragraphs you wrote in Activity 4, question 2 using similar notes to those given below. If you have forgotten to include anything in your paragraphs, add it in.

3. Using the mark schemes on pages 166 and 171, decide which band your paragraphs would fall into.

┌─ A clear point   Evidence to support the point ─┐

The narrator, the Duke, has a great deal of self-confidence: 'since none puts by / The curtain I have drawn for you, but I'. The language here illustrates the Duke's power and control. Throughout the poem he repeatedly uses 'I'. This suggests his self-obsession and his power. Browning is using the voice of a controlling narrator to show how completely he ruled over his wife – even to the extent of managing who could see her portrait.

Explanation of the effect of the quotation   How it reflects the poet's point of view   Focus on the writer's choice of language

---

Glossary

Frà Pandolf: fictional painter

countenance: face

earnest: showing serious feelings

mantle: a cloak

flush: blush

courtesy: politeness

favour: small token gift from a loved one or suitor

bough: branch

trifling: small in value or importance

wits: intelligence

forsooth: in truth, indeed

stoop: bend down, lower oneself (often with negative association)

munificence: extreme generosity

ample: large, quite enough

warrant: guarantee

dowry: property or money given by a bride's family to her husband when she marries him

avowed: acknowledged openly

Neptune: Roman god of the sea

Claus of Innsbruck: fictional sculptor

Comparing Poems

To prepare for your English Literature exam:

- explore specific comparisons and links between St. Vincent Millay's 'Pity me not because the light of day' and other poems in the collection, for example the way the writer presents a view of love in 'One Flesh' or 'Sonnet 116', or the way the writer explores relationships in 'Kissing'
- practise comparing in detail and evaluating the ways in which two poets express their ideas and achieve effects.

Pity me not because the light of day
by Edna St. Vincent Millay

First thoughts
Activity 1

1. Look at the first eight lines of the poem. What do you think has happened? Find a quotation to support your ideas.

2. Now look at the last six lines of the poem.
   a. List the type of images the poet uses to describe love.
   b. Why do you think she uses such images?

Looking more closely
Activity 2

1. a. List all the lines in the poem where change or the passing of time is mentioned.
   b. For each line, explain why you think the words or phrases have been used.
   c. What effect do they have on the reader? For example:

   > She describes the moon as 'waning.' This means getting smaller. She appears to link the idea of love changing with the changes in the natural world. This suggests that changes are inevitable.

2. In the first line we hear the situation from the narrator's perspective. What do you imagine has just happened?

3. Write down the number of lines in the poem, then mark up the *rhyme scheme*.
   a. What *form* is the poem written in?
   b. Is this form significant to the purpose or effect of the poem? Give reasons for your answer.

4. The poet uses imagery to convey her feelings about love. Look carefully at the poem again. Copy and complete the grid below.

What we think is true	Quotation to support this	What this means	Why the word choice is important	What we don't know
The narrator has been told that her lover no longer cares for her:	'And you no longer look with love on me.'	That she was loved once, but now he feels differently.	The direct address to the narrator, 'you' makes it sound as if she is talking to him.	Why he has changed his feelings towards her.
She is realistic believing that time causes all love to pass:				
She knows that love has ended, but she still feels upset by this:				
The relationship between the couple was relatively short lived:				

5. The poem is organised in two distinct parts. Look carefully at the poem. Where is the main change?

6. The poet uses several poetic techniques such as *alliteration* and *onomatopoeia*. Find examples of these and discuss their effect on the reader. For example:

> The poet uses the word 'hushed'. This use of onomatopoeia makes the word sound soft and quiet, this echoes the fact that the man's love has gradually died.

Glossary

thicket: shrubs and small trees growing close together

waning: the lit area of the moon becoming smaller

ebbing: the moving of the tide out to the sea

assails: attacks

strewing: scattering things over a surface

beholds: sees

Developing your ideas   Activity 3

1. What sort of mood or atmosphere do you think the poem captures? In pairs, discuss which words below best describe the poem's mood and why.

happy   solemn   depressing   melancholy   regretful   realistic

disappointed   guilty   tragic   joyful   wistful   tender   serious

carefree   disturbing   thoughtful   unhappy   controlled

2. This poem is written after the end of the relationship. What evidence can you find for what the relationship was like?

3. Look again at the final two lines of the poem. They are written as a *rhyming couplet*. Why do you think the poet decided to end the poem this way? What effect does it have on you as a reader?

Developing your response   Activity 4

1. Look at the two opinions about the poem expressed below. Which one do you agree with most? Support your ideas with quotations.

Student A

This poem is really moving because the narrator starts off by explaining that she knows love will end. She lists many beautiful short-lived images from nature to support her ideas. However at the end she admits that even though she knows this, she still feels great hurt at the end of her relationship.

Student B

This poem is realistic. It is more about time passing rather than about a particular love affair ending. The poet spends longer discussing nature, and beauty ending rather than looking at the relationship. This means that the poem's focus is on the passing and brief nature of life.

2. Look at this example of an examination-style question:

Explore how St. Vincent Millay presents her ideas about love and relationships in 'Pity me not because the light of day'.
Use evidence from the poem to support your answer.

Write one section on language and structure that could be included in your answer.

Results Plus
Self/Peer assessment

1. Look at the paragraphs you wrote in Activity 4 and at the mark schemes on pages 166 and 171. Which band would your answer fall into?

2. What could you change or add to improve your answer?

Use the mark scheme to identify the two things most likely to improve your mark.

3. Redraft your answer, making these changes.

4. Look again at the mark scheme. Check that your work has moved into a higher band.

The Habit of Light
by Gillian Clarke

First thoughts

Activity 1

In 'The Habit of Light' Clarke creates a strong impression of a woman using only one description of her actual physical appearance.

1. **a.** Think about somebody you know well. How would you describe their physical appearance to a stranger?

    b. How would you describe the things they do in a way that puts across their personality?

    c. Which of your two descriptions tells a stranger more about the person you are describing?

2. Read the poem aloud. Try using different tones of voice to create a suitable mood. Are there any particular lines that stand out?

Comparing Poems

To prepare for your English Literature exam:

• explore specific comparisons and links between Clarke's 'The Habit of Light' and other poems in the collection, for example the way the writer presents a picture of an individual in 'My Last Duchess', the way the writer presents ideas in 'Sonnet 116' or how the writer explores relationships in 'One Flesh'

• practise comparing in detail and evaluating the ways in which two poets express their ideas and achieve effects.

Looking more closely

Activity 2

1. There is a lot of description of the poem's setting.

    a. If you were drawing the setting for a book what items would you need to include? Look carefully at the poem and make a list.

    b. Find two examples of imagery related to the setting and describe the effect they have on the reader. For example:

    > The poet uses the image of the pots and pans moving and celebrating: 'saucepans danced their lids'. This **personification** of the pots dancing makes the kitchen sound lively and joyful.

2. Make a list of the activities that the woman in the poem undertakes and look at the language the poet uses. Why do you think the poet includes such detail about ordinary events?

3. **a.** What times of day are mentioned in the poem?

    b. Why do you think the narrator chose these times to describe the woman and her habits?

4. Look up the word 'habit' in the dictionary. How could its double meaning be related to the poem?

5. The poet uses various techniques to put her ideas across. In the grid below, match the writer's technique, an example from the poem and its intended effect.

Writer's technique	Example	Intended effect
Personification	'the palest potatoes in a colander, her red hair bright'	The pattern of sound in these words create a soothing harmonious atmosphere.
Rhyme	'to show off her brass … her silver and glass,'	This creates a very visual image for the reader. It also explains the amount of things she was carrying.
Listing	'saucepans danced their lids'	This makes the setting sound lively and creates a happy atmosphere, as even objects have come alive in the cheerful atmosphere of the house.
Detailed description	'her pinny full of strawberries, a lettuce, bringing / the palest potatoes'	The detail here and the focus on colour conjure up a vivid image for the reader. It means we can visualise the woman.

Developing your ideas

1. The poem uses a lot of description of light and colour. Make a note of where this occurs and explain why you think she does this.

2. It is unclear who the woman is in relation to the poet, and why she has been written about.

   a. Who do you think the woman might be?

   b. Does it matter who she is? Could the poet have had a different reason for describing the woman?

Developing your response

1. Some people think that the atmosphere and setting of the poem are as important as the character.

   a. How would you describe the poem's setting?

   b. Why do you think the poet has described it in such detail? Identify her use of two poetic devices in your answer.

2. Look at this example of an examination-style question:

   Explain how Clarke creates a relationship between the woman in the poem and her home.
   Use evidence from the poem to support your answer.

   Write one section on language or imagery that could be included in your answer.

> ### Glossary
>
> **opulence:** richness
> **Aga:** a cooker
> **pinny:** apron
> **colander:** container with holes for straining water from food
> **habit:** custom; or attire/dress

  ResultsPlus
Self/Peer assessment

These sentences are all taken from different students' writing in response to the task above.

1. Use some of these sentences, and the mark schemes on pages 166 and 171, to create a paragraph which you think would achieve a high band mark.

2. **a.** Look again at the paragraphs you wrote in Activity 4, question 2. Use the mark schemes to identify the two things most likely to improve your work.

   b. Redraft your answer, making those changes. Check that your new answer has moved up to the next band.

> There is a great deal of energy in the poem. Both the woman and her surroundings merge together: 'her pinny full of strawberries'. The poem is very visual so that you can really imagine what is taking place. The use of fruit imagery and the lush descriptions of nature make it seem a very joyful place.

> The woman has a cosy relationship with her home. This is shown by her number of possessions and the way they are described.

> The woman is busy in her surroundings. She has a lot of things to do.

> The atmosphere is happy and cheerful. This is created by the use of light and colour: 'a glimpse of the cloud-lit sea'. The word 'glimpse' suggests that she can just see the sea, and the idea of it being 'cloud-lit' gives us a very visual image of the clouds being reflected on water.

> The poet creates a cheerful, happy atmosphere. This is illustrated in the use of light and colour used in the poem: 'At dawn she'd draw all the curtains back for a glimpse / of the cloud-lit sea.'

> The poet creates a cosy atmosphere. The woman and her surroundings are seen as relaxed and happy: 'saucepans danced their lids,' even the objects are personified as dancing and enjoying themselves.

- to explore and develop my response to 'Nettles' by Vernon Scannell
- to understand how Scannell uses imagery and metaphor to convey his feelings about parenthood.

Comparing Poems

To prepare for your English Literature exam:

- explore specific comparisons and links between Scannell's 'Nettles' and other poems in the collection, for example the writer's view of family in 'Lines to my Grandfather', the ways in which the writer presents her ideas in 'The Habit of Light' or '04/01/07'
- practise comparing in detail and evaluating the ways in which two poets express their ideas and achieve effects.

Nettles
by Vernon Scannell

First thoughts

Activity 1

1. What are your first impressions of the poem? Did the last line change your initial thoughts?

2. What did you notice most about the poem? What is the poet describing?

3. This poem is spoken by a narrator. What do we learn about this narrator and why is he so angry?

Looking more closely

Activity 2

1. The young boy in this poem has had a typical childhood accident, but his father becomes very upset by it. Look through the poem and identify quotations that show the child is suffering pain.

2. There are clues throughout the poem that show it is about more than just a childhood accident – there is a deeper meaning. Make notes around each of the quotations below to show what they suggest. The first has been done for you.

   a.

   'And then I lit
   A funeral pyre to bury the fallen dead,'

   This makes it sound serious and significant. A pyre is a ceremonial burning. Perhaps this is an image of how he wishes to protect his son against all difficulties.

   This personifies the nettles, making them sound like enemies. Perhaps it hints at the future danger the son will have in his life.

   b. 'My son would often feel sharp wounds again.'

   c. 'But in two weeks the busy sun and rain.
   Had called up tall recruits behind the shed':

3. What poetic techniques does the writer use in the quotations above to create strong images in the reader's mind? Choose two of the following and explain how the poet uses them.

   - *similes*
   - *metaphors*
   - *alliteration*
   - *personification*

Developing your ideas

Activity 3

1. Many of the *verbs* in the poem give a clue about the emotions of the characters. Some of them are violent and others are more loving.

   a. Note all the different action verbs.

   b. Place them on a continuum line like the one below, according to how violent they are. Give a reason for your placement of each. Two examples have been done for you.

   Loving ◄————————×————————————×————► **Violent**
   　　　　　　　　　fell　　　　　　slashed

2. This is a poem about a father/son relationship. What can you discover about the relationship between them? Copy and complete the grid opposite.

Clue from text	What it suggests	Comment on the language
'White blisters beaded on his tender skin.'	The father feels great sympathy for his son's injury.	'white blisters,' sounds very painful. It is also a detailed description of his injury. The **adjective** 'tender' suggests great love for the son, and reminds us that he is young and his skin will be very soft.
'We soothed him till his pain was not so raw.'		
'And then I took my billhook, honed the blade'		
'My son would often feel sharp wounds again.'		

Glossary

regiment: an army unit
billhook: tool with curved blade for cutting vegetation
honed: sharpened
pyre: funeral bonfire for burning a dead body

Developing your response

Activity 4

1. Students have written the following notes on their responses to the poem. Select one you agree with and one you disagree with. For each, find evidence from the poem to support your view.

Student A
The poem depicts a devoted father desperate to protect his son but who realises that his son will face further pain and challenges.

Student B
It is a moving poem. The nettles are a metaphor for all the dangers and difficulties of life.

Student C
The poem is depressing. The last line is despondent as it hints that the child's future will be hard.

Student D
The imagery is interesting – the nettles are like an army which will triumph. It suggests that the boy may become a soldier.

2. Look at this example of an examination-style question:

   Explore how Scannell conveys his feelings about parenthood in 'Nettles'.
   Use evidence from the poem to support your answer.

   Write one section on imagery and metaphor that could be included in your answer.

 ResultsPlus
Self/Peer assessment

1. Read this paragraph written in response to the task above.

2. Annotate the paragraphs you wrote using similar notes to those given on the right. If you have forgotten to include anything in your paragraphs, add it in.

3. Using the mark schemes on pages 166 and 171, decide which band your paragraphs would fall into.

— A clear point ————————————— Evidence to support the point —

The narrator of this poem has a great deal of strong emotion and love towards his young son: 'And went outside and slashed in fury with it'. The language here reflects the way he tried to destroy all of the nettles. The word 'slashed' sounds violent and shows how he sees the nettles as metaphors for all the difficulties his child will face. This word suggests great unpleasantness and harm. The narrator describes the nettles as if they are the enemy, thereby personifying them and showing how he wishes to defend his son against them.

— An explanation of the effect of the quotation   Focus on the writer's choice of language   How it reflects the poet's point of view

My learning objectives

- to explore and develop my response to 'At the border, 1979' by Choman Hardi
- to understand how Hardi uses narrative structure to explore her relationship with her home country.

Comparing Poems

To prepare for your English Literature exam:

- explore specific comparisons and links between Hardi's 'At the border, 1979' and other poems in the collection, for example the way the writers present their thoughts and feelings in 'Our Love Now' or 'The Habit of Light', or the way the writer presents a picture of relationships in 'Lines to my Grandfathers'
- practise comparing in detail and evaluating the ways in which two poets express their ideas and achieve effects.

At the border, 1979

by Choman Hardi

First thoughts

Activity 1

Choman Hardi was born in Iraqi Kurdistan in 1974. Her family fled to Iran, but returned to Iraq after the amnesty in 1979, when she was five years old.

1. The opening line is unusual:

   'It is your last check-in point in this country!'

   What three questions would you like to ask about what is happening at the opening?

2. This appears to be an autobiographical poem about the author's return to her country. Find three pieces of evidence that suggest this.

Looking more closely

Activity 2

1. There are indications in the poem that there has been conflict and unhappiness in the past. Find two words that show this.

2. The people in the poem appear to be very excited about returning home. Find three examples that demonstrate this.

3. Find three things that interest you about the following lines, and note them down:

   'A man bent down and kissed his muddy homeland.
   The same chain of mountains encompasses all of us.'

4. The poem is structured as a narrative (story) and it uses various poetic devices to emphasise the structure. Copy and complete the following grid.

Poetic device	Quotation	Effect on the reader	Why it has been written like this?
Uses the inclusive 'we'	'We grabbed a drink –' 'We are going home.' 'We waited while our papers were checked,'	Reader feels sympathy for the group; and also feels involved.	The use of the pronoun 'we' adds interest, as well as involving the reader, as it is unclear at the start what exactly in happening.
Detailed descriptions			
Use of exclamation mark			
Use of lots of **verbs**			
References to a range of different senses			
Different length **stanzas**			
Direct speech			

Developing your ideas
Activity 3

1. The bubbles below show three different types of relationships found in the poem.

> *the relationship of the five-year old with her family*

> *the relationship of the refugees with the guards*

> *the relationship of the poet as an adult with herself aged 5*

   a. Identify at least two more types of relationship in the poem. Think about place and home as well as people.

   b. Discuss why the different relationships are important.

2. Look at the different descriptions of people in the poem. Select two lines of description and comment on them. For example:

> The people are described as being like a group.
>
> 'Dozens of families waited in the rain.'
>
> The word 'dozens' makes it sound as if there are a great many of them. The fact they are in the rain shows the unpleasant conditions and their patience.

Developing your response
Activity 4

1. Look at this example of an examination-style question:

   Explain how Hardi shows the importance of people's relationships with their homeland in 'At the border, 1979'.
   Use evidence from the poem to support your answer.

   Write one section that could be included in your answer.

ResultsPlus
Self/Peer assessment

1. Look at the paragraphs you wrote in Activity 4 and at the mark schemes on pages 166 and 171. Which band would your answer fall into?

2. What could you change or add to improve your answer? Use the mark schemes to identify the two things most likely to improve your mark.

3. Redraft your answer, making these changes.

4. Look again at the mark schemes. Check that your work has moved into a higher band.

Lines to my Grandfathers
by Tony Harrison

My learning objectives

- to explore and develop my response to 'Lines to my Grandfathers' by Tony Harrison
- to understand how Harrison conveys thoughts and feelings about his grandfathers through the use of structure, form and imagery.

Comparing Poems

To prepare for your English Literature exam:

- explore specific comparisons and links between Harrison's 'Lines to my Grandfathers' and other poems in the collection, for example the way writers present their ideas in 'Nettles', 'The Habit of Light' or 'At the border, 1979'
- practise comparing in detail and evaluating the ways in which two poets express their ideas and achieve effects.

First thoughts

Activity 1

1. Think about a family member who you admire. Describe a memory that illustrates their personality.

2. Now look at Harrison's poem. Note down your first impressions of the grandfathers.

Looking more closely

Activity 2

1. **a.** This poem is narrated by Harrison himself reflecting on his grandfathers and his memory of them. Select three lines that show a vivid memory of them.

   b. Annotate your chosen lines. Which words stand out and add to the descriptions of the men? Think about why Harrison chose these words and what impression he is trying to create. For example:

   a violent *verb* that suggests great energy and hostility   suggests that a strong pressure has been exerted on it

   'booted it to pulp and squashed it flat.'

   this creates an unpleasant image of the rat as a shapeless mess of blood

2. Write a sentence that explains the effect of one of the words you have annotated.

Developing your ideas

Activity 3

1. Look carefully at the descriptions of the men.

   a. How many do you think are being described?

   b. What do you think is the relationship between each man and Wilkinson?

2. Look at the structure of the poem. Why do you think Harrison divided it into two separate parts?

3. There are many references to 'lines' in the poem. For example, 'Ploughed parallel as print', which shows the grandfather's great skill in ploughing in straight lines. What other references to lines can you find? Make a note of each one and explain why you think they have been included.

4. Harrison gives some information about himself in the poem. For example he holds on to the men's possessions. Look at the details he has included. Copy and complete the grid with ideas on why Harrison included such details.

Detail	Quotation	Comment on language	Poet's feeling on this
He describes what his Grandfather carried: a cane and money. A guinea was a coin worth a great deal in those days.	'He carried cane and *guineas*, no coin baser!'	'guineas' has been written in italics to stress it. It appears as if it is an unusual thing. This is also reinforced by the exclamation mark.	He perhaps appears a little shocked that his Grandfather had such riches or that he showed them off. It could also be that he is proud of him.
	'but took his knuckle duster, 'just in case'.'		
	'He cobbled all our boots.'		
	'drunk as a lord could foot it on straight lines.'		

Developing your response

Activity 4

1. This poem records a man's memories and efforts to find out more about his past. How successfully do you think Harrison conveys this?

2. The poem considers several relationships. How successfully do you think it depicts Harrison's feelings about his grandfathers?

3. Look at this example of an examination-style question:

   Explore how Harrison presents relationships between the past and present in 'Lines to my Grandfathers'.
   Use evidence from the poem to support your answer.

   Write one section on structure, *form* or imagery that could be included in your answer.

ResultsPlus
Self/Peer assessment

1. Read this paragraph written in response to the task above.

2. Annotate the paragraphs you wrote in Activity 4, question 3, using similar notes to those given on the right. If you have forgotten to include anything in your paragraphs, add it in.

3. Using the mark schemes on pages 166 and 171, decide which band your paragraphs would fall into.

— A clear point   Evidence to support the point —

Harrison shows the importance of his grandfathers through the amount of detail he uses describing them: 'with waxed moustached, gold chain, his cane' There is some pride in the way he recalls his grandfather's possessions, he explains that the chain of his watch is 'gold' suggesting that he is successful. He 'waxes' his moustaches suggesting that he takes great care in keeping them in place. Recalling this amount of detail suggests that they are important to him even though they are probably not living. All of the objects are considered old fashioned now, however the amount of detail Harrison uses describing them shows he has detailed knowledge of them . It shows how close he feels to his relations and the links with the objects are one way of keeping this connection alive.

— Explanation of the quotation   How it reflects the poet's point of view   Close focus on language —

My learning objectives

- to explore and develop my response to '04/01/07' by Ian McMillan
- to understand how Ian McMillan uses imagery and structure to communicate emotions related to the loss of his mother.

Comparing Poems

To prepare for your English Literature exam:

- explore specific comparisons and links between McMillan's '04/01/07' and other poems in the collection, for example how the writers present their thoughts on relationships in 'Nettles' and 'Song for Last Year's Wife', or the way in which the writer expresses feelings in 'Lines to my Grandfathers'

- practise comparing in detail and evaluating the ways in which two poets express their ideas and achieve effects.

04/01/07
by Ian McMillan

First thoughts

Activity 1

1. Experiment with reading this poem aloud in different ways, capturing different moods. Try changing the pace and emphasis until you have a reading you feel is effective.

2. This poem seems to describe a true event in the narrator's life. Pick out three details that make it sound like a real memory.

3. In the first *stanza* the narrator is suddenly awoken and his life is changed. Find two different words in this verse that suggest pain and sudden change.

Looking more closely

Activity 2

1. The poet seems to be in shock.

   a. Look for examples where the poet shows that some of his senses are more alert owing to the shock of the situation.

   b. How does this add to our understanding of the poet's experience?

2. Look at the grid below and match the writer's technique to an example, and the intended effect on the reader.

Writer's technique	Example	Effect on the reader
Violent vocabulary	'I'm suddenly awake in the new year air'	The longer sentence draws out the increase in tension in the poem. The following shorter sentence creates a state of suspense.
Use of *first person*	'The telephone shatters the night's dark glass.'	Helps the reader imagine the real hurt and emotional pain of the narrator.
Use of *onomatopoeia*	'The stream dried up,'	Makes us imagine that we are sharing the experience, hearing what is happening.
Use of very physical description	'Outside a milk float clinks and shines'	Makes the experience seem vivid and creates empathy for the narrator.
Uses visual imagery from nature	'And I feel tears slap my torn face;'	This reflects the ending of the natural bond between child and mother. The natural image highlights how important this bond is.
Use of varying sentence length	'Outside a milk float clinks and shines / And a lit plane drones in the night's dark blue, / And I feel the tears slap my torn face; /The light clicks on. I rub my eyes.'	Shocks and surprises the reader and indicates all is not right.

Developing your ideas   Activity 3

1. Look at the poem's *rhymes* and stanza structure. What do you notice about them? Why do you think the poet has crafted his poem in this way?

2. People react differently to this poem. How does it make you feel? Look at the *adjectives* below and select two that describe how you feel. Then use them in a sentence. For example:

> *The poem makes me feel sympathetic towards the narrator because very quickly his whole life has changed.*

despondent	confused	sad	pessimistic	nervous	emotional
hopeless	happy	entertained	thoughtful	disappointed	guilty
empathetic	despairing	hopeful	surprised	reflective	relieved

Developing your response   Activity 4

1. What impression do you get of the importance of the relationship between mother and son in this poem? Support your answer with evidence from the poem.

2. The final *couplet* appears particularly significant. Discuss what you think it means. Think about its significance to the form of the poem.

3. Look at this example of an examination-style question:

   Explore how McMillan conveys his feelings about the news of his mother's death in '04/01/07'.
   Use evidence from the poem to support your answer.

   Write one section on structure or language that could be included in your answer.

ResultsPlus
Self/Peer assessment

1. Answer true or false to the following statements.

   I can find evidence for and comment on:

   a. the way the narrator experiences shock in the poem

   b. the way the mother's death is seen as very significant to the poet

   c. the way the poet uses violent words and imagery to make his point

   d. how the poet makes us feel sympathy towards his situation

   e. how the poem suggests the mother/child bond is important

   f. my response to the poem.

2. If you answered 'false' to any statement, compare your ideas with a partner. Look again at the poem and your answers to the questions to help you.

3. Look again at the paragraphs you wrote in Activity 4, question 3. What could you change or add to improve your answer? Use the mark schemes on pages 166 and 171 to identify the two things most likely to improve your mark.

Comparing the 'Relationships' poems

When you compare two poems, it can be helpful to think about three different areas:

• Language: the words, images or techniques (such as simile or metaphor) used
• Structure: the shape, rhyme and rhythm of the poem
• Viewpoint: the writer's attitude to the subject of the poem

Read the poems 'Our Love Now' and 'Valentine', then complete the activities below.

Making comparisons and links between poems

Activity 1

1. Look again at 'Our Love Now' and then answer the following questions:
   a. What clues are there about what the couple's relationship is like?
   b. What signs are there to suggest a conflict in the relationship?
2. Look again at 'Valentine' and then answer the same questions.
3. Write one sentence about each poem, summing up what the poem is about and the writer's attitude towards the relationship.

Evaluating ways of expressing meaning and achieving effects

Activity 2

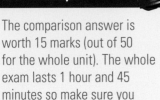

1. **a.** The poet of 'Valentine' uses images to suggest feelings about love and a relationship. Think about why the poet has selected each of the images below. How has the poet used each image to make her point about the relationship?

   red rose   satin heart   onion   wedding-ring

   b. Now look at the images below which the poet of 'Our Love Now' uses to suggest his feelings about love and a relationship. For each image say why the poet selected it and how he uses it to make his point about the relationship.

   storm   hair cut   burn   cut

   c. Compare the use of imagery in each poem. What do you notice about the similarities and differences in the way each poet uses imagery?

2. **a.** Compare the shape and structure of the two poems by writing a sentence or two for each of the bullets below:
   • compare the way stanzas are structured
   • compare how each poet makes the start of the poem engaging
   • compare how each poet uses punctuation for effect
   • compare how the poet uses a speaker or narrator in the poem.

   b. For each poem, choose **one** effect from the list of possible effects on the reader below that most closely matches your personal response. Then, for each poem, write one or two sentences explaining the features that create the effect you have chosen.
   • Makes the reader feel that the relationship is unhappy.

   • Makes the reader feel sympathy towards the person speaking in the poem.
   • Suggests that relationships inevitably cause pain and suffering.
   • Shows that the ending of relationships are abrupt and final.
   • Creates a sense that you are observing a real relationship.

Selecting appropriate examples

Activity 3

1. Copy and complete the grid below to help you compare the two poems:

	Language	Structure	Viewpoint
Valentine			First person monologue on a relationship.
	Quotation:	Quotation:	Quotation:
Our Love Now	Conversational speech, including lots of images		
	Quotation:	Quotation:	Quotation:

2. **a.** Look at this quotation from 'Valentine': | it will blind you with tears red rose |

   b. Now look at your completed grid. Which of your points do you think this quotation supports? Add the quotation to your grid.

   c. Choose five more quotations from the poems: one to support each of the three areas in each of the poems.

Developing your response

Activity 4

1. Look at the paragraphs below written in response to the examination-style question:

   Explain how the writer of 'Our Love Now' presents different thoughts and feelings about relationships from those given in 'Valentine'.

   ┌─── A clear point   Evidence to support it ───┐

   'Our Love Now' describes the end of a relationship. 'it leaves damage in its wake which can never be repaired.'
   It is as if the storm represents an argument and the poem suggests that the damage caused by it has ruined the relationship. The writer reflects the seriousness of the situation by using different images connected with change and ending with a violent storm. Words such as 'damage' and 'wake' suggest the destruction and damage done.
   However, in 'Valentine' we are presented with one main central image that reflects the relationship. 'Its fierce kiss will stay on your lips possessive and faithful'
   The image of an onion reflects love as a mixture of positive and negative attributes. Its strong kiss is 'faithful' but there is also the sense that it could overpower the lover. Like 'Our Love Now' the writer ends the poem on a very strong violent final image. The strong words 'knife' and 'forever dead' highlighting the abrupt ending of each relationship.

   └─ An explanation of the   Exploration of the   Words and phrases   Close focus on language,─┘
      effect of the quotation   writer's intention   to show comparison   structure or tone

2. Now try writing four paragraphs giving your response to a different examination-style question:

   Explain how the writer of 'Nettles' presents different ideas about love from those given in 'Sonnet 116'.

   Use the same structure as in the paragraphs above.

3. Annotate your paragraphs using the same annotations as above. If you've forgotten to include anything in your paragraphs, add it in.

4. Using the mark schemes on pages 166 and 171, decide which band your paragraphs would fall into.

Build better answers

Here are some extracts from student answers to Higher Tier English Literature examination questions. Read the answers together with the examiner comments to help you understand what you need to do to build better answers.

(a) Explore how the writer conveys his attitudes towards remembered love in 'Song for Last Year's Wife'.

Use **evidence** from the poem to support your answer.

(15 marks)

Student 1 – Extract typical of a grade C answer

This shows an awareness of the tone of the wording used in the title, with its suggestion that she is like a former possession.

> The writer is thinking about his wife who has left him. In the title he says she is 'last year's wife'. This is like you might talk about an old mobile phone or games console. It makes you think he is not feeling very warm about her. But in the poem you can see he does still think about her quite a lot. When he says 'I imagine you', he obviously has a clear picture of her in his mind. He also talks about 'loss', which still hits him, and he feels angry that she left him. 'Love had not the right to walk out of me'.

There is certainly anger and bitterness in the poem, which the student has identified with an appropriate quotation.

Examiner summary

This part of the answer is typical of grade C performance. The student obviously understands some of the deep feelings the narrator shows, and is able to use relevant quotations from the poem to support the points they have made. These are drawn from different parts of the poem, so there is a definite sense that the student has understood the poem as a whole.

Student 2 – Extract typical of a grade A answer

The fact that he is still desperate to know what she is doing, even though it is a year since she left, is shown clearly by the reference to 'spying' on her.

> This poem conveys how someone whose wife has left him feels a year later. He addresses her ('Alice') by name: he is conscious of her presence though she has gone. However, the rhetorical question 'Have you noticed?' suggests that he doubts whether she still thinks of him. His own memories are vivid, and he can almost feel her absent body next to him ('your body's as firm... as warm and inviting'). Because of his strong feelings, he sends 'spies to discover' how she is. It seems that he cannot get her out of his life or thoughts. Even though he acknowledges that she is gone and that he now has a new lover ('another mouth feeding / from me'), he feels a strong sense of 'loss'.

The point about the rhetorical question is focused and supported.

Examiner summary

This part of the answer is typical of grade A performance. There is a confident and mature grasp of the complex emotions which the narrator is feeling, and the quotations from the text are well integrated into the response. This ensures that the points the student makes are based securely on evidence. There is astute reference to his sense that perhaps Alice has now forgotten about him.

(b) (i) Compare how the writers explore different ideas about love in 'Kissing' and 'Song for Last Year's Wife'.

Use **evidence** from the poems to support your answer.

You may include material you used to answer (a).

(15 marks)

Student 1 – Extract typical of a grade C answer

This is a relevant comment on the setting of the poem and there is an awareness of the contrast between the two stanzas.

The two poems are both about couples who are or were in love. The two stanzas of 'Kissing' show different scenes. Young people show feelings in public places 'walking on the riverbank', a romantic place. Secondly, middle-aged people have just as powerful feelings as he says their kisses are 'as moist as ever', but use slightly more private places such as taxis. The people in 'Kissing' seem very much in love at the present moment, but in 'Last Year's Wife' the relationship has been over for 'a year', and there is a much less happy atmosphere. In this poem the person speaking thinks more about the past and how he feels about his wife now.

The student comments appropriately on the use of the present tense the whole way through 'Kissing' and the contrast between past and present in 'Last Year's Wife'.

Examiner summary

This part of the answer is typical of grade C performance. It shows a secure grasp of the subject matter of the two poems and compares them in an appropriate way. There is more on 'Kissing', which is fine, but the points that are made on 'Last Year's Wife' are also reasonable ones, and the quotations are relevant. To improve the answer there would need to be closer analysis and greater use of examples.

Student 2 – Extract typical of a grade A answer

This is a very apt point about the similarities and differences in the two poems.

'Kissing' is written by someone observing lovers, but the narrator in 'Last Year's Wife' is one of the two central figures. Both poems focus on how love is shown, but Patten accentuates the persistence of his feelings after the relationship has ended. In 'Kissing', the title underlines the preoccupation with physical shows of love, often in public. The poets' purposes in writing also seem different: 'Kissing' considers how young and older people alike express physical love: it emphasises the intensity of their feelings and how they seize the moment. Both stanzas end with a reference to time: 'They've got all day'; 'They too may have futures'. 'Last Year's Wife', however, looks backwards and explores the narrator's complex emotions when reflecting on his wife's departure.

The student is clearly developing a strong interpretation of what the two poems are aiming to achieve, and shows very well the difference in the two writers' perspectives.

Examiner summary

This part of the answer is typical of grade A performance. The points the student makes are very well grounded in a thoughtful and well-judged reading of the two poems, and there is an evident and strong ability to draw out meanings and make comparative points in a convincing way.

Clashes and Collisions

My learning objectives

- to explore and develop my response to 'Half-caste' by John Agard
- to understand how Agard uses linguistic and grammatical features to influence the reader and challenge perceptions of race.

Comparing Poems

To prepare for your English Literature exam:

- explore specific comparisons and links between Agard's 'Half-caste' and other poems in the collection, for example the way the writer presents his thoughts and feelings about conflict in 'Catrin', the ways a writer presents ideas in 'Exposure', or how the poet explores tension between different groups of people in 'Parade's End'

- practise comparing in detail and evaluating the ways in which two poets express their ideas and achieve effects.

Half-caste by John Agard

First thoughts

Activity 1

1. Practise reading 'Half-caste' in different ways. What sort of *tone* and attitude do you think the speaker has? Experiment with making the narrator sound serious, then humorous and then angry. Which approach do you think is best suited to this poem?

2. **a.** What impression do you get of the narrator's life from the poem?
   b. How do other people treat him?
   c. How does he react when they call him 'half-caste'?

Looking more closely

Activity 2

1. Agard uses a range of different images to put across his feelings, for example:

'Excuse me
standing on one leg
I'm half-caste'

> It appears as if he is asking for forgiveness, but really he is mocking the listener.

> This presents a ridiculous visual image, and highlights how he feels about people who treat him, as if he is only half a person. He wants to mock them.

> This is blunt and direct and shows he is challenging the reader's view of him, as half a person.

Explore the following lines as above. Pick out words that you think have an impact on the reader, and explain their effect.

'Explain yuself
wha yu mean
when yu say half-caste
yu mean when picasso
mix red an green
is a half-caste canvas'

2. The poet uses many images in the poem. Look carefully at the details he has included. Copy and complete the chart with ideas on why Agard included such imagery. Add some more images from the poem.

Image	Quotation	Why this has been used?	Comment on language used
Overcast sky	'yu mean when light an shadow / mix in de sky / is a half-caste weather /'	It is a humorous image of British weather. It is used to create amusement and ridicule this aspect of Britain.	Agard puns on the idea of 'overcast' weather relating to 'half-caste,' he also continues the image connected with painting.
Tchaikovsky creating music			

Developing your ideas

1. Read the poem again, noticing where Agard uses *rhyme*. Why do you think he uses rhyme in the poem? What effect would it have if the poem lacked rhyme when it was read aloud?

2. Look at the *dialect* words and ways that Agard constructs sentences. Pick out three things you notice. Why do you think the poet decided to write the poem in this way?

Developing your response

1. This poem shows a man's protest against the way he is treated through humour. How successfully do you think Agard puts this across? Support your comments with evidence from the poem.

2. How effective do you think 'Half-caste' is as a title? Support your comment by reference to at least one quotation from the poem. What could be an alternative title?

3. Look at this example of an examination-style question:

   Explain how Agard uses language and form to put forward his point of view in 'Half-caste'.
   Use examples from the poem to support your answer.

   Write one section on Agard's use of varying tone to challenge the reader's perspective that could be included in your answer.

Glossary

half-caste: old-fashioned term to describe people of mixed racial origins, but now regarded as offensive

Picasso: Spanish painter (1881–1973) who pioneered Cubism, putting elements together in unexpected ways to produce beautiful results

canvas: strong coarse cloth to paint on

ah rass: mild West Indian expletive

Tchaikovsky: Russian composer (1840–93) whose works included Swan Lake

symphony: long piece of music for an orchestra, often composed on a piano

---

ResultsPlus
Self/Peer assessment

1. Read this paragraph written in response to the task above.

2. Annotate your paragraphs written in Activity 4, question 3, using similar notes to those given on the right. If you have forgotten to include anything in your paragraphs, add it in.

3. Using the mark schemes on pages 166 and 171, decide which band your paragraphs would fall into.

— A clear point

Evidence to support the point —

Agard shows both anger and humour in the way he responds in 'Half Caste'. He speaks very aggressively to the reader. He uses the first person narrative to make this more direct: 'Explain yuself / wha yu mean / Ah listening to yu wid de keen / half of mih ear'. The words 'Explain yuself' are a direct challenge to the reader, as Agard asks them to give an account of their behaviour. He then softens this by using a ridiculous image to highlight how illogical they are being treating him differently because he is of mixed race. It is clearly impossible for him to choose to listen only in one ear, but he is making a serious point – he is one person and should be treated fairly and with respect.

An explanation of the effect of the quotation

How it reflects the poet's point of view

Clear focus on the writer's choice of language

My learning objectives

- to explore and develop my response to 'Parade's End' by Daljit Nagra
- to understand how Nagra uses vocabulary and narrative structure to engage the reader and explore issues of racial and cultural tension with a community.

Comparing Poems

To prepare for your English Literature exam:

- explore specific comparisons and links between Nagra's 'Parade's End' and other poems in the collection, for example the way the writer presents conflict in 'Half-caste', or the ways the writers convey thoughts and feelings in 'Exposure' or 'Hitcher'

- practise comparing in detail and evaluating the ways in which two poets express their ideas and achieve effects.

Parade's End
by Daljit Nagra

First thoughts

Activity 1

1. This poem is about the various injustices a family experiences.
   a. List the things that happen to them.
   b. How does the poem make you feel about these incidents?

2. This poem is very visual. Imagine you were drawing the shop and its immediate environment. List what you would include in the setting and how it would be organised. Add quotations from the poem to support particular points in your list.

Looking more closely

Activity 2

1. Look at the title. It could have several meanings. How many can you think of?

2. This poem includes a lot of detail to show what everyday life was like for the family living in Yorkshire, running a local supermarket. Copy and complete the grid below, explaining what the quotations mean, then commenting on the language and what the poet is trying to convey.

Quotation	What it means	Comment on language
'swilling kidneys, liver and a sandy block / of corned beef,'	A detailed description of some of the meat for sale. The types of meat are cheap cuts, which links to the setting of the poem.	It is a detailed list. The words make us vividly imagine the meat 'swilling', suggesting that the kidneys are pooling in blood. The adjective 'sandy' brings to mind the crumbly texture and colour of the fat around the corn beef.
'Spread trolleys / at ends of the darkened aisles.'		
'Thundering down the graffiti of shutters'		
'In the unstoppable pub-roar / from the John O'Gaunt across the forecourt,'		
'we swept away the bonnet-leaves / from gold to the brown of our former colour.'		

Developing your ideas

Activity 3

1. Some of the poem is written in a Yorkshire *dialect*. It is the voice of some local people responding to the family. Read it aloud. What do you notice about how it sounds and what it adds to the poem?

2. Throughout the poem there is a menacing atmosphere. The threat of violence is never far away. Look closely at the following three quotations, and explain how they convey this sense of danger and violence.

a. 'Bolted / two metal bars across the back door / (with a new lock).'

b. 'Ready for the getaway to our cul-de-sac'd / semi-detached'

c. 'and rushed / the precinct to check it was throbbing red.'

For example, for the first quotation you might say:

> The poet uses the word 'bolted' to suggest the strength and defence the family need to put up against their tormentors. 'Bolted' suggests firm action, securing the door with a firm bolt, but it also shows the mental threat they feel. The detail 'two metal bars' makes it sound like they really need to make the defences to their shop really strong, and the brackets around 'new lock' suggests the previous one had been broken by a robbery.

Developing your response

Activity 4

1. The poem describes one day from the perspective of the shop owner's son.
   a. Find evidence to show that it has been written from this viewpoint.
   b. Why do you think the poet decided to use this narrative structure?

2. This poem protests against the unfairness and racism experienced by many families who tried to set up businesses. Look at the following students' comments. Find a quotation from the poem to support each of their ideas.

Student A

This poem highlights the unfairness of racism. The family are creating a shop that is clearly used and needed by the local people, yet they are badly treated because of it. The 'local' men are actually not working and yet they are abusing a family who is just trying to make a living. The poem highlights their jealousy.

Student B

The family are shown as resilient, hardworking and caring. The poem shows that they try hard and are united in their attempt to make a successful life for themselves.

3. Look at this example of an examination-style question:

   Explain how Nagra presents conflict in 'Parade's End'.
   Use examples from the poem to support your answer.

   Write one section on Nagra's use of mood and vocabulary to express fear that could be included in your answer.

Results Plus
Self/Peer assessment

1. Answer true or false to the following statements. **I can find evidence for and comment on:**
   a. the way the family are seen as hardworking in the poem
   b. the way the family are victims of crime
   c. the way the poet uses violent words to highlight tension
   d. the way the setting is described as being in a poor area
   e. how the poet encourages the reader to sympathise with the family
   f. how the poem suggests racism is unjust
   g. my response to the poem.

2. If you answered 'false' to any statement, compare your ideas with a partner's. Look again at the poem and your answers to the questions on these pages to help you.

3. Look again at the paragraphs you wrote in Activity 4, question 3. What could you change or add to improve your answer? Use the mark schemes on pages 166 and 171 to identify the two things most likely to improve your mark.

Glossary

parade: row of shops; showy or vain display; a formal or public procession

Granada: make of car

dole: (informal) money paid by the State to unemployed people

precinct: enclosed area free from traffic

pucker: wrinkle

John O'Gaunt: pub whose name is an historical figure Shakespeare famously used first to praise England and then to criticise it for its shameful faults

forecourt: enclosed area in front of a building

My learning objectives

- to explore and develop my response to 'Belfast Confetti' by Ciaran Carson
- to understand how Carson uses punctuation and form to create an image of conflict.

Comparing Poems

To prepare for your English Literature exam:

- explore specific comparisons and links between Carson's 'Belfast Confetti' and other poems in the collection, for example the writer's view of conflict in 'Exposure', or the presentation of violence in 'Hitcher'
- practise comparing in detail and evaluating the ways in which two poets express their ideas and achieve effects.

Belfast Confetti
by Ciaran Carson

First thoughts

Activity 1

1. Look at the title of the poem.
   a. What do you associate with each of these words?
   b. What clues do they give the reader about the content of the poem?

2. The poem is about a violent conflict.
   a. What seems to have happened?
   b. Write down three things you would like to ask about the situation.

3. a. Read the poem aloud. Try using different tones of voice to create a suitable mood.
   b. Which particular words or lines benefit from being emphasised?

Looking more closely

Activity 2

1. a. Who do you think is the narrator of the poem?
   b. What has he observed happening? Find quotations to support your ideas.

2. The poem shows the impact of an IRA bomb. Look at the first *stanza*. Pick out three words that suggest violence and conflict.

3. a. What do you think happens in the second stanza?
   b. Why is the narrator feeling under pressure? Pick out three words that show his feelings.

Developing your ideas

Activity 2

1. This poem is a narrative; it tells a story.
   a. How does this narrative grip the reader's attention? (Think about the line length and layout of the poem.)
   b. The poem creates a strong visual image for the reader as the story develops. Select three lines of the poem that you think are very descriptive and explain why they are effective. For example:

   'Nuts, bolts, nails, car-keys. A fount of broken type.'

   These objects are small, but sharp and metal. They suggest a lot of injury and pain will be inflicted on people.

   This creates an image of lots of small objects raining down on people. Perhaps from a distance all these objects look like punctuation marks.

2. The poet uses images not usually linked with violence such as:
   a. confetti
   b. rain
   c. punctuation.
   For each of these images find out where the poet has used them and explain how the image has been adapted to add violence in the poem.

3. The writer has used various techniques to put his ideas across. Match the writer's techniques opposite to the effect created.

Techniques	Effects created
Highly visual descriptions, including precise details, e.g. 'I know this labyrinth so well – Balaclava, Raglan, Inkerman, / Odessa Street –'	This captures the reader's attention straight away. It also hints that the violence was very sudden and quick to start.
A narrative told in the *first person*.	Builds up a clear picture in the reader's mind, so that they can imagine the scene.
Dramatic language such as starting with 'Suddenly', and using violent images 'a burst of rapid fire...'	These create various effects, for example the question marks show the narrator's fear and confusion. The shrapnel is also described as punctuation marks, so the fact that there is a lot in the poem reflects the bomb showering its punctuation (nails) on the people.
Use of a wide range of punctuation, such as question marks, ellipsis, commas and full stops.	It allows the reader to imagine that they are experiencing the situation firsthand. It also makes us wonder how far the narrator was involved in the incident. It makes it difficult to get a clear picture of what is happening because we see it through the confused eyes of the narrator.

Glossary

Belfast: capital city of Northern Ireland and centre of some of the worst violence during the Irish troubles

confetti: small pieces of coloured paper thrown at celebrations, but here a nickname for the shrapnel in the IRA bombs

fount: source, fountain

asterisk: * a punctuation mark designed to draw attention to something

labyrinth: complicated arrangement of paths or passageways

Balaclava, Inkerman: famous battles in the Crimean War (1853–56)

Raglan: famous Crimean commander

punctuated: to put punctuation marks into a text, to break something up at various points

Saracen: armoured personnel carrier

Kremlin-2 mesh: anti-rocket mesh

Makrolon face shields: protection for the face made from thermo-plastic

fusillade: great outburst of firing guns or questions

Developing your response

Activity 4

1. Only the narrator and the riot police are directly mentioned in the poem. It is unclear whether the narrator is just a bystander or whether he is more involved. What do you think? Find evidence to support your ideas.

2. Look at how the riot police have been presented. What techniques are used and why are they effective?

3. Summarise the poem and its effect on you in ten words.

4. Look at this example of an examination-style question:

   Explain how Carson presents conflict in 'Belfast Confetti'.
   Use examples from the poem to support your answer.

   Write one section on Carson's use of punctuation or the narrative form that could be included in your answer.

ResultsPlus
Self/Peer assessment

1. Read this paragraph written in response to the task above.

2. Annotate your paragraphs, using similar notes to those given on the right. If you have forgotten to include anything in your paragraphs, add it in.

3. Using the mark schemes on pages 166 and 171, decide which band your paragraphs would fall into.

— A clear point

Evidence to support the point —

Carson presents the conflict as being very quick to start and very violent: 'Suddenly as the riot squad moved in, it was raining / exclamation marks.' Here the narrator is presented as an onlooker. The bomb explodes and from a short distance the shrapnel raining out of the bomb appears to look like a range of punctuation marks. This is effective because the bombs were packed with small, different pieces of metal and they would have looked like this. The idea of them 'raining down' suggests their large number and how they covered a large area. The poet uses the image to reinforce the scale of the attack and also the confusion of the victims.

An explanation of the effect of the quotation

How it reflects the poet's point of view

A clear focus on the writer's word choice

My learning objectives

- to explore and develop my response to 'Our Sharpeville' by Ingrid de Kok
- to understand how de Kok uses imagery and language to explore a significant event in South Africa's history.

Comparing Poems

To prepare for your English Literature exam:

- explore specific comparisons and links between de Kok's 'Our Sharpeville' and other poems in the collection, for example the way the poet presents his life in 'Half-caste', the writer's attitude to violence in 'Belfast Confetti', or the ways in which the poet presents a picture of people's lives in 'Parade's End'

- practise comparing in detail and evaluating the ways in which two poets express their ideas and achieve effects.

Our Sharpeville
by Ingrid de Kok

First thoughts   Activity 1

The Sharpeville Massacre occurred on 21 March 1960, when white South African police opened fire on a crowd of black protesters, killing 69 people and injuring at least 130.

1. Why do you think the poem is written from a child's perspective?

2. The poet reinforces the girl's innocence in the first *stanza*. Find a line that highlights this and explain why you have selected it.

Looking more closely   Activity 2

1. Re-read the first stanza. It describes groups of workers.
   a. What language does de Kok use that makes them sound threatening to the girl?
   b. Why do you think the men are noisy and excited?

2. In the second stanza the girl watches the men. Find three words that show that she is comparing them to ideas she has heard from Sunday School.

3. a. Pick out an example of imagery that you feel adds impact to the poem.
   b. What does it tell you and why do you think the poet uses it?

4. Look at what the Grandmother says to the little girl:

   'Then my grandmother called from behind the front door,
   her voice a stiff broom over the steps:
   'Come inside; they do things to little girls'.'

   a. Find three words which suggest Grandmother's tension in these lines.
   b. Do you think the men are a real threat to the narrator? Find evidence from later in the poem to support your ideas.

Developing your ideas   Activity 3

1. Students have made the following comments. Decide whether you agree or disagree with each, and find evidence to support your opinion.

Student A

The poem shows a huge amount of fear and suspicion – the watching eyes behind curtains and dogs pacing in the yard. The whole town anticipates violence.

Student B

The conflict within the narrator is interesting. She glamorises the men, imagining rich biblical images. This shows her innocence. She eventually realises the horrific reality, reinforced by the image of the 'deep jade pool' turning to blood.

Student C

The Grandmother seems fearful and concerned for the girl's safety, telling her to stay away from the men because they might harm her, but this is a 'lie'. Why is the Grandmother hiding the reality of the situation?

Student D

There is an atmosphere of guilt and secrecy – the town is hiding from what they know will happen. The girl becomes part of this, pretending to believe the lie.

2. The poet has included a range of poetic devices. Copy and complete the grid below. Think about the choices de Kok has made and why. The first example has been done for you.

Feature of the poem	Its effect	Why it has been chosen
Imagery such as 'night falling, its silver stars just like the ones / you got for remembering your Bible texts'.	The imagery at the beginning of the poem is associated with childish and innocent ideas. Here the girl compares real stars with the shiny ones she gets at Sunday school.	This makes the reader see the incident through the eyes of the child. It also shows that the poem appears to start off pleasantly but the images become harsher as she realises the truth of the situation.
The narrator is depicted as a young girl, speaking in the *first person*.		
The last stanza has many words that are connected with secrecy and concealment: 'drawn tightly', 'locked', 'closed rooms'.		
There is some grotesque and sinister imagery: 'a pool of blood that already had a living name'.		

Glossary

veld: area of open grassland in South Africa

arteries: tubes that carry blood away from the heart to all parts of the body; important roads or routes.

Transvaal: a region north of the river Vaal in South Africa

oasis: a fertile place in a desert, with a spring or well of water

jade: a rich green colour based on the semi-precious stone of the same name

maules: people who injure by handling or clawing

brocade: heavy material woven with raised patterns

Developing your response

Activity 4

1. How successful do you think de Kok is in capturing a child's view of a violent conflict?

2. Summarise this poem and its effect on you in ten words.

3. Look at this example of an examination-style question:

Explore how de Kok depicts conflict through the eyes of a child in the poem 'Our Sharpeville'.
Use examples from the poem to support your answer.

Write one section on language and imagery that could be included in your answer.

ResultsPlus
Self/Peer assessment

1. Answer true or false to the following statements.
   I can find evidence and comment on:
   a. the childish view of the narrator
   b. the town's fear and secrecy
   c. violence in the poem
   d. how the girl knows she has been lied to
   e. how the poet creates tension in the poem
   f. how the poet creates child-like imagery.

2. If you answered 'false' to any statements, compare your ideas with a partner's. Look again at the poem and your answers on these pages to help you.

3. Look again at the paragraphs you wrote in Activity 4. What could you change or add to improve your answer? Use the mark schemes on pages 166 and 171 to identify the two things most likely to improve your mark.

- to explore and develop my response to 'Exposure' by Wilfred Owen
- to understand how Owen uses poetic devices to reflect the horror of war and what effect these have on a reader.

Comparing Poems

To prepare for your English Literature exam:

- explore specific comparisons and links between Owen's 'Exposure' and other poems in the collection, for example the writer's view of conflict in 'Belfast Confetti', or in 'Parade's End' or the way the writer reflects on war in 'O What is that Sound'
- practise comparing in detail and evaluating the ways in which two poets express their ideas and achieve effects.

Exposure
by Wilfred Owen

First thoughts

Activity 1

Wilfred Owen was a soldier and poet in the First World War. The poem 'Exposure' describes the horrific experience of soldiers enduring terrible conditions on the edges of the battlefields.

1. What is your reaction to the poem?

2. Look carefully at the first two *stanzas*. How does Owen make the physical experience of the soldiers sound terrible? Find quotations to support your ideas.

Looking more closely

Activity 2

1. Owen uses a range of techniques to convey the feelings and emotions of being at war. Look at the quotations below. Copy and complete the grid by identifying the poet's techniques, the emotions suggested and their effect on the reader.

Key image or description	Technique	Emotion it suggests	Effect on the reader
'the merciless iced east winds that knive us…'	Personification	A great deal of pain and almost hopelessness about their situation.	It makes us sympathise with the soldiers. The idea of the wind attacking the soldiers helps us to realise how physically painful it was for them.
'we hear the mad gusts tugging on the wire, / Like twitching agonies of men among its brambles.'			
'Pale flakes with fingering stealth come feeling for our faces –'			
'Slowly our ghosts drag home:'			
'All their eyes are ice,'			

2. Look at the sixth stanza, when the men remember home. Pick out the descriptions of home. What do you notice about how Owen has described the mood here?

3. Re-read the last stanza of the poem. How does the poet feel at this stage? Pick one line that you feel is most effective in describing the suffering of the men and say why.

Developing your ideas

Activity 3

1. Make a note of all the actions that occur in the poem. Why do you think the poet included such actions?

2. How effective is the title 'Exposure'? Support your comments with evidence.

3. Owen uses the weather to highlight the harshness of the men's situation. Below is one student's ideas map about this device and its uses. Discuss their ideas, and add at least four ideas of your own.

> The weather appears spiteful and hostile towards the men. It is like the weather is their real enemy.

> Owen uses personification to make the weather seem like a real person who is attacking the men. For example the wind 'knives' us.

Owen's use of weather

> Frost appears to be used as an image of death. It is used throughout the last verse. Does this signify death for all of the men?

> Are the men more afraid of the weather than the opposing army? The bullets are described as 'less deadly than the air that shudders black with snow'. Why is snow being described as black?

Developing your response

Activity 4

1. How do you think the narrator feels about God and religion after his experiences in the trenches? Find a line that refers to this and explain what you think his views are.

2. Some people have commented that this poem has the feeling of utter defeat and hopelessness and that the weather reflects the soldiers' feeling of isolation, cut off from home and all comfort. How do you respond to the poem? Summarise your feelings in ten words.

3. Look at this example of an examination-style question:

   Explain how Wilfred Owen presents the horror of war in 'Exposure'. Use examples from the poem to support your answer.

   Write one section on imagery and emotive language that could be included in your answer.

ResultsPlus
Self/Peer assessment

1. Answer true or false to the following comments. **I can find evidence for:**
   a. the narrator's feeling of pain and suffering
   b. the horror experienced by men in the trenches
   c. Owen's use of personification, *metaphor, alliteration* and *simile*
   d. how the narrator feels that God has abandoned them
   e. my response to the poem.

2. If you answered 'false' to any statements, compare your ideas with a partner's. Look again at the poem and your answers on these pages to help you.

3. Look again at the paragraphs you wrote in Activity 4. What could you change or add to improve your answer? Use the mark schemes on pages 166 and 171 to identify the two things most likely to improve your mark.

Glossary

salient: the front military line that protects against the enemy; noticeable or striking

sentries: soldiers guarding something

poignant: penetrating, effective, sharp

nonchalance: casual lack of concern

glozed: made smaller

loath: unwilling

burying party: the group of soldiers responsible for burying the dead

My learning objectives

- to explore and develop my response to 'Catrin' by Gillian Clarke
- to understand how Clarke uses language and structural features to present the mixed feelings involved in the parent-child relationship.

Comparing Poems

To prepare for your English Literature exam:

- explore specific comparisons and links between Clarke's 'Catrin' and other poems in the collection, for example the writer's attitude towards authority in 'Your Dad Did What?', or the way in which the writer reflects on conflict in 'Parade's End,' or 'Half-caste'
- practise comparing in detail and evaluating the ways in which two poets express their ideas and achieve effects.

Catrin
by Gillian Clarke

First thoughts

Activity 1

1. This poem is about the relationship between a mother and her child. With a partner, find all the negative comments in the poem about the relationship.

2. What do you think the mother's attitude towards her daughter is? Find evidence from the poem to support your ideas.

Looking more closely

Activity 2

1. Re-read the first *stanza* of your poem, It describes the birth and the hospital environment. Look at the language the poet uses.
   a. How does the poet describe the hospital?
   b. How does the mother react when she is in pain?

2. In the second stanza the baby is born and the poem shifts in time to the present. Find two words that show this.

3. Discuss the following line with a partner:
   'Neither won nor lost the struggle
   In the glass tank clouded with feelings
   Which changed us both.'
   Write down three questions that you would like to ask about these lines.

4. The baby grows up into a young girl. Look at the words used in the description of the child.
   'Still I am fighting
   You off, as you stand there
   With your straight, strong, long
   Brown hair and your rosy,
   Defiant glare,'
   a. How do you think the mother feels about her daughter?
   b. Pick one *adjective* used to describe her and explain why you think it has been used. For example: Why do you think the mother describes her daughter's hair in so much detail? Why does she use the word 'strong'?
   c. Select one example of a poetic technique used in the poem, such as *alliteration*. Write a sentence about why it has been used.

Developing your ideas

Activity 3

1. Think about the poem as a whole. Look at the student comments below and opposite. Decide whether you disagree or agree with each comment and find evidence to support your own opinion.

Student A
This poem shows a huge amount of pain and unhappiness. There does not seem to be any benefits shown in having a daughter.

Student B
This poem is really realistic. Clarke shows that parent/child relationships are often hostile.

Student C
Clarke may dislike her daughter at times, but the poem still shows that she loves her.

Student D
The setting of the poem in the hospital sets a really depressing mood.

Student E
This poem shows that a parent / child relationship has to be about compromise and meeting each other half way.

2. The poet has structured the poem in order to create specific effects for the reader. She has also included various poetic devices. Think about the following choices Clarke has made. Copy the grid and make notes on why she has written the poem in this way. The first one has been done for you.

Structure and poetic devices	The effect	Why has it been written like this
The poem has been divided into in two very different stanzas.	It divides the poem into the past (giving birth) and the present (the ongoing conflict with her daughter)	It emphasises that her conflict with the daughter is ongoing, it happened in the past but it is still taking place. It shows a clear divide between the past and the present.
Many lines run onto the next line. 'I can remember you, our first / Fierce confrontation, the tight / Red rope of love which we both / Fought over'	When I read this is makes me feel…	
The end of each stanza ends with a full stop.	This makes the ending seem…	
The poet uses violent words 'shouted', 'wild', 'fierce confrontation', 'fighting you off'. Sometimes words are repeated: '**We** want, **we** shouted'.	These words make the narrator seem…	
The narrator addresses the daughter directly in the poem. She does this by calling her 'you', rather than by giving her a name or talking about her.	The effect this has is that…	

Developing your response

Activity 4

1. How successful do you think Clarke has been in capturing the conflict between parents and children?

2. Look at this example of an examination-style question:

   Explore how the conflict between a mother and daughter is presented in 'Catrin'. Use examples from the poem to support your answer.

   Write one section on language that could be included in your answer.

ResultsPlus
Self/Peer assessment

1. Answer true or false to the following comments.
   I can find evidence for:
   a. the narrator's feeling of hostility towards her daughter
   b. the pain experienced by the woman in childbirth
   c. Clarke's use of **metaphor**, imagery and emotive language
   d. the woman feels proud of her daughter
   e. my response to the poem.

2. If you answered 'false' to any statements, compare your ideas with a partner's. Look again at the poem and your answers on these pages to help you.

3. Look again at the paragraphs you wrote in Activity 4, question 2. What could you change or add to improve your answer? Use the mark schemes on pages 166 and 171 to identify the two things most likely to improve your mark.

My learning objectives

- to explore and develop my response to 'Your Dad Did What?' by Sophie Hannah
- to understand how Hannah uses language, grammatical features and form to portray misunderstanding.

Comparing Poems

To prepare for your English Literature exam:

- explore specific comparisons and links between Hannah's 'Your Dad Did What?' and other poems in the collection, for example the ways in which the writers present their attitude towards childhood in 'Our Sharpeville' or 'Catrin', or how the writer presents strong feelings in 'Half-caste'
- practise comparing in detail and evaluating the ways in which two poets express their ideas and achieve effects.

Your Dad Did What?
by Sophie Hannah

First thoughts

Activity 1

1. The poem is about a misunderstanding between a child and an adult.

   a. How do you feel about the teacher's treatment of the pupil in the poem?

   b. Think about a time when you were misunderstood. What happened and how did it make you feel?

2. a. What do you think has really happened to the child?

   b. Why do you think they did not explain this fully to the teacher?

Looking more closely

Activity 2

1. a. Read the poem aloud. Try using different tones of voice to create the character of the teacher and express his/her feelings.

   b. Which particular lines or words do you think benefit from being emphasised?

   c. Look at the **adjectives** below and pick out two that seem most appropriate to describe the teacher's **tone**. Make sure that you can support your choice with evidence from the text. (Use a dictionary to check the meaning of any words you are unsure of.)

   sympathetic   frustrated   annoyed   thoughtless   determined   harsh

   impatient   relaxed   confused   stressed   callous   thoughtful

   happy   spiteful   remorseful   worried   proud   cheerful   caring

2. The writer has used various techniques to put her ideas across. Match the writer's techniques below to the effect created.

Technique	Effect created
The poem has a clear *rhyme scheme*, whereby alternate lines rhyme. The rhyme scheme is less clear in the last *stanza* where the final words appear to jar.	We realise that the teacher does not really take much notice of the children as individuals; they are just 'essays' to her. It also suggests that there might be many children who are experiencing difficulties that teachers do not know about.
The poet uses question marks as the teacher marks the child's work.	It gives the child a 'voice'. The reader can understand the confusion the teacher has in first reading the work. When we understand what it means we sympathise with the child.
The poet does not add much information about the child, except that he 'seems bright' but that he wrote very little.	This explains what has happened to the child. We feel sympathy that his father had died yet he still had to write about his holiday. It is unclear if the teacher finally realises what the child means.

The twist at the end of the poem. The poet puns on the letter 'E', the teacher gives the child an 'E' grade for the work, and it is the missing letter that makes the child's experience clear to the reader.	This creates a child-like atmosphere during the poem. The reader realises that 'did' should be read 'died' and this shocks us.
The poet includes the lines from the child's work in italics.	These show the teacher's confusion and her growing frustration at the child.

Glossary

bar one: except one

reams: a large quantity, often referring to paper

Developing your ideas

Activity 3

1. **a.** This poem is written from the teacher's viewpoint. Find evidence from the poem to support this.

   b. Why do you think the poet decided to write the poem this way?

2. Look carefully at the teacher's actions. What can you find out about his/her attitude towards his/her pupils? Select a line from the poem to support your ideas.

3. How would you describe the mood of the poem? Find a line from the poem to support your ideas.

Developing your response

Activity 4

1. Is the poet unfairly critical of the teacher, or does she have a valid point? Use evidence from the poem to support your ideas.

2. **a.** Imagine you were asked to describe this poem to somebody who had not read it. What would you say about it?

   b. Why do you think it has been included in 'Clashes and Collisions?'

3. Look at this example of an examination-style question:

   Explain how Hannah creates a sense of sadness in 'Your Dad Did What?'. Use examples from the poem to support your answer.

   Write one section on language or structure that could be included in your answer.

ResultsPlus
Self/Peer assessment

1. Read this paragraph written in response to the task above.

2. Annotate your paragraphs from Activity 4, question 3 using similar notes to those given on the right. If you have forgotten to include anything in your paragraphs, add it in.

3. Using the mark schemes on pages 166 and 171, decide which band your paragraphs would fall into.

Evidence to support the point ——— A clear point

Hannah presents the conflict between adult and child largely through the teacher's voice: 'One writes My Dad did. What? Your Dad did what?' Here the poet presents the teacher as fairly annoyed and frustrated at the child's lack of detail in his essay. However the reader sees the real sadness behind the comment after they have read the whole poem. The teacher's anger is reinforced by the repetition of questions marks as the teacher struggles to understand what the child means. The tone of the teacher's comment sounds frustrated and angry, as if she can't be bothered to really think about what the child has written, she is just angry that there is a lack of detail. This makes the reader feel really sorry for the child. The poet shows the teacher's lack of concern for the individual child is also signalled by the fact she does not use his name – she just calls him 'One.'

An explanation of the effect of the quotation | How it reflects the poet's view | Close focus on the writer's word choice

My learning objectives

- to explore and develop my response to 'The Class Game' by Mary Casey
- to evaluate how effectively Casey has used vocabulary and poet devices to portray differences in social class and her attitudes towards these.

Comparing Poems

To prepare for your English Literature exam:

- explore specific comparisons and links between Casey's 'The Class Game' and other poems in the collection, for example the ways in which the writers present their attitude towards unfair treatment in 'Half-caste' or 'Cousin Kate', or the way the writer presents her thoughts and feelings about a particular incident such as 'Catrin'
- practise comparing in detail and evaluating the ways in which two poets express their ideas and achieve effects.

The Class Game
by Mary Casey

First thoughts

Activity 1

1. **a.** This poem considers somebody's reaction to being judged on how they speak. Read it aloud, trying different tones of voice to create a suitable mood.

   b. Are there particular words that you think should be emphasised?

2. The narrator is angry about how she is judged. Do you think people today are judged on the way they speak and the *accent* they use? Give reasons for your answer.

Looking more closely

Activity 2

1. How would you describe the narrator's language? Is it formal/colloquial/informal/standard English? Give examples to support your answer.

2. The narrator speaks as if she is replying to something someone has said.

   a. What do you think might have been said to her?

   b. Why do you think the poet decided to write the poem in this way? How does it make you feel?

3. What are your impressions of the narrator? Support your ideas with quotations from the text.

4. The poet uses several poetic devices to enhance the poem. Select two of the following devices, find examples of where they are used and comment on what effect they add to your understanding of the poem:

   - *rhyme*   • slang   • *dialect* phrases   • use of contrast.

Developing your ideas

Activity 3

1. This poem includes a lot of detail about how people speak, the vocabulary they use and how they are judged. Copy and complete the grid below, looking at how Casey uses detail in the poem.

Example	What this means	Why Casey chooses these words
'With me second-hand clothes.'	Her clothes are not new. There is a suggestion that the listener is looking down on her because of this.	'With me', is grammatically incorrect, it should be 'with my', so the example shows her use of language. She is making the point that you shouldn't judge somebody because of their clothes or how they speak.
'Me say 'Tara' to me 'Ma' instead of 'Bye Mummy / dear"		
''Cos we live in a corpy,'		
'Or did I drop my unemployment card'		
'Bread pudding is wet nelly'		

2. What information do we learn about the **listener** in the poem? Make a list of how she acts, speaks and what you can assume about her lifestyle.

Developing your response

Activity 4

1. People have different reactions to this poem and its meaning.

   a. Decide which of the comments below you agree with, and find evidence from the poem to support your ideas.

> **Student A**
> This poem highlights the unfairness of judging people and making assumptions about them (e.g. their job) because of the way they speak.

> **Student B**
> The narrator of this poem is angry and attacks the listener for making assumptions. Throughout the poem she uses *rhetorical questions* to unsettle the reader and reveal preconceptions.

> **Student C**
> This poem is not meant to be taken too seriously. It is a humorous look at how people speak differently despite being the same underneath. This is shown in the examples she uses such as the different way people say goodbye. The final lines show the narrator's self-confidence; others might judge her but she is happy.

> **Student D**
> The narrator of this poem obviously has low self esteem because other people's views of her depress her. She clearly feels jealous of the better off people with their 'pretty little semi,' and 'patio'. She comes across as somebody without any power to change her situation.

   b. Write two sentences of your own indicating what you think about the narrator of the poem. Do you think it is a serious protest or do you feel it is much more light-hearted? Give reasons for your answer.

2. Look at this example of an examination-style question:

> **Explore how effectively Casey has used vocabulary and poetic devices to portray differences in social class and her attitudes towards them. Use examples from the poem to support your answer.**

Write one section that could be included in your answer.

Results Plus
Self/Peer assessment

1. Read this paragraph written in response to the task above.

2. Annotate the paragraphs you wrote in Activity 4, question 2 using similar notes to those given on the right. If you have forgotten to include anything in your paragraphs, add it in.

3. Using the mark schemes on pages 166 and 171, decide which band your paragraphs would fall into.

— A clear point

Evidence to support the point —

Casey presents attitudes towards social class in a serious way at the start of the poem. This is shown by using a direct address to the reader: 'How can you tell what class I'm from?' Throughout the poem she continually questions the reader's assumptions about what somebody is like by how they talk and the words they choose. There are a great number of rhetorical questions used in the poem, this is because she is constantly questioning and challenging the reader to think for themselves.

— An explanation of the effect of the quotation

How it reflects the poet's point of view

Clear focus on the writer's use of language —

My learning objectives

- to explore and develop my response to 'Cousin Kate' by Christina Rossetti
- to understand how Rossetti has used narrative form and language to explore relationships and evoke sympathy in the reader.

Comparing Poems

To prepare for your English Literature exam:

- explore specific comparisons and links between Rossetti's 'Cousin Kate' and other poems in the collection, for example the writer's view of family conflict in 'Catrin', or the ways in which the writers present violence in 'Our Sharpeville' and 'Hitcher'
- practise comparing in detail and evaluating the ways in which two poets express their ideas and achieve effects.

Cousin Kate
by Christina Rossetti

First thoughts

Activity 1

1. The first **stanza** ends with the following lines:

   'Why did a great lord find me out
       To fill my heart with care?'

   Think of three questions you would like to ask the person speaking this line. For example: 'Who is the great lord?'

2. Look carefully at what happens to the girl. Who do you feel is to blame for her situation?

Looking more closely

Activity 2

1. This poem was written in the 19th century so contains many words that are less common today. Look at the following words from the poem. Think about what their meaning might be. Use a dictionary if you are unsure of any.

   | maiden | fair | lured | palace-home | joy | dove | outcast | howl |

   | dust | gold | sand | spit | clothes | gift | shame pride |

   Place the words on a continuum line like the one below according to how positive or negative the words are. Give reasons for your placement of each.

   positive ◄─────────── neutral ──────────► negative

2. **a.** Rossetti uses many words connected with wealth and status. Why do you think this is?

   b. There are also a great number of words connected with pain and dirt. Why do you think this is?

3. The ending of the poem is interesting:

   'My fair-haired son, my shame, my pride,
       Cling closer, closer yet:
   Your sire would give broad lands for one
       To wear his coronet.'

   a. Pick out any words that suggest the woman is pleased that she has a son.

   b. Why would her feelings about having a son be mixed?

   c. Why could the ending of the poem be seen as a triumph for the narrator?

Developing your ideas

Activity 3

1. Two women are described in the poem – the narrator and her cousin, Kate. Copy and complete the grid opposite, finding information about each girl and her behaviour. Make it clear whether it is a similarity or difference between the girls.

The first one has been done for you.

The narrator	Cousin Kate	Similarity	Difference
She is described as 'Hardened by sun and air'	She is described as: 'You grow more fair than I'		Cousin Kate is described as being more attractive than the narrator. The narrator is suggested as being perhaps older, or that exposure to the weather has slightly faded her beauty.
			The narrator has been treated badly by the lord, but her cousin has received marriage and great riches.

2. This poem is a *ballad*.

   a. What do you notice about the structure of this poem?

   b. Why do you think Rossetti decided that the ballad form was the best for presenting her ideas?

3. Ballads were often spoken aloud as a form of storytelling and frequently relate tragic events. They often have a particular *rhythm* and *rhyme scheme*. Read the poem aloud. What do the rhythm and rhyme add to the poem?

Glossary

cottage-maiden: a girl born and brought up in a rural cottage

flaxen: pale yellow

woe: sorrow or misfortune

thereof: of this

cast me by: throw off

sport: playing

rye: cereal used to make bread, biscuits, etc.

mean estate: poor home / background

sire: father

coronet: crown

Developing your response

Activity 4

1. Look at the way the lord is described in the poem.

   a. What impression do you receive of him?

   b. How did he treat each of the girls?

2. This poem deals with the narrator being shunned by society after her experiences with the lord. Do you think she should feel shamed by her experiences? Give reasons for your answers.

3. Some think that the narrator feels more betrayed by her cousin than the lord. What do you think? Whose behaviour in the poem do you think is most cruel?

4. Look at this example of an examination-style question:

   Explain how Rossetti creates sympathy for the narrator in 'Cousin Kate'. Use examples from the poem to support your answer.

   Write one section on Rossetti's use of narrative *form* that could be included in your answer.

ResultsPlus
Self/Peer assessment

1. Read this paragraph written in response to the task above.

2. Annotate the paragraphs you wrote in Activity 4, using similar notes to those here. If you have forgotten to include anything in your paragraphs, add it in.

3. Using the mark schemes on pages 166 and 171, decide which band your paragraphs would fall into.

— Evidence to support the point

A clear point—

Rossetti indicates the narrator's pain and suffering after being abandoned by her lover: 'Even so I sit and howl in dust / You sit in gold and sing'. The narrator describes the extreme mental pain she is experiencing in being abandoned. The images in the poem conflict with each other showing how her life is so different to her cousin's. The image of 'dust' connects to the real poverty of her life, and also the way she is seen as dirty and soiled by society. This contrasts with the richness and happiness her cousin experiences when she marries the lord. The image of 'gold' suggests wealth and singing indicates happiness and contentment.

— An explanation of the effect of the quotation

How it reflects the poet's point of view

Close focus on the—writer's word choice

My learning objectives

- to explore and develop my response to 'Hitcher' by Simon Armitage
- to understand how Armitage uses first-person narrative and vocabulary to build character profiles and explore motivation.

Comparing Poems

To prepare for your English Literature exam:

- explore specific comparisons and links between 'Hitcher' and other poems in the collection, for example the ways in which the writer presents ideas about conflict between people in 'Catrin', or the ways writers reflect on violence in society in 'Belfast Confetti' and 'Our Sharpeville'
- practise comparing in detail and evaluating the ways in which two poets express their ideas and achieve effects.

Hitcher
by Simon Armitage

First thoughts
Activity 1

1. **a.** Read the poem and make a note of what happens.

    b. Are you surprised by any parts of the poem?

2. The poem has been written with a particular narrative voice.

    a. Who is the narrator?   **b.** What do we find out about his life?

    c. Why do you think Armitage decided to write the poem from his viewpoint?

3. Imagine you are a middle-aged man in an average job. List the stresses and aspects of your everyday life that might make you angry.

4. **a.** Read the poem aloud to yourself a few times. Experiment with different ways of reading it.

    b. What tone works best?

    c. Which particular words do you think should be emphasised?

Looking more closely
Activity 2

1. The poem is called 'Hitcher.' What do you find out about the hitchhiker in the poem? Find quotations to support your ideas.

2. Re-read the third and fourth *stanzas*. Consider the narrator's attitude towards the hitchhiker.

    a. How does he react towards him?   **b.** What might be his motivation?

3. Look at the vocabulary the narrator uses. Why do you feel Armitage deliberately selected everyday colloquial word choices, even though he is describing a violent crime?

4. Are the following statements true or false? Use evidence from the poem to support your answer.

    The narrator feels:

    - violent anger towards the hitchhiker
    - proud of his behaviour
    - that his behaviour towards the hitchhiker is amusing
    - that he is similar to the hitchhiker is some ways
    - superior towards the hitchhiker.

5. The poet uses the word 'I' a great deal in the poem. Why do you think this is?

Developing your ideas
Activity 3

1. Each stanza has a different action in it. Most actions are performed by the narrator. Look carefully at the actions and how they are described. Explore some of these by copying and completing the grid opposite.

2. The narrator shares some similarities with the hitchhiker.

    a. What are they?

    b. Why do these similarities make the poem more effective?

3. Many of the lines in the poem are striking. Pick out two lines that you find particularly interesting and explain how the poet has made them effective.

Action	What it suggests	Why the language is effective?
'I thumbed a lift to where the car was parked. / ... It was hired'.	Perhaps he planned the attack, so he hired a car? Perhaps his car had broken down therefore making him angry? He is also hitchhiking here, linking him further with the man he attacks.	The start of the poem uses everyday, normal language. This is important because it does not prepare us for the later violence. It sounds as if he is just telling us a typical story about his day.
'I picked him up in Leeds.'		
'I let him have it / ... then six times with the krooklok'		
'and leant across / to let him out, and saw him in the mirror'		
'He'd said he liked the breeze / to run its fingers / through his hair.'		

Glossary

ansaphone: a machine to record telephone messages

krooklok: a heavy metal device to prevent car theft

verge: soft ground by the edge of the road

stitch that: an expression to show a lack of concern or a term for violently head butting someone

Developing your response

Activity 4

1. The reason for the narrator's attack on the hitchhiker is never made completely clear. Why do you think Armitage decided to leave this unclear?

2. Some people find this a very disturbing poem. How do you respond to it? Use examples from the poem to support your ideas.

3. One interpretation of the poem is that the hitchhiker is actually the narrator's free will, that he fights on his way to work. Find evidence to support this idea.

4. Look at this example of an examination-style question:

   Explain how Armitage presents conflict and violence in the poem 'Hitcher'. Use examples from the poem to support your answer.

   Write one section on Armitage's use of language or the narrative structure that could be included in your answer.

ResultsPlus
Self/Peer assessment

1. Read this paragraph written in response to the task above.

2. Annotate the paragraphs you wrote in Activity 4, using similar notes to those on the right. If you have forgotten to include anything in your paragraphs, add it in.

3. Using the mark schemes on pages 166 and 171, decide which band your paragraphs would fall into.

— Evidence to support the point   A clear point —

Armitage makes the violence in the poem appear shocking because it is so unexpected: 'I let him have it / on the top road out of Harrogate – once'. The words sound conversational, and it takes a moment for the reader to realise that the narrator has violently assaulted his passenger. The words 'let him have it' are deliberately *ambiguous*, and it is only when we read the following lines and realise that he has hit him with the krooklok that we realise he has tried to kill the man. Armitage has shocked and surprised the reader, particularly because it has been written about in such a matter-of-fact way.

— An explanation of the effect of the quotation   How it reflects the poet's point of view   Clear focus on the writer's choice of words —

The Drum
by John Scott

First thoughts

Activity 1

1. Look at the opening lines:

   'I hate that drum's discordant sound,
   Parading round, and round, and round:'

   a. What do you think is happening? What is 'the drum' here?

   b. Make an ideas map of all the connections you can think of for the word 'drum'. Which do you feel are relevant to the context of the poem?

2. What happens to the people who become involved in war in the poem? List their experiences.

Looking more closely

Activity 2

1. Re-read the first *stanza* of the poem. It describes the reasons young people join the army.

   a. How does the poet describe the way in which they are persuaded to join up?

   b. What do you think the poet's view is about the objects they receive for joining up?

2. In the second stanza, the poet describes the effects of war. Pick out two lines that show the horror and waste of war.

3. Note down three things that interest you about the following lines:

   'And when Ambition's voice commands,
   To march, and fight, and fall, in foreign lands.'

4. Look at the vocabulary in the poem. Select two lines that show how the poet uses contrasting negative and positive words.

5. The poet uses various poetic techniques to express his view. Copy and complete the grid below, exploring the choices that Scott has made.

Technique	Example	Why has it been written like this?
Very graphic vocabulary	'mangled limbs' and 'dying groans'	These are vivid and descriptive. They make the reader really imagine the agony and pain that the people are experiencing.
Rhyme		
Repetition		
Rhythm		
Personification		

Developing your ideas

1. Students have made the following comments on the poem. Find evidence from the poem to support the idea that each student makes.

Student A
This poem shows the horror and violent nature of war. There are many grotesque images showing how war ruins individual lives, communities and destroys cities and towns. The poet creates a vivid picture of why war should be avoided at any cost.

Student B
The narrator's attitude is very one sided and biased. He lists in graphic detail the atrocities and horrifying effects of war, but he does not consider the alternative. He does not consider the fact that sometimes war might be a solution, and if people are unable to take part in a just war, they may face worse suffering and oppression.

Student C
The poem is interesting because the way the poet uses the image of a drum to show his hatred and disgust about the effects of war. The drum is an interesting device to use because it represents the call to war and it is often used to rouse and encourage troops. Here it is being used in a very different way as an image of all that is wrong with war.

Glossary

discordant: a harsh unpleasant sound

yields: gives

tawdry: cheap and ugly

arms: weapons

ravaged: greatly damaged

plains: a large area of flat country

swains: country lads, or a man courting a woman

bestows: gives to someone

Developing your response

1. How successful do you think Scott is in presenting his attitude towards war?

2. Explain what this poem is about in a couple of sentences. Which line of the poem best reflects the theme, do you think?

3. The poem ends with a strong image. Why do you think Scott ended the poem in such a way?

> 'And all that Misery's hand bestows,
> To fill the catalogue of human woes.'

4. Look at this example of an examination-style question:

   Explore how Scott uses negative language to convey his attitude towards war. Use examples from the poem to support your answer.

   Write one section on Scott's contrasting language that could be included in your answer.

ResultsPlus
Self/Peer assessment

1. Answer true or false to the following comments.
   I can find evidence for:
   a. the narrator's feeling of hostility towards war
   b. the way that war is presented as causing suffering to all types of people
   c. how Scott uses violent words and emotive language to prove his point
   d. how Scott uses rhyme and rhythm to make the poem effective
   e. my own response to the poem.

2. If you answered 'false' to any statements, compare your ideas with a partner's. Look again at the poem and your answers on these pages to help you.

3. Look again at the paragraphs you wrote in Activity 4, question 4. What could you change or add to improve your answer? Use the mark schemes on pages 166 and 171 to identify the two things most likely to improve your mark.

My learning objectives

- to explore and develop my response to 'O What is that Sound' by W.H. Auden
- to understand how Auden uses dialogue and the narrative form to build tension, explore repercussions and express emotions connected with war.

Comparing Poems

To prepare for your English Literature exam:

- explore specific comparisons and links between Auden's 'O What is that Sound' and other poems in the collection, for example how the writers present their thoughts and feelings on violent conflict in 'Exposure' or 'Our Sharpeville', or the way in which the writer expresses feelings in 'The Drum'
- practise comparing in detail and evaluating the ways in which two poets express their ideas and achieve effects.

O What is that Sound
by W.H. Auden

First thoughts
Activity 1

1. Who do you think the narrators of the poem are? What clues can you find in the poem?

2. One narrator is speaking to another *persona* in the poem. What clues are there to the identity of the second persona? Find a line from the poem to support your ideas.

3. What time period do you think this poem is from? Find details in the poem that give you an idea about the historical setting.

Looking more closely
Activity 2

1. This poem is a *ballad*. It often has a distinctive *rhyme* or *rhythm*.
   a. What do you notice about the structure of this poem?
   b. Why do you think W.H. Auden decided that the ballad structure was the best form to use for his poem?

2. List the different actions that the soldiers are undertaking. What do you notice about these actions as the poem progresses?

3. The main narrator discusses other local people in the poem. What do we find out about each of them?

4. *Dialogue* is used throughout the poem. Find one example and explain the effect it has on the reader.

Developing your ideas
Activity 3

1. Plot the level of tension in each *stanza* on the graph below. For example, if you think there is a low level of tension in the first stanza because the narrator is just interested in the sound he can hear, mark it as 1.

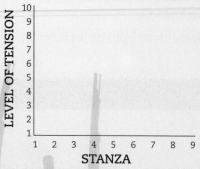

2. Explore the poetic techniques Auden uses to build up tension in the poem. Match each technique listed in the grid opposite with an appropriate example and explanation of effect. (Some examples from the poem can be used more than once.)

Poetic techniques	Example	Effect on the reader
Use of dialogue	'O what...'	This reinforces the uncertainty and fear the narrator feels.
Use of direct address	'O what is that sound which so thrills the ear...?'	This gives an indication of the violence and brutality of the men. It suggests that they will deal violently with the speaker of the poem.
Use of different senses	'splintered the door'	We can imagine we are being addressed.
Repetition of words and phrases	'Only the sun on their weapons, dear, / As they step lightly.'	This adds to the sense of fear, as the soldiers are getting ever nearer. It also adds to the steady rhythm of the poem, we can almost hear the soldiers marching towards us.
Violent words	'Haven't they reined their horses, their horses?'	It draws the reader into the conversation.
Use of questions	'O what is that light I see flashing so clear'	These make the reader feel as if they can see, hear and fully experience the situation.

Glossary

manoeuvres: planned and organised movement of troops

wheeling: moving in a curve or circle, changing direction

reined: slowed a horse with reins

parson: a member of the clergy, especially a rector or a vicar

cunning: skilful at deceiving

splintered: broken into thin sharp pieces of wood

Developing your response

Activity 4

1. Look again at the last couple of lines of the poem.
   a. What happens?
   b. How effective do you think this is as an ending of the poem?

2. a. How effective is the title of the poem?
   b. Think of an alternative title. Use evidence from the text to support your title.

3. Look at this example of an examination-style question:

   Explore how Auden builds tension, explores repercussions and expresses emotions connected with war.
   Use examples from the poem to support your answer.

   Write one section on Auden's use of dialogue or the narrative form that could be included in your answer.

ResultsPlus
Self/Peer assessment

1. Read this paragraph written in response to the task above.

2. Annotate the paragraphs you wrote for Activity 4, using similar notes to those on the right. If you have forgotten to include anything in your paragraphs, add it in.

3. Using the mark schemes on pages 166 and 171, decide which band your paragraphs would fall into.

A clear point — Evidence to support the point

Auden uses dialogue to create tension in the poem. The narrator constantly questions the second person about what is happening: 'O where are you going? Stay here with me!' Here the questioning reaches a new level of tension as the speaker demands that their lover stay with them. Their fear is shown in the use of short sentences and the exclamation mark. This shows the person's surprise since not only are the soldiers running towards the house, but her lover appears to be abandoning her too.

An explanation of the effect of the quotation | How it reflects the poet's point of view | Clear focus on the writer's choice of words

My learning objectives

- to explore and develop my response to 'Conscientious Objector' by Edna St. Vincent Millay
- to evaluate the effectiveness of the personification of Death in the poem to help convey the persona's stance as a conscientious objector.

Comparing Poems

To prepare for your English Literature exam:

- explore specific comparisons and links between St. Vincent Millay's 'Conscientious Objector' and other poems in this collection, for example the writer's view of war in 'Exposure' or 'August 6, 1945', or the way the writer conveys his feelings in 'O What is that Sound'
- practise comparing in detail and evaluating the ways in which two poets express their ideas and achieve effects.

Conscientious Objector
by Edna St. Vincent Millay

First thoughts   Activity 1

1. **a.** The first line has been placed on its own. Why do you think this is?

   'I shall die, but that is all that I shall do for Death.'

   b. Why has death been given a capital letter?

2. In the second *stanza*, the poet lists Death's actions. Why do you think he calls killing 'business'?

Looking more closely   Activity 2

1. The poet *personifies* Death by describing him throughout the poem as being a real figure. Find three examples of this.

2. **a.** The narrator makes Death appear sinister and frightening. Find two pieces of evidence to prove this and explain each one. For example:

   > Death is described as a knight on a horse: 'With his hoof on my breast, I will not tell him'. This is a very painful and violent image. The man's breast is a very vulnerable part of him. The idea of the 'hoof' sounds painful, as it is suggesting that he is being trampled or tortured by Death because he refuses to join him.

   b. Do you find the poet's use of such violent images effective in the poem? Support your ideas with a different reference to the text.

3. The narrator uses the word 'I' a great deal in the poem. Why do you think this is? What effect does it have?

Developing your ideas   Activity 3

1. The poet explains why he refuses to go to war and why he refuses to become involved in any actions that might result in people's deaths. Are you persuaded by the poet's point of view?

2. Think about the poem as a whole and look at the student comments below and opposite. Decide whether you agree or disagree with each comment and find evidence to support your ideas.

Student A

This poem shows how difficult it was for conscientious objectors to hold onto their beliefs. Death is described as very persuasive and powerful. This shows that any individuals who refused to go to war because of their beliefs were really strong and brave. Conscientious objectors were badly treated by society; they were ridiculed and imprisoned.

Student B

St. Vincent Millay's use of personification is very effective. The image of Death on horseback has been used for hundreds of years, but she develops it throughout the poem to show the wide range of wars Death is involved in. It suggests the brutality of war on both civilians and soldiers.

Student C

One of the most effective things about this poem is the use of a first person narrator. The reader can really experience the person's determination to stand up for their beliefs even though Death is powerful and dangerous. The repeated use of 'I' throughout the poem shows the person's confidence in their own beliefs.

Student D

I think the personification of Death in this poem is unconvincing. In the modern day we know that death does not exist in this manner and the image of a man on a horse to represent death is outdated. It does not reflect the modern horror of war. I think this poem would make its point more effectively if the war was described more graphically and realistically, rather than by using an outdated symbol of death.

3. How do you respond to this poem? Write your opinion in a paragraph and include at least one quotation to support your ideas.

Developing your response

Activity 4

1. Find two parts of the poem where the narrator makes his stand against Death very clearly and shows his determination not to become involved in any actions. Give reasons for your choices.

2. Imagine you could ask the speaker in the poem two questions about his beliefs. What would you ask?

3. This poem's title is 'Conscientious Objector'.

    a. How suitable a name do you think this is for the poem?

    b. Suggest an alternative name and explain the reasons for your choice.

4. Look at this example of an examination-style question:

    Explore how St. Vincent Millay uses the personification of Death within the poem to help convey the persona's stance as a conscientious objector. Use examples from the poem to support your answer.

    Write one section that could be included in your answer.

ResultsPlus
Self/Peer assessment

1. Read this paragraph written in response to the task above.

2. Annotate the paragraphs you wrote for Activity 4, question 4 using similar notes to those given on the right. If you have forgotten to include anything in your paragraphs, add it in.

3. Using the mark schemes on pages 166 and 171, decide which band your paragraphs would fall into.

— A clear point —

Evidence to support the point —

St. Vincent Millay presents being a conscientious objector as a difficult challenge: 'Though he flick my shoulders with his whip, I will not / tell him which way the fox ran.' The personification of Death as a hunter is threatening and makes him appear very dangerous to the narrator. The 'whip', that Death holds indicates the awful power that leaders of countries hold, and potentially the violence that is threatened to the conscientious objector for refusing to be part of it all.

— An explanation of the effect of the quotation

How it reflects the poet's point of view

Clear focus on the writer's choice of words

My learning objectives

- to explore and develop my response to 'August 6, 1945' by Alison Fell
- to explain how Fell uses imagery, vocabulary and form to convey the horror of a nuclear attack.

Comparing Poems

To prepare for your English Literature exam:

- explore specific comparisons and links between Fell's 'August 6, 1945' and other poems in this collection, for example the writers' presentation of war in 'The Drum' or 'Exposure', or the way in which the writer conveys thoughts and feelings in 'Parade's End'
- practise comparing in detail and evaluating the ways in which two poets express their ideas and achieve effects.

August 6, 1945
by Alison Fell

First thoughts

Activity 1

1. Look at the first three lines of the poem and the title.
   a. What clues do you have about what sort of poem it is?
   b. What does it suggest will happen?

2. Read over the whole poem. It focuses on how the bomb affects two particular people.
   a. Who are they?
   b. Over 120,000 people were killed by the bomb. Why do you think the poet focused mainly on two people?

Looking more closely

Activity 2

1. This poem is particularly striking because of its use of visual imagery. Copy and complete the following grid, explaining what each image suggests and the effect it has on the reader.

Example of visual imagery	What this might suggest	Effect on reader
'bees drizzle over / hot white rhododendrons'	The beautiful nature in the countryside before the impact of the explosion. It could suggest peace and happiness.	The reader feels sorry that such a beautiful place will be ruined. The 'hot white' of the flowers suggest beauty and innocence. But 'hot white' could also suggest the heat of the explosion.
'went up like an apricot ice'		
'saw Marilyn's skirts / fly over her head for ever'		
'a scarlet girl / with her whole stripped skin'		
'people are become / as lizards'		

2. Look at the last **stanza** of the poem:

   'Later in dreams he will look
   down shrieking and see
   ladybirds
   ladybirds.'

   a. Why is this an interesting ending to the poem?
   b. Why do you think the poet decided to end the poem describing the pilot rather than the victims of the bomb?

Developing your ideas

1. The pilot's feelings and emotions change as the poem develops. Copy the graph below and plot the pilot's emotions. Make sure you have evidence from the text to back up your decisions.

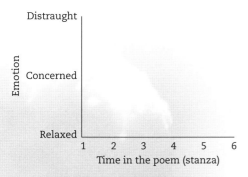

2. Look at the description of the victims of the attack. How are they described?

3. **a.** How does the poet try to build up a pleasant atmosphere before the attack?

   b. Why do you think she does this?

   c. Look at what happens to the girl and how she is described. Why do you think Fell described the girl in such detail?

Developing your response

1. The poet uses repetition towards the end of the poem. Why do you think this is?

2. What else do you notice about the form of this poem?

3. The poem considers the horror of war from the perspective of the innocent civilians and the pilot.

   a. Find two lines that suggest sympathy for the people caught up in the explosion.

   b. Do you think the poet expects us to have any sympathy for the pilot as well? Give reasons for your answer.

4. Look at this example of an examination-style question:

   Explain how Fell uses imagery, vocabulary and form to convey the horror of a nuclear attack.
   Use examples from the poem to support your answer.

   Write one section that could be included in your answer.

Glossary

Enola Gay: the USA B-29 Superfortress bomber that dropped the first atomic bomb on Hiroshima, Japan on 6th August 1945. It was named after the pilot's mother

impact: collision

Marilyn: Marilyn Monroe, iconic 1960s film star, famous for a photograph of her with her skirts billowing up

rhododendrons: a large plant with dramatic flowers, originally from the Far East

salamanders: a lizard-like amphibian, once thought to live in fire

ResultsPlus
Self/Peer assessment

1. Read this paragraph written in response to the task above.

2. Annotate the paragraphs you wrote in Activity 4, using similar notes to those given on the right. Add in anything you have forgotten.

3. Using the mark schemes on pages 166 and 171, decide which band your paragraphs would fall into.

— Evidence to support the point   A clear point —

Fell uses imagery to show the horror and pain felt by the victims of the attack: 'a scarlet girl/with her whole stripped skin'. The poet's use of language creates a great deal of sympathy for the victims. The word 'girl' shows her innocence and youth, the fact that she does not have a name means that she is representative of many girls who will have suffered. The image of skin being 'stripped' is exceptionally painful and unpleasant. The poet's use of detailed description shocks and appals the reader.

An explanation of the   How it reflects the   Clear focus on the writer's
effect of the quotation   poet's point of view   choice of words

My learning objectives

- to explore and develop my response to 'Invasion' by Choman Hardi
- to analyse how Hardi uses vocabulary and verb tense to create an ominous sense of impending conflict.

Comparing Poems

To prepare for your English Literature exam:

- explore specific comparisons and links between Hardi's 'Invasion' and other poems in this collection, for example the presentation of conflict in 'August 6, 1945' or 'O What is that Sound', or the ways the writer presents his ideas in 'The Drum'
- practise comparing in detail and evaluating the ways in which two poets express their ideas and achieve effects.

Invasion
by Choman Hardi

First thoughts

Activity 1

1. The poem is describing an approaching invasion. What can you tell about the sort of conflict it will be?

2. How do you react to the poem? Does the title give you certain expectations?

Looking more closely

Activity 2

1. Find two lines that make the approaching conflict sound threatening.

2. Look at the descriptions of what will happen. Why do you think the poet describes events in the way she does? Copy and complete the following grid.

Description	What it means	Why has it been written this way?
'Soon they will come.'	The community will be invaded soon.	It is a very short sentence which creates tension. The word 'soon' indicates that they have very little time. The fact that the enemy are unnamed, described as 'they', makes them seem more threatening.
'then they'll appear through the mist.'		
'In their death-bringing uniforms'		
'their guns and tanks pointing forward.'		
'with rusty guns and boiling blood.'		

3. Look at the following lines:

   'We will lose this war, and blood
   will cover our roads,'

   Why has the poet used this *tense*? Which words emphasise the hopelessness?

4. The narrator uses a range of devices to show the horror of what will happen, and how they are powerless to prevent it. In the grid below, match the description of her techniques with the appropriate quotation and its effect.

Narrator's technique	Quotation	Effect
Using the future tense	'We will lose this war,'	It makes it sound like he is predicting the future. It makes it sound unavoidable.
Using repetition of some key phrases	'We will lose this war… we've lost this war'	The use of 'we' means that the reader feels directly involved in the situation. It draws them into the poem.
Uses words connected with death	'and blood / will cover our roads,'	This reinforces the message and the hopelessness of the situation.

Addresses the reader directly	'First we will hear'	This highlights the death and destruction that will occur. It creates a grim picture to make the reader imagine the horror of invasion.

Glossary

confronted: came or brought face to face, especially in a hostile way

Developing your ideas

Activity 3

1. In the last part of the poem what advice does the narrator give? Do you agree with it?

2. The poet builds up the tension in the poem very carefully. Pick three different parts of the poem where you feel the poet does this particularly effectively and explain how it is done.

3. Choose and discuss one line from the poem that you find effective.

Developing your response

Activity 4

1. Students have given the following responses to the poem. Select two you agree with and one you disagree with. For each, find evidence from the poem to support your view.

Student A
The poet has described the incident as if they had been present. It is very vivid and realistic.

Student B
The poem shows the hopelessness of trying to defend your country against an invader. The poet suggests the people should just give in.

Student C
We admire the young men who will fight for their freedom – even though they are presented as having no hope of success.

Student D
The most frightening thing about this poem is that it is predicting what will happen, rather than describing a past event. This suggests that the pain and violence is still to come, but they are powerless to prevent it.

2. Look at this example of an examination-style question:

Explain how Hardi uses vocabulary and verb tense to create an ominous sense of impending conflict.
Use examples from the poem to support your answer.

Write one section that could be included in your answer.

ResultsPlus
Self/Peer assessment

1. Read this paragraph written in response to the task above.

2. Annotate the paragraphs you wrote in Activity 4 using similar notes to those given on the right. Add in anything you have forgotten.

3. Using the mark schemes on pages 166 and 171, decide which band your paragraphs would fall into.

A clear point ——— Evidence to support the point ———

The poem is written in a very tense way: 'the sound of their boots approaching at dawn / then they'll appear through the mist.' The poet focuses in on the frightening sound of the soldiers arriving. This builds up a great deal of tension, they appear stealthy and cunning as they can't be seen. The fear is linked to the fact that the poem is describing not what has happened, but what will happen. This makes it seem frightening and unavoidable.

An explanation of the effect of the quotation | How it reflects the poet's point of view | Clear focus on the writer's choice of words

Comparing the 'Clashes and collisions' poems

When you compare two poems, it can be helpful to think about three different areas:

- Language: the words, images or techniques (such as simile or metaphor) used
- Structure: the shape, rhyme and rhythm of the poem
- Viewpoint: the writer's attitude to the subject of the poem

Read 'Exposure' and 'O What is that Sound', then complete the activities below.

Results Plus
Examiner tip

The comparison answer is worth 15 marks (out of 50 for the whole unit). The whole exam lasts 1 hour and 45 minutes so make sure you spend an appropriate amount of time answering the comparison question.

Making comparisons and links between the poems — Activity 1

1. Look again at 'Exposure' and then answer the following questions:

   a. What is the writer's attitude towards war?

   b. What does the writer describe in the poem?

   c. Why do you think the writer ends the poem in the way he does?

2. Look again at 'O What is that Sound' and then answer the same questions.

3. Write one sentence about each poem, summing up what the poem is about and the writer's attitude towards war.

Evaluating ways of expressing meaning and achieving effects — Activity 2

1. a. The poet of 'Exposure' uses vivid descriptions to suggest feelings about war. How has the poet used each description below to make his point about war?

   'iced east winds that knive us'   'mad gusts tugging on the wire'

   'shivering ranks of grey.'   'flights of bullets streak the silence.'

   b. Now look at the descriptions below from 'O What is that Sound'. For each one say how the poet uses it to make his point about war.

   'their eyes are burning'   'broken the lock and splintered the door'

   'what is that light I see flashing so clear'   'their boots are heavy on the floor.'

   c. Compare the vivid descriptions in each poem. What do you notice about the similarities and differences in the way each poet uses description?

2. a. Compare the shape and structure of the two poems by writing a sentence or two for each bullet point below:

   - compare the length of the two poems
   - compare how each poem starts
   - compare the use of rhyme and rhythm in each poem
   - compare the way the incident is related – such as the use of the narrator
   - compare the length of the lines of the poem.

   b. For each poem, choose **one** effect from the list of possible effects on the reader below and on page 73 that most closely matches your personal response. Then, for each poem, write one or two sentences explaining the features that create the effect you have chosen.

   - Makes the reader feel that the war is frightening.
   - Makes the reader feel sympathy towards the people in the poems.
   - Suggests that violent conflict is inevitable.

- Shows that waiting for a conflict to start is tense and frightening.
- Makes the end of the poem memorable and dramatic.

Selecting appropriate examples

Activity 3

1. Copy and complete the grid below to help you compare the two poems:

	Language	Structure	Viewpoint
Exposure	Detailed description of the weather Quotation:	Quotation:	Quotation:
O What is that Sound	Quotation:	Quotation:	Appears to be a woman talking to her lover. He responds in the penultimate stanza Quotation:

2. **a.** Look again at this quotation from 'O What is that Sound':

   > No, I promised to love you, dear,
   > But I must be leaving.

   b. Now look at your completed grid. Which of your points do you think this quotation supports? Add the quotation to your grid.

   c. Choose five more quotations from the poems: one to support each of the three areas in each of the poems.

Putting it into practice

Activity 4

1. Look at the paragraphs below written in response to the examination-style question:

   Explain how the writer of 'Exposure' presents different thoughts and feelings about war from those given in 'O What is that Sound'.

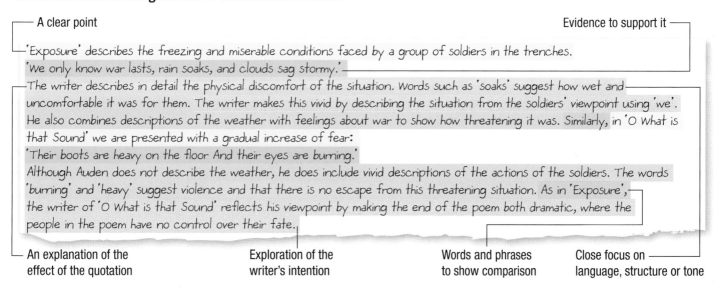

A clear point — Evidence to support it

'Exposure' describes the freezing and miserable conditions faced by a group of soldiers in the trenches.
'We only know war lasts, rain soaks, and clouds sag stormy.'
The writer describes in detail the physical discomfort of the situation. Words such as 'soaks' suggest how wet and uncomfortable it was for them. The writer makes this vivid by describing the situation from the soldiers' viewpoint using 'we'. He also combines descriptions of the weather with feelings about war to show how threatening it was. Similarly, in 'O What is that Sound' we are presented with a gradual increase of fear:
'Their boots are heavy on the floor And their eyes are burning.'
Although Auden does not describe the weather, he does include vivid descriptions of the actions of the soldiers. The words 'burning' and 'heavy' suggest violence and that there is no escape from this threatening situation. As in 'Exposure', the writer of 'O What is that Sound' reflects his viewpoint by making the end of the poem both dramatic, where the people in the poem have no control over their fate.

An explanation of the effect of the quotation — Exploration of the writer's intention — Words and phrases to show comparison — Close focus on language, structure or tone

2. Now try writing four paragraphs giving your response to a different examination-style question:

   Explain how the writer of 'Half-caste' presents different ideas about divisions in society from those given in 'The Class Game'.

   Use the same structure as in the paragraphs above.

3. Annotate your paragraphs using the same annotations as above. If you've forgotten to include anything in your paragraphs, add it in.

4. Using the mark schemes on pages 166 and 171, decide which band your paragraphs would fall into.

Here are some extracts from student answers to Higher Tier English Literature examination questions. Read the answers together with the examiner comments to help you understand what you need to do to build better answers.

(a) Explore how the writer presents her ideas about Twentieth century war in 'August 6, 1945'.

Use **evidence** from the poem to support your answer.

(15 marks)

Student 1 – Extract typical of a grade C answer

The student makes the point securely, but for a higher grade would need more development on why this particular simile was chosen: for example, there is a stark contrast between the pleasant associations of an ice cream and the horror of the scene.

> This poem is unusual as it presents ideas about war through looking at two people, the pilot of the plane that dropped the atom bomb and a girl who was a victim of the bomb which killed many people in Japan. The pilot gives a vivid description of what it looked like when the bomb exploded, with the colourful simile 'the whole blooming sky went up like an apricot ice'. The pictures of the girl are also very strong. At first, the pilot found it a sight that affected him, 'the eye of his belly', but later he fully realised the dreadful effects that the bomb had had on so many innocent people.

This shows some awareness of this unusual phrase, but the point is not developed.

Examiner summary

This part of the answer is typical of grade C performance. The student has shown a clear grasp of some of the main ideas in the poem and has commented on some effects, with sensible comments about the simile and an awareness of the pilot's changing emotions. There is a definite understanding that the writer has brought out horrific aspects of dropping the bomb.

Student 2 – Extract typical of a grade A answer

The student makes a very good point about this juxtaposition.

> This powerful poem highlights the horror of the atom bomb falling on Japan, through focusing closely on individuals, not the shocking number of casualties. Fell shows us the pilot immediately before and after the bomb's release: he 'whistles a dry tune' as he approaches his target – the dryness was perhaps inside his mouth. His complex reaction is shown by juxtaposing two contrasting emotions: 'laugh' and 'tremble'. The poem then examines the fate of the girl who made him recall Marilyn Monroe in the iconic picture. The description is horrifying, with her flayed skin and lost sight, compared to blind creatures, 'lizards or salamanders'. At the end, we learn just how great the effect on him has been, as he shrieks in vivid nightmares.

There is very good awareness of the context for this reference.

Examiner summary

This part of the answer is typical of grade A performance. This student writes powerfully and with a real grasp of the poet's intentions. Key words from the text are used extremely well to illustrate some detailed analysis, which deals thoughtfully with the way the pilot becomes haunted by memories, despite his initial reaction. The point about the juxtaposing of emotions shows strong engagement with the poet's language.

(b) (i) Compare how the writers of 'August 6, 1945' and **one** poem of your choice from the 'Clashes and Collisions' collection reflect on attitudes to war.

Use **evidence** from the poems to support your answer.

You may include material you used to answer (a).

(15 marks)

Student 1 – Extract typical of a grade C answer

The student makes a relevant choice of quotation to show the people's mounting fears.

I think another interesting poem about war to compare with 'August 6, 1945' is 'Invasion'. Both poems start by looking at a forthcoming attack. However, in 'Invasion', Choman Hardi writes about the views of people in a town or village who are waiting for the fighting to begin, 'first we will hear the sound of their boots'. They imagine the soldiers getting nearer and nearer. Just like 'August 6, 1945', war is shown to destroy lives and lands. War also gives people bad dreams afterwards in both poems as 'will creep into our dreams', and 'later in dreams' show.

This comparison brings out the effects of war, whether conventional or nuclear.

Examiner summary

This part of the answer is typical of grade C performance. The student has justified solidly the choice of 'Invasion' as the comparative poem, and has focused on points of similarity as well as on key differences. The point about nightmares is brought out by quoting the two poems side by side. While in this extract there is comparatively little on the language of 'August 6, 1945', the approach demonstrates a grasp of both poems.

Student 2 – Extract typical of a grade A answer

The candidate shows good awareness of the contrasting forms of the two poems.

'O What is that Sound' at first seems very different from the atomic attack of 'August 6, 1945'. The lone bomber contrasts with the cavalry regiment. Auden builds tension and suspense as a man or woman asks a lover for reassurance about the soldiers' approach, but is betrayed and abandoned. The ominous build-up as the soldiers approach is emphasised by the repetition of key words such as 'drumming, drumming'. Auden uses a ballad form, while Fell uses short, broken lines; both poems focus on the plight of a single victim. The girl in 'August 6, 1945' is just one person caught up in the bomb's fall-out; however, Auden's soldiers are hunting their victim, with the powerful climax 'And their eyes are burning'.

This is a very neatly made point, summarising the context of the two poems well.

Examiner summary

This part of the answer is typical of grade A performance. This student has chosen two poems which look at war in very different ways. The answer includes excellent comparative points, with extremely thoughtful contrasts, while also underlining a key similarity. Although ideas are not completely developed in the extract, the writer has engaged really well with the poem, and sees how important language and form are in conveying intentions.

Comparing Poems

To prepare for your English Literature exam:

- explore specific comparisons and links between Corbett's 'City Jungle' and other poems in this collection, for example the writer's view of city life in 'City Blues', or 'London', or the way the writer presents her ideas in 'Our Town with the Whole of India!'
- practise comparing in detail and evaluating the ways in which two writers express their ideas and achieve effects.

City Jungle *by Pie Corbett*

First thoughts

Activity 1

1. Look again at the title of the poem. What is being described in the poem: a city or a jungle?

2. What general mood and *tone* does the poem create? Is it friendly, threatening or indifferent?

Looking more closely

Activity 2

1. **a.** Make a list of all the *nouns* and *verbs* in the poem.

   b. What do you notice?

2. Corbett has used *personification* throughout the poem. For example, in line 4 he describes the cars as if they are human:

   'Thin headlights stare'

   a. What does the word 'stare' suggest about the cars in this city? Select one of the words below (or one of your own choice):

interested	intimidating	bored	fascinated	aggressive

   b. Pick out three more examples of the writer's use of personification. Note the different ideas that each image suggests and their effect on the reader. Copy and complete the table below.

Example of personification	Ideas it suggests	Effect on the reader?
'Lizard cars cruise by.'	cars as animals, reptilian, smooth and slinky, cold-blooded, unhurried	Perhaps a bit threatening? Or maybe rather self-satisfied and smug? Emphasises jungle atmosphere of predators and prey

3. A *metaphor* describes something *as* something else. The writer of 'City Jungle' uses an *extended metaphor*: he describes the city as a jungle throughout the poem.

   a. Identify three images from the poem in which elements of the city are described as elements of the jungle.

   b. What does each comparison with the jungle suggest about the city? Briefly explain the effect of each image.

Developing your ideas

1. Read the poem aloud and make notes about:
   - the sound of the words in the poem
   - the techniques the writer has used to create these sounds
   - their effect on the reader.

   For example,

   > 'The gutter gargles' uses both personification and onomatopoeia to describe the sound of water in the gutters and drains. The repetition of initial sounds emphasises the actual sound of gurgling / bubbling of water, bringing echoes of jungle sounds to the reader.

   a. Pick out three more lines or phrases from the poem in which you think the sound of the words is as important as their meaning.

   b. What techniques has the writer used to create the sound of the words? (Is it **alliteration**, **onomatopoeia**, **assonance**, **sibilance**, or another technique?)

   c. What effect does each example have on the reader? Hint: think about how it contributes to the mood or atmosphere of the poem.

2. **a.** How would you describe the overall mood or atmosphere of the poem? Select one of the words below (or your own choice):

   miserable   dangerous   unloved   violent   exciting

   b. Write a short paragraph explaining your answer. Remember to support your ideas with evidence from the poem.

Developing your response

1. Look at these lines from the poem:

   'Hunched houses cough.
   Newspapers shuffle by,'

   The words 'hunched', 'cough' and 'shuffle' sound like they are describing people. What might these words suggest is happening to human life in the city?

2. Look at this example of an examination-style question:

   **Explain how Corbett creates an image of the city in 'City Jungle'.
   Use examples from the poem to support your answer.**

   Write one section on Corbett's use of personification and extended metaphor that could be included in your answer.

ResultsPlus
Self/Peer assessment

1. Look at the paragraphs you wrote in Activity 4 and at the mark schemes on pages 166 and 171. Which band would your answer fall into?
2. What could you change or add to improve your answer? Use the mark schemes to identify the two things most likely to improve your mark.
3. Redraft your answer, making these changes.
4. Look again at the mark schemes. Check that your work has moved into a higher band.

Glossary

hunched: bent into a hump

tarmac: a mixture of black tar and broken stone used for making a hard surface on roads

My learning objectives

- to explore and develop my response to 'City Blues' by Mike Hayhoe
- to explain how Hayhoe uses language and form to present alternative images of a city.

Comparing Poems

To prepare for your English Literature exam:

- explore specific comparisons and links between Hayhoe's 'City Blues' and other poems in this collection, for example the writer's view of city life in 'City Jungle', or the way the writers express their feelings in 'Cape Town morning' or 'Sea Timeless Song'
- practise comparing in detail and evaluating the ways in which two writers express their ideas and achieve effects.

City Blues
by Mike Hayhoe

First thoughts
Activity 1

1. Re-read the first line of the poem. Why do you think the writer decided to set his poem at this time, day and month?

2. Look carefully at the unusual *form* of the poem, particularly at the words joined by lines, for example:

/light\
\sun/

   a. What do you notice about the pairs of words linked inside these lines?

   b. Why do you think the writer chose to set out the poem in this way?

Looking more closely
Activity 2

1. List the different things the writer describes. For example:

   the sun rising
   _____
   _____
   _____
   _____

2. **a.** Choose three lines in which pairs of words are linked. Explain briefly the effect of each word on the reader.

   b. For each of the lines you have chosen, decide which of the paired words you prefer and explain why.

3. Throughout the poem, Hayhoe refers to nature. For example in the first six lines he writes about the sun, wind and trees.

   a. Identify all the references to nature in the poem.

   b. Choose three quotations which show how nature is presented in the poem. For example, the sun is described as a 'bully'. What effect do you think the writer is trying to create in each of your chosen quotations?

Developing your ideas
Activity 3

1. Look at these words and phrases taken from the poem:

   - 'wades in'
   - 'not big enough to take it'
   - 'knows its place'

   - 'comes to the point'
   - 'more than can be said / for'
   - 'lousy'

a. Choose one of the words below (or another of your choice) to describe the phrases above:

aggressive   informal   friendly   cruel

b. How do these words and phrases contribute to the mood or atmosphere of the poem?

c. Look at the title of the poem. What does it show about the writer's attitude to the city?

2. Why do you think the writer describes the sun as 'lousy' at the end of the poem? Try to think of at least two possible reasons.

Glossary

napalm: highly flammable liquid used in fire bombs

Developing your response   **Activity 4**

1. Look at these two *metaphors* from the poem.

a. the bully ⟨light / sun⟩ wades in

sets glass aflame

b. A sheet of paper...

⟨floats / flaps⟩ into the sunlight

is a ⟨swan / bird⟩

Is this poem about beauty in the city or cruelty and violence, or all three? Or do you think the poem is about something else altogether? Use the quotations above, and at least one other, to support your ideas.

2. Look at this example of an examination-style question:

Explain how Hayhoe creates images of a city in 'City Blues'.
Use examples from the poem to support your answer.

Write one section on the poet's use of this unusual form that could be included in your answer.

ResultsPlus
Self/Peer assessment

1. Look at the paragraphs you wrote in Activity 4 and at the mark schemes on pages 166 and 171. Which band would your answer fall into?

2. What could you change or add to improve your answer? Use the mark schemes to identify the two things most likely to improve your mark.

3. Redraft your answer, making these changes.

4. Look again at the mark schemes. Check that your work has moved into a higher band.

Postcard from a Travel Snob
by Sophie Hannah

Comparing Poems

To prepare for your English Literature exam:

• explore specific comparisons and links between Hannah's 'Postcard from a Travel Snob' and other poems in this collection, for example the way the writer expresses her feelings in 'My mother's kitchen', or the way the writers present their ideas in 'City Blues' or 'A Major Road for Romney Marsh'

• practise comparing in detail and evaluating the ways in which two writers express their ideas and achieve effects.

First thoughts

Activity 1

1. The poem describes two very different types of holiday.
   a. What general impression do you get of each type of holiday?
   b. Which does the writer seem to prefer?

Looking more closely

Activity 2

1. 'Wish you were here!' is a *cliché* often used on postcards.
   a. How does the writer use cliché in the first line and what effect does it have?
   b. What impression does the first line give of the narrator's character and mood?

2. Look at the following lines:
   • 'When you're as multi-cultural as me,'
   • 'not like your seaside-town-consumer-hell.'

   What information do these lines give us about how the narrator sees herself and how she sees other people?

3. In the first *stanza*, there is a dash in the final line.
   a. Why has the writer used a dash here and what effect does it create?
   b. Pick out two other places where the writer has used a dash. Explain the effect each has.

4. Some of the words and phrases in the poem describe the people that go on the sort of holidays that the narrator dislikes.
   a. Pick out two examples that describe these people and explain how they show the narrator's attitude to them.
   b. The narrator describes herself as 'multi-cultural' and her friends as 'connoisseurs'. What do these words suggest about the narrator's opinion of herself and her friends?
   c. Look at the title of the poem. What is the writer's opinion of the narrator? Remember that the *narrator* or *speaker* of a poem can express a point of view that the *writer* does not necessarily share themselves.

5. Look at the final two lines of the poem. What is the difference between

'a British tourist in the sea'   and

'an anthropologist in trunks'?

(Think about how they might see themselves and also how others might see them.)

Developing your ideas

Activity 3

1. List the words and phrases that describe the two types of holiday in the poem. Try to link up pairs to show the contrast between the two types of holiday. For example:

> 'karaoke nights' can be paired with the contrasting 'peaceful place'.

2. How would you describe the *tone* of the poem? Select one of the words below or choose your own:

pompous   mocking   *ironic*   critical   superior

Give reasons for your answer.

Developing your response

Activity 4

1. Sophie Hannah has said that she really enjoys package holidays and laughs at people who 'go out of their way to have an uncomfortable time'. Why do you think she wrote this poem?

2. Look at this example of an examination-style question:

Explain how Hannah creates attitudes to holidays in 'Postcard from a Travel Snob'.
Use examples from the poem to support your answer.

Write one section on language that could be included in your answer to communicate different attitudes to the theme of holiday destination.

ResultsPlus
Self/Peer assessment

1. Read this paragraph written in response to the task above.

2. Annotate your paragraphs using similar notes to those given on the right. If you've forgotten to include anything in your paragraphs, add it in.

3. Using the mark schemes on pages 166 and 171, decide which band your paragraphs would fall into.

— A clear point

Evidence to support it —

The narrator in the poem contrasts two very different kinds of holiday: 'This place is not a holiday resort / with karaoke nights and pints of beer / for drunken tourist types – perish the thought.' The narrator clearly dislikes and dismisses this kind of package holiday as something for drunken tourists, seeing himself as superior to tourists because he prefers somewhere more 'peaceful' and remote. The final phrase really emphasises how much he despises the idea of a package holiday, and the dash before it creates a pause to give it additional dramatic effect. Hannah seems to be mocking both people who love package holidays and people who hate them.

An explanation of the effect of the quotation

Explores the writer's intention

Close focus on word choice and punctuation

Sea Timeless Song
by Grace Nichols

Comparing Poems

To prepare for your English Literature exam:

- explore specific comparisons and links between Nichol's 'Sea Timeless Song' and other poems in this collection, for example the way the writer presents her ideas in 'Our Town with the Whole of India!', or how the writer reflects on the passing of time in 'The Stone Hare' or the power of nature in 'London Snow'

- practise comparing in detail and evaluating the ways in which two writers express their ideas and achieve effects.

First thoughts

Activity 1

1. Think about words and ideas connected with the sea in the poem.

   a. Which words do you think are particularly effective?

2. Make a list of the linguistic features a poet could use to help with sea imagery.

Looking more closely

Activity 2

1. Why does the writer use so much repetition in the poem? Think about the look and sound of the poem as well as its meaning.

2. Look at the title of the poem. In what ways is this poem like a song? Think about the *form* of the poem and the writer's choice of language.

3. Throughout the poem, Nichols repeats the phrase 'sea timeless'. What effect does this create?

4. There are only four *nouns* in the poem: 'hurricane', 'hibiscus', 'tourist' and 'sea'.

   a. In what way is the sea the 'odd one out' in this poem? Briefly explain your answer.

   b. There are more differences than similarities between a hurricane, a hibiscus plant and a tourist. Why do you think Nichols chose three such different things to structure the three *stanzas* of the poem?

Developing your ideas

1. Look at lines 8 and 9 of the poem:

   'Hibiscus bloom / then dry-wither so'

   Nichols uses a hyphen to join the two words 'dry' and 'wither' forming a *compound word*.

   a. What is the effect of this hyphenation?

   b. How does the compound word contrast with the word 'bloom'?

2. Grace Nichols is originally from Guyana, a small county in the northern coast of South America that is part of the English-speaking Caribbean. Nichols has said that she feels at home both in Guyana and in England, where she now lives. How does this poem connect those two places?

3. *Sea Timeless Song* is written using features of Caribbean *dialect*. For example, if it were written in standard English, the first three lines of the poem might be:

   > Hurricanes come / and hurricanes go / but the sea... the sea is timeless

   Why do you think Nichols chose to write the poem using dialect?

Glossary

hibiscus: a plant from warm or tropical regions known for its bright, flamboyant flowers

Developing your response

1. Look at this example of an examination-style question:

   Explain how Nichols creates her attitudes to nature in 'Sea Timeless Song'. Use examples from the poem to support your answer.

   Write one section that could be included in your answer.

ResultsPlus
Self/Peer assessment

These sentences are all taken from different students' writing in response to the task above.

1. Use some of these sentences, and the mark schemes on pages 166 and 171, to create a paragraph which you think would achieve a high band mark.

2 a. Look again at the paragraphs you wrote in Activity 4. Use the mark schemes to identify the two things most likely to improve your mark.

   b. Redraft your answer, making those changes. Check that your new answer has moved up to the next band.

> In each of the three stanzas, Nichols begins by highlighting elements of her Guyanan culture which are only temporary.

> While much of Guyana life comes and goes with the passing of time, the sea is highlighted as something permanent and eternal.

> She writes about a 'hurricane', the 'Hibiscus bloom', and the 'tourist' trade.

> 'but sea ... sea timeless'. Every stanza ends in the same way, with the same repetition of this phrase suggesting not only the sea's permanence but also the rhythm of its waves and tides.

> Choosing these three varied aspects of Guyanan life suggests that so much of our lives is temporary: the natural violence of the hurricane, the natural beauty of the hibiscus and not only the visits of tourists but the lives of all humans.

> The image of the sea suggests something that connects all lands and all lives.

> Nichols writes using a non-standard Caribbean dialect to reflect her Guyanan culture which is at the heart of this poem.

My learning objectives

- to explore and develop my response to 'My mother's kitchen' by Choman Hardi
- to explain how Hardi uses language and structure to convey her ideas about what makes a home.

My mother's kitchen
by Choman Hardi

Comparing Poems

To prepare for your English Literature exam:

- explore specific comparisons and links between Hardi's 'My mother's kitchen' and other poems in this collection, for example how the writers present their thoughts and feelings on the relationship between people and places in 'London' or 'Orkney / This Life', or the way in which the writer expresses her feelings in 'Postcard from a Travel Snob'
- practise comparing in detail and evaluating the ways in which two writers express their ideas and achieve effects.

First thoughts **Activity 1**

Choman Hardi was born in Iraqi Kurdistan. Her family was forced to move frequently due to political upheavals: from Kurdistan to Iran, back to Iraq, and eventually to the United Kingdom.

1. **a.** Why do you think Hardi has written this poem about her mother's home?

   b. Hardi could have written about any member of her family and any room in the house. Why does she focus on her mother and the kitchen?

2. Do you think Hardi is looking forward to inheriting her mother's kitchen? Explain your answer, briefly.

Looking more closely **Activity 2**

1. The narrator's mother is moving for the ninth time.

   a. Pick out three quotations which show how moving so many times has affected the narrator's mother's life and belongings.

   b. For each quotation, write a sentence or two explaining how each links to her mother's experiences.

   For example:

   suggests they are old, useless

   'rusty pots she can't bear throwing away.'

   suggests there has been so much change and disruption in her life,
   she wants to hang onto anything familiar even if they are useless

2 **a.** List the things which the writer's mother still owns, despite all her moves.

   b. Now list the things which the writer's mother had to leave behind when she moved.

3. Look carefully at the two lists.

   a. Firstly look at the list of things the writer's mother still owns. Write briefly about the way they are described. Use quotations to support your ideas.

   b. Now look at the list of things which were left behind. Write briefly about the way they are described. Remember to use quotations from the poem.

   c. Are there any similarities or differences in the ways in which things from the two lists are described?

Developing your ideas

Activity 3

1. Look at these lines from the first *stanza*:

   "Don't buy anything just yet… soon all of this will be yours."

   a. What does it suggest about how the mother is feeling?

   b. How does it suggest the past experiences of her life have affected her?

2. Now look at these quotations from the second and third stanzas.

   •   'she is excited about
   starting from scratch.
   It is her ninth time.'

   • 'She never talks about her lost furniture'

   • 'She never feels regret for things,
   only for her vine in the front garden'

   Explain briefly what you think each quotation suggests about how the mother feels about her life and past.

3. Re-read the final line of the poem.

   a. Why will the narrator never inherit these trees?

   b. Why do you think Hardi has chosen to end the poem with this image?

Developing your response

Activity 4

1. Select one of the following words (or another of your choice) to describe the mood of this poem:

   depressing   optimistic   reflective   excited   regretful

   Explain your choice of word, using a quotation from the poem to support it.

2. Look at this example of an examination-style question:

   How does Hardi explore the theme of 'Somewhere, anywhere' in this poem? Use examples from the poem to support your answer.

   Write one section on language or structure that could be included in your answer.

ResultsPlus
Self/Peer assessment

1. Look at the paragraphs you wrote in Activity 4 and at the mark schemes on pages 166 and 171. Which band would your answer fall into?

2. What could you change or add to improve your answer? Use the mark schemes to identify the two things most likely to improve your mark.

3. Redraft your answer, making these changes.

4. Look again at the mark schemes. Check that your work has moved into a higher band.

Cape Town morning
by Ingrid de Kok

Comparing Poems

To prepare for your English Literature exam:

• explore specific comparisons and links between de Kok's 'Cape Town morning' and other poems in this collection, for example the way in which the writer presents a picture of city life in 'London', or the ways in which the writers convey their thoughts and feelings in 'Assynt Mountains', or 'Our Town with the Whole of India!'

• practise comparing in detail and evaluating the ways in which two writers express their ideas and achieve effects.

First thoughts
Activity 1

1. The poem describes Cape Town in South Africa. What impression do you get of the city from this poem?

Looking more closely
Activity 2

1. The poem is divided into four *stanzas*. What is the main subject of each stanza? (Hint: look at the key *nouns*.)

2. Look at this line in the first stanza:

   'Window panes rattle old rust,'

   How does this help to create your first impression of Cape Town?

3. In the second stanza the street children are described as

   'shaven mummies in sacks,'

   with 'eyelids weighted by dreams of coins,'

   and 'beneath them treasure of small knives.'

   Briefly explore each quotation. What impression is the reader given of the street children through these images?

4. Look at the third stanza. What impression is the reader given of the flower sellers?

5. Look at the final stanza. Pick out two words used to describe the appearance and action of the trucks. Why do you think the writer has described them in this way?

Developing your ideas

Activity 3

1. **a.** In what season is the poem set?

   b. What does this season usually *symbolise*?

   c. Identify three details from the poem which are either in keeping with or in contrast to our expectations of this season.

   d. What effect does this have on the *tone* of the poem?

2. Some of the language in the poem could be put into matching or contrasting pairs. For example: 'Winter' could be paired with 'Summer'; 'fresh' could be paired with 'sour'.

   a. What other pairings can you pick out?

   b. For each one, write a sentence or two exploring the ideas and the effect that they have on the reader.

Developing your response

Activity 4

1. How would you describe Ingrid de Kok's view of Cape Town? Try to think of at least three different answers, and find a quotation from the poem to support each one.

2. Look at this example of an examination-style question:

   Explain how de Kok creates a view of Cape Town.
   Use examples from the poem to support your answer.

   Write one section on the poet's use of imagery and vocabulary that could be included in your answer.

Glossary

sediment: material that settles to the bottom of a liquid; the dregs

municipal: to do with the government of a town or city

Our Town with the Whole of India! *by Daljit Nagra*

My learning objectives

- to explore and develop my response to 'Our Town with the Whole of India!' by Daljit Nagra
- to evaluate the ways in which Nagra uses language and imagery to explore Indian culture in England.

Comparing Poems

To prepare for your English Literature exam:

- explore specific comparisons and links between Nagra's 'Our Town with the Whole of India!' and other poems in this collection, for example the way the writers present their ideas in 'Sea Timeless Song', 'Cape Town morning' or 'City Jungle'.
- practise comparing in detail and evaluating the ways in which two writers express their ideas and achieve effects.

First thoughts

Activity 1

1. The poem describes the suburb of Southall in West London. What are your first impressions of this place?

2. **a.** What do you notice about the shape of this poem, its length and structure?

   b. Why might Nagra have decided to write the poem in this way?

Looking more closely

Activity 2

1. **a.** What is the first word of each *stanza* and the first word of every sentence in the first stanza?

   b. What is Nagra emphasising by using this word?

2. **a.** Identify all the words in the first stanza which are associated with traditional Indian culture.

   b. Now pick out all the words in the first stanza that are associated with traditional Western culture.

   c. What is the effect of *juxtaposing* words associated with different cultures in this way? What is Nagra suggesting about the differences between the cultures?

3. Look carefully at the second stanza.

   a. Which part of Southall is Nagra describing here?

   b. What do you learn about the different people who live or have lived in Southall?

4. Look carefully at the third stanza.

   a. Make a list of the different things Nagra describes in this stanza.

   b. Without repeating yourself, sum up the image of Southall which Nagra creates in this stanza:
   - in one sentence
   - in three words
   - in one word.

5. Re-read the final three lines of the poem. What is the final image which Nagra leaves us with? Why do you think he chose to do this?

Developing your ideas

1. Look at the phrases below, taken from the third stanza:

   • 'syrup-tunnelled / jalebis'
   • 'familied clumps.'
   • 'point for poled yards of silk'

   a. Briefly explain each phrase. Use the following questions to help you:
      • What does it suggest to you as a reader?
      • What effect might the writer have wanted it to have?
      • How might each phrase help the reader to understand Indian culture within England?

   b. Choose at least three other phrases from the poem which intrigue and appeal to you as a reader. Use the bullet-pointed questions above to help you write briefly about each of your chosen phrases.

Developing your response

1. How do you think Nagra wants to present Indian culture in the United Kingdom? Write four or five sentences, supporting your ideas with quotations from the poem.

2. Look at this example of an examination-style question:

   Explain how Nagra creates an image of an Indian culture within an English town in 'Our Town with the Whole of India!'

   Use examples from the poem to support your answer.

   Write one section on the poet's use of language and imagery that could be included in your answer.

ResultsPlus
Self/Peer assessment

1. Look at the paragraphs you wrote in Activity 4 and at the mark schemes on pages 166 and 171. Which band would your answer fall into?

2. What could you change or add to improve your answer? Use the mark schemes to identify the two things most likely to improve your mark.

3. Redraft your answer, making these changes.

4. Look again at the mark schemes. Check that your work has moved into a higher band.

sundering: breaking

mandirs: Hindu temples

tridents: a three-pronged spear

Vasaikhi: a Sikh harvest festival held in April

Eidh: a Muslim festival

Diwali: a Festival of Light, important in Hinduism and Sikhism, falling in October/November

Odysseus: a hero of Greek mythology who underwent a series of trials on his long journey home from the Trojan Wars

Rama: a Hindu god who spent fourteen years in exile undergoing a series of trials

Penelope: the faithful wife of Odysseus

Sita: the faithful wife of Rama

emporium: a large shop

bhangra: a type of music, begun as a Punjabi Sikh folk dance to celebrate the coming of Spring

sitar: a type of Indian stringed instrument

furbishly: an *adverb* created by the poet and derived from the verb to furbish which means to renovate, polish or modernise

Teddy Boys: the name given to young men in the 1950s who were associated with rock 'n' roll music

saffron: an expensive spice made from the stamens of crocus flowers, used to give food flavour and yellow colour

jalebis: a fried, sticky sweet, traditionally eaten in celebration

karela: bitter melon or bitter gourd

okra: known as 'lady's fingers', a green fruit

posse: a group of people

My learning objectives

- to explore and develop my response to 'In Romney Marsh' by John Davidson
- to explore how Davidson uses form, imagery and language to convey his admiration for Romney Marsh.

Comparing Poems

To prepare for your English Literature exam:

- explore specific comparisons and links between Davidson's 'In Romney Marsh' and other poems in this collection, for example how the writer presents a picture of Romney Marsh in 'A Major Road for Romney Marsh' or the ways in which the writers convey their thoughts and feelings in 'Composed upon Westminster Bridge' or 'Assynt Mountains'
- practise comparing in detail and evaluating the ways in which two writers express their ideas and achieve effects.

In Romney Marsh
by John Davidson

First thoughts

Activity 1

1. Using your first impressions of the poem, describe Romney Marsh to a partner.

2. How does the narrator in the poem feel about Romney Marsh?

Looking more closely

Activity 2

1. **a.** Read the first *stanza* aloud to yourself or a partner. What do you notice about:
   - its structure?
   - its *rhyme scheme*?
   - its *rhythm*?

   b. Is the structure, rhyme scheme and rhythm the same in all the other verses? What effect does this have?

2. Imagine the narrator in the poem walking across Romney Marsh as he describes what he sees and hears. What does the rhythm of the poem suggest to you?

3. Look at the second stanza.
   a. What is the wire which the narrator describes, do you think?
   b. How is it affected by the wind?

4. Throughout the poem, the narrator describes the different colours of the scene.
   a. List all the colours he mentions.
   b. What is the effect of referring to so many different colours?

5. The narrator uses **similes** and **metaphors** to compare different elements of the marshland to things of great value.
   a. Make a list of all these comparisons. What effect do they have?

6. Look at this line from the fourth stanza:

   'The swinging waves pealed on the shore;'

   The word 'pealed' usually describes the ringing of bells.
   a. Why do you think Davidson chose to use this word? Think about occasions when bells are 'pealed'.
   b. How does the word 'swinging' reinforce the image of the waves as ringing bells?

Developing your ideas

1. Compare line 1 of the poem with line 17.

   a. What happens in the narrator's walk across Romney Marsh at line 17, do you think?

   b. Pick out any similarities in the first half of the poem (lines 1–16) and in the second half (lines 17–28).

   c. Choose two specific similarities. Briefly explain how the sights and sounds of Romney Marsh change in the second half of the poem.

2 **a.** List the different sights the narrator sees, then list the sounds he hears. For each sight and sound you have identified, choose one or two words which Davidson uses to describe it. Record your answers in a table like the one below:

Sight	Descriptive word	Sound	Descriptive word
sunlight	yellow	wind	ringing shrilly

   b. Which do you think is more effective in conveying the narrator's experience: the visual or the *aural* descriptions? Write four or five sentences explaining your answer using quotations from the poem to support it.

Developing your response

1. Select a word from the ones listed below (or another of your choice) to describe the mood or atmosphere of the marsh in the poem.

   beautiful   dangerous   noisy   violent   peaceful   dramatic

2. Look at this example of an examination-style question:

   Explain how Davidson creates a picture of Romney Marsh.
   Use examples from the poem to support your answer.

   Write one section on the poet's use of imagery and *form* that could be included in your answer.

ResultsPlus
Self/Peer assessment

1. Read this paragraph written in response to the above task.

2. Annotate your paragraphs using similar notes to those given on the right. If you've forgotten to include anything in your paragraphs, add it in.

3. Using the mark schemes on pages 166 and 171, decide which band your paragraphs would fall into.

— A clear point

Evidence to support it —

Davidson describes a walk across a landscape which he thinks is both beautiful and powerful: 'The saffron beach, all diamond drops / And beads of surge, prolonged the roar.' Davidson creates an image of visual beauty, by describing not only the physical appearance of the beach and waves but also suggesting their immense worth in comparing them to saffron and diamonds. The verb 'roar' contrastingly emphasises the physical power of nature. In this landscape the thoughts and feelings of the narrator are overwhelmed by physical and metaphorical description as though he is lost in the beauty and power of this place.

— An explanation of the effect of the quotation

Explores the writer's intention

Close focus on particular word choice —

Glossary

Romney Marsh: a salt marsh of about 100 square miles in the south-east of England

knolls: small round hills

offing: the area of sea between the shore and the horizon; close by, near

saffron: an expensive spice made from the stamens of crocus flowers, used to give food flavour and yellow colour

A Major Road for Romney Marsh
by U.A. Fanthorpe

My learning objectives

- to explore and develop my response to 'A Major Road for Romney Marsh' by U.A. Fanthorpe
- to explore how Fanthorpe uses form and language to persuade readers against the planned developments in Romney Marsh.

Comparing Poems

To prepare for your English Literature exam:

- explore specific comparisons and links between Fanthorpe's 'A Major Road for Romney Marsh' and other poems in this collection, for example the way the writer presents a picture of Romney Marsh in 'In Romney Marsh', the way the writer presents her ideas in 'Sea Timeless Song', or how the writer explores the relationship between man and nature in 'City Blues'
- practise comparing in detail and evaluating the ways in which two writers express their ideas and achieve effects.

First thoughts

Activity 1

1. What are your first impressions of Romney Marsh from this poem?
2. What is the writer's attitude to the major road that is planned for Romney Marsh?

Looking more closely

Activity 2

1. Fanthorpe describes the Marsh as:

   'a kingdom, a continent.'

   What does the writer's choice of language suggest about her view of this place?

2. Look at lines 4–6. Pick out the words and phrases which create an image of Romney Marsh in your mind. Briefly describe each one.

3. Some of the lines in the poem are enclosed in brackets and aligned on the right of the page.

   a. What is the difference between the lines in brackets and those not in brackets?

   b. Why do you think Fanthorpe has set the poem out in this way?

   c. Which point of view do you think Fanthorpe agrees with? Explain your answer.

4. In line 18, Fanthorpe uses abbreviations to refer to three cities near Romney Marsh: T'DEN (Tenterden), F'STONE (Folkestone) and C'BURY (Canterbury).

   a. Identify the other abbreviations in the poem and write them out in full.

   b. What do these abbreviations suggest about:
   - the narrator's attitude to Romney Marsh?
   - Fanthorpe's view of the narrator's attitude?

Developing your ideas

1. Look at these phrases taken from the poem:

   - 'obstinate hermit trees.'
   - 'truculent churches'
   - 'the Military Canal
     Minding its peaceable business,'

   a. Comment on the effect of each of the highlighted words.

   b. How do these language choices contribute to our overall impression of Romney Marsh?

2. The voice in *parentheses* repeats the phrase 'It wants' each time it speaks. What does this suggest about the voice's attitude to the Marsh?

3. Fanthorpe uses *alliteration* and repetition in lines 4 to 8. How do these techniques help to convey the writer's views on Romney Marsh?

Glossary

Romney Marsh: a salt marsh of about 100 square miles in the south-east of England

Happy Eaters: a fast food 'chain' like McDonalds

truculent: aggressively resisting authority

Kwiksaves: supermarkets

artics: articulated lorries

Levels: a large flat area of land in Romney Marsh, crossed by drainage ditches

Developing your response

1. How would you describe the two different voices in the poem? Select from the words below or come up with your own choice.

naive	conservationist	environmentalist	sympathetic	hostile

greedy	relentless	threatening	romantic	in favour of progress

2. Look at this example of an examination-style question:

   Explain how Fanthorpe creates different attitudes to Romney Marsh. Use examples from the poem to support your answer.

   Write one section on the poet's use of *form* and language that could be included in your answer.

ResultsPlus
Self/Peer assessment

1. Look at the paragraphs you wrote in Activity 4 and at the mark schemes on pages 166 and 171. Which band would your answer fall into?

2. What could you change or add to improve your answer? Use the mark schemes to identify the two things most likely to improve your mark.

3. Redraft your answer, making these changes.

4. Look again at the mark schemes. Check that your work has moved into a higher band.

My learning objectives

- to explore and develop my response to 'Composed upon Westminster Bridge' by William Wordsworth
- to explore how Wordsworth uses language, literary devices and form to express his feelings on the view of London from Westminster Bridge.

Comparing Poems

To prepare for your English Literature exam:

- explore specific comparisons and links between Wordsworth's 'Composed upon Westminster Bridge' and other poems in this collection, for example the writer's view of the city in 'London', the writer's attitude to city life in 'City Jungle', or the ways in which the writer presents a picture of a particular place in 'In Romney Marsh'

- practise comparing in detail and evaluating the ways in which two writers express their ideas and achieve effects.

Composed upon Westminster Bridge, September 3, 1802
by William Wordsworth

First thoughts

Activity 1

1. **a.** What is being described in the poem?
   b. What time of day is this poem describing?

2. Wordsworth was one of the Romantic writers. They often wrote about the beauty of nature. For example, Wordsworth wrote this poem about daffodils:

> **Daffodils**
> I wander'd lonely as a cloud
> That floats on high o'er vales and hills,
> When all at once I saw a crowd,
> A host, of golden daffodils;
> Beside the lake, beneath the trees,
> Fluttering and dancing in the breeze.

   a. In what way might Wordsworth's choice of subject in 'Composed upon Westminster Bridge' be surprising?
   b. In what way is his use of language and description less surprising?

Looking more closely

Activity 2

1. Look at these three extracts from the poem:

   - 'Earth has not anything to show more fair:'
   - 'Dull would he be of soul who could pass by
     A sight so touching in its majesty;'
   - 'Never did sun more beautifully steep
     In his first splendour, valley, rock, or hill;'

   For each one, write a sentence explaining what you think Wordsworth means. Use the glossary opposite to help you.

2. Look at line 6. What is the effect of this list of everything that Wordsworth can see?

3. In lines 9 and 10, Wordsworth compares this view of London to a view of the countryside. What is the effect of this?

4. How does Wordsworth feel at the end of the poem? Choose a quotation from the poem to support your answer.

Developing your ideas

1. Think about how Wordsworth described London in 1803. Might a writer use any of the same language or images to describe London today?

2. Wordsworth uses *personification* throughout the poem. Copy and complete the table below. Find the relevant quotation for each aspect of the city, then add your thoughts on the effect of this personification. An example has already been completed to help you.

Aspect of city personified	What it does	Effect
The city (line 4)	Wears the morning 'like a garment'	Sounds like a woman in a beautiful dress
The sun (line 9)		
The river (line 12)		
The houses (line 13)		
The city as a whole (line 14)		

3. Think about Wordsworth's emotions as he looks at London. How does he convey what he feels to the reader? Think about:
   - the use of exclamation marks in the poem
   - the use of personification
   - the imagery at the end of the poem
   - anything else which gives you a sense of the writer's emotions.

Developing your response

1. 'Composed upon Westminster Bridge' is a *sonnet* – a poem with fourteen lines and a regular *rhyme scheme*, often about love. Why do you think Wordsworth chose this form for his poem?

2. Look at this example of an examination-style question:

   How does Wordsworth's 'Composed upon Westminster Bridge' convey a sense of place?
   Use examples from the poem to support your answer.

   Write one section on the poet's use of imagery, language and *form* that could be included in your answer.

ResultsPlus
Self/Peer assessment

1. Read this paragraph written in response to the task above.

2. Annotate your paragraphs using similar notes to those given on the right. If you've forgotten to include anything in your paragraphs, add it in.

3. Using the mark schemes on pages 166 and 171, decide which band your paragraphs would fall into.

— A clear point ————————————————— Evidence to support it —

Throughout the poem, Wordsworth sounds more as if he is describing a natural landscape than a city: 'Never did sun more beautifully steep / In his first splendour, valley, rock or hill'. Wordsworth is emphasising that London on this morning is equally as beautiful as any landscape. The word 'splendour' emphasises not only the beauty of the view but Wordsworth's reaction to it: he seems truly moved by its beauty and wants the reader, if they are not 'dull... of soul', to respond in the same way to the poem.

— An explanation of the effect of the quotation   — Explores the writer's intention   — Close focus on particular word choice

Glossary

fair: beautiful
majesty: regal, being dignified and imposing, stately
doth: does
steep: to soak or immerse
ne'er: never

Comparing Poems

To prepare for your English Literature exam:

- explore specific comparisons and links between Blake's 'London' and other poems in this collection, for example the writer's view of the city in 'Composed upon Westminster Bridge', the ways in which the writer presents his ideas in 'City Jungle', or how the writer presents his thoughts and feelings on the relationship between people and places in 'Orkney / This Life'

- practise comparing in detail and evaluating the ways in which two writers express their ideas and achieve effects.

London
by William Blake

First thoughts   Activity 1

1. Write a list of words that could be used to describe Blake's feelings about London.

2. In the first *stanza*, Blake writes about the streets, the river and people's faces in London. Note down the different aspects of city life which Blake describes in the rest of the poem.

3. Why do you think Blake writes about so many different aspects of the city and its people?

Looking more closely   Activity 2

1. Most of the language in the poem is very negative.

   a. Write down the five most negative words in the poem.

   b. Why has Blake used the words 'youthful' and 'newborn' in the poem?

2. Look at these lines from the first stanza:

   'And mark in every face I meet
   Marks of weakness, marks of woe.'

   a. What effect does London life seem to be having on the people who live there?

   b. Read these two lines aloud. Think about the words Blake has used and their sound. Which poetic techniques has Blake used to make these two lines stand out for the reader?

   c. Find other examples in the poem where poetic techniques are used to affect the sound of the peom. Explain their effect on the reader.

3. Look carefully at the third stanza.

   a. How does Blake describe the following:

   - a chimney sweep
   - a soldier
   - the Church
   - a palace?

   b. Look at each description in turn. What is Blake suggesting about each of these people and places?

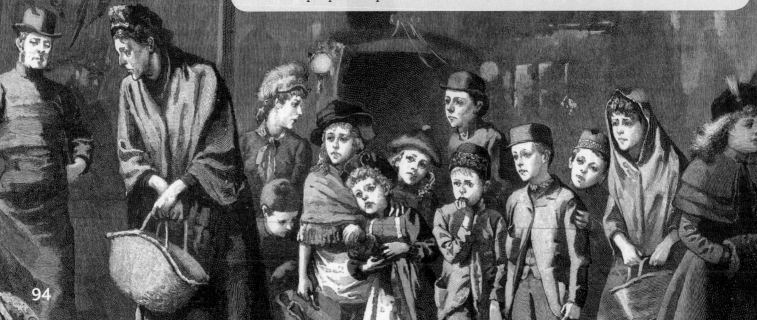

Developing your ideas

Activity 3

1. In the final stanza, Blake writes about a new-born infant and about marriage.

   a. What point is Blake trying to make in the final stanza, do you think?

   b. Why do you think Blake chose to place these two images at the end of the poem?

2. Look at this phrase from the second stanza:

   'mind forg'd manacles'

   a. In what ways are the people of the city imprisoned?

   b. How could these manacles be 'mind forg'd'?

Developing your response

Activity 4

1. Blake seems to be horrified by the city of London.

   a. Who or what do you think he holds most responsible for the problems he describes and who do you think are the main victims?

   b. Find evidence from the poem to support at least three of your choices.

2. Look at this example of an examination-style question:

   Explain how Blake conveys his attitude to the poor in London.
   Use examples from the poem to support your answer.

   Write one section on the poet's use of imagery and language that could be included in your answer.

Glossary

charter'd: charted or mapped; also suggests they are under the control of the wealthy

woe: sorrow or misfortune

manacles: chains or handcuffs

appalls: fills with horror

hapless: having no luck

harlot: a prostitute

blights: spoils

hearse: a vehicle for taking a coffin to a funeral

ResultsPlus
Self/Peer assessment

These sentences are all taken from different students' writing in response to the task above.

1. Use some of these sentences, and the mark schemes on pages 166 and 171, to create a paragraph which you think would achieve a high band mark.

2 **a.** Look again at the paragraphs you wrote in Activity 4. Use the mark schemes to identify the two things most likely to improve your mark.

   b. Redraft your answer, making those changes. Check that your new answer has moved up to the next band.

> Blake is appalled by the city of London.

> Even the most innocent are vulnerable in this terrible place.

> Throughout the poem, Blake describes what he sees and hears in the most negative language.

> The contrast of our expectations and Blake's description emphasises just how degraded these people are.

> Blake describes a huge variety of the city's sights, sounds, places and people.

> Blake's use of repetition not only emphasises his point but the relentlessness of the degradation suffered by the people of London.

> 'And mark in every face I meet / Marks of weakness, marks of woe.'

> 'the youthful Harlot's curse / Blasts the new-born Infant's tear'

> Blake focuses our attention on the most innocent and vulnerable in society.

London Snow
by Robert Bridges

First thoughts | Activity 1

1. How does London react to the snowfall described in the poem? Pick out five words that show the range of different effects that the snow has on people and their lives.

2. Read aloud the first four lines of the poem. What do you notice about:
   • the *rhyme scheme*
   • the use of *alliteration*
   • the use of *onomatopoeia* in these lines?

Looking more closely | Activity 2

1. At what time of day did the snow fall on London? Why is this important in the poem?

2. Look at lines 1–9 of 'London Snow'. Pick out at least two ways in which the snow affected the city when it first fell.

3. On line 14, the 'strange unheavenly glare' of this morning is described. In what way is this light 'unheavenly?' Try to think of two or three possible explanations.

4. On lines 19–24, Bridges describes a group of boys playing in the snow. How does he convey their excitement?

5. Look at line 31:

   'doors open, and war is waged with the snow;'

   a. Who is Bridges referring to here?
   b. In what way are they waging war with the snow?

6. In the last line of the poem, Bridges refers to people and
   'the charm they have broken.'

   What do you think he means?

7. What do you think are the four most striking or memorable images in the poem?
   a. Choose a quotation to illustrate each one.
   b. Explain briefly how Bridges has made each image striking or memorable.

   Write your answers in a table like the one below.

Quotation	Effect
'When men were all asleep the snow came flying.'	The contrast of the people being still and quiet in their sleep with the snow flying in makes the snow seem as if it is being rather sneaky, full of energy and mischief.

My learning objectives

• to explore and develop my response to 'London Snow' by Robert Bridges
• to explain how Bridges uses language and form to convey how snowfall transforms the appearance and atmosphere of a familiar place.

Comparing Poems

To prepare for your English Literature exam:

• explore specific comparisons and links between Bridges' 'London Snow' and other poems in this collection, for example the ways in which the writers present their attitude towards London in 'Composed upon Westminster Bridge' or 'London', or the ways in which the writer reflects on the power of nature in 'Sea Timeless Song'

• practise comparing in detail and evaluating the ways in which two writers express their ideas and achieve effects.

Developing your ideas

Activity 3

1. Look closely at the *verbs* Bridges uses in lines 1–9 of 'London Snow'. For example:

   'flying'   'falling'   'settling'

   'muffling'   'stifling'   'lying'

   'hushing'   'deadening'

   a. What do you notice?

   b. Pick out any other similar verbs in the poem.

   c. What effect has Bridges created?

2. Look closely at the *adverbs* Bridges uses in the same lines, for example:

   'stealthily'   'perpetually'   'loosely'   'lazily'   'incessantly'

   a. Pick out any other adverbs in the poem.

   b. What image of the snow is created by these adverbs?

3. Re-read the poem, picking out examples of images which use one of the five senses to create a feeling of place and atmosphere. Copy and complete a table like the one below, noting the sense used (sight, sound, smell, taste, touch), the specific image and its effect.

Sense	Image from the poem	How it builds up a sense of place and atmosphere
Sight	'Large white flakes falling on the city brown,'	The writer describes how the snow slowly transforms the city from its usual ordinary brown appearance, to its new pure white image.

Developing your response

Activity 4

1. Look again at the last two lines of the poem. How do they reflect the attitudes and feelings that Bridges explores in the rest of the poem?

2. Look at this example of an examination-style question:

   Explain how Bridges creates images of a snowfall in a city in 'London Snow'.
   Use examples from the poem to support your answer.

   Write one section on the poet's use of language that appeals to the senses and evokes a sense of awe that could be included in your answer.

ResultsPlus
Self/Peer assessment

1. Look at the paragraphs you wrote in Activity 4 and at the mark schemes on pages 166 and 171. Which band would your answer fall into?

2. What could you change or add to improve your answer? Use the mark schemes to identify the two things most likely to improve your mark.

3. Redraft your answer, making these changes.

4. Look again at the mark schemes. Check that your work has moved into a higher band.

My learning objectives

- to explore and develop my response to 'Assynt Mountains' by Mandy Haggith
- to explore how Haggith uses extended metaphor to create a picture of a distinctive landscape

Comparing Poems

To prepare for your English Literature exam:

- explore specific comparisons and links between Haggith's 'Assynt Mountains' and other poems in this collection, for example the ways in which the writer presents his thoughts and feelings about a particular place in 'In Romney Marsh', 'City Jungle' or 'Cape Town morning'
- practise comparing in detail and evaluating the ways in which two writers express their ideas and achieve effects.

Assynt Mountains
by Mandy Haggith

First thoughts

Activity 1

1. Identify any words or phrases in the poem which suggest this is a poem describing a range of mountains in the far north of Scotland.

2. Think of an alternative title for the poem that does not use any *proper nouns*.

Looking more closely

Activity 2

1. The poem is written using two *extended metaphors*: describing the mountains as if they were something else. Look at this phrase taken from the poem:

   'rugs on knees'

   This phrase could suggest smooth flat ledges a little way up the mountain covered with snow or with trees. What image of the mountains does it create in your mind?

2. Look carefully at other key phrases taken from the poem:
   - 'the row of crones'
   - 'the coalfire dawn'
   - 'Canisp, nearest the blaze, grins'
   - 'between blackened stumps'
   - 'ancient Lewisian gums'

   What does each phrase contribute to the picture that the poem builds up in the reader's mind?

3 a. What two different things are the mountains compared to in the poem?

   b. How are these two things connected?

   c. What does this suggest about the Assynt Mountains?

Developing your ideas

1. Why do you think Canisp might be described as grinning?

2. Look at the central, single line of the poem. Why do you think that Haggith set the poem out in this way? What effect do you think Haggith wanted this to have?

3. Do you think Haggith's use of imagery in the poem is effective? Briefly explain your answer, using evidence from the poem.

Developing your response

1. Does the poem give any clues to the writer's feelings about Assynt Mountains? Use quotations from the poem to support your answer.

2. Look at this example of an examination-style question:

   Explain how Haggith describes a mountain range in 'Assynt Mountains'. Use examples from the poem to support your answer.

   Write one section on the poet's use of *metapor* and imagery that could be included in your answer.

Glossary

Assynt: a region of natural beauty in north-west Scotland

crones: old women

Canisp: one of the mountains in the Assynt mountain range

Lewisian: the Lewisians are a collection of metamorphic and igneous rocks, which are the oldest rocks in the British Isles. They are in north-west Scotland, where Assynt parish is located

ResultsPlus
Self/Peer assessment

These sentences are all taken from different students' writing in response to the task above.

1. Use some of these sentences, and the mark schemes on pages 166 and 171, to create a paragraph which you think would achieve a high band mark.

2 **a.** Look again at the paragraphs you wrote in Activity 4. Use the mark schemes to identify the two things most likely to improve your mark.

   b. Redraft your answer, making those changes. Check that your new answer has moved up to the next band.

> Haggith describes the mountains as if they were elderly women. Every feature of physical description in the poem is presented as a metaphor.

> Describing the mountains as old women makes them sound like giants or ogres, taking this landscape out of the everyday and into a world of mythology.

> Haggith is emphasising the way that time has changed and aged this landscape.

> The word 'crone' suggests something ancient, perhaps even magical about the mountains – but with their rugs on their knees in front of the fire, there is also something harmless, almost friendly, about these decrepit old women.

> Haggith uses an extended metaphor to describe the mountains.

> The 'blackened stumps' suggests not only trees perhaps growing on the mountain but also rotten teeth.

Orkney / This Life
by Andrew Greig

First thoughts

Activity 1

1. The writer wrote this poem to reflect on and explore why Orkney is so important to him. List some of the reasons he gives.

2. From your first impression of the poem, name three things that seem to be important in the writer's life. Use evidence from the poem to support your ideas.

Looking more closely

Activity 2

1. Re-read the first *stanza*. What impressions are you given of Orkney? Briefly explain your ideas.

2. Look again at the second stanza.
   a. Who do you think the narrator is talking to here?
   b. How would you describe their relationship? Use a quotation from the poem to support your ideas.

3. In the third stanza, the narrator gives us a hint of what it is like to live in the community of Orkney. What impressions does it give you of life on the island?

4. Variations of the phrase 'It is the way...' are used throughout the poem. What effect does the repeated use of this phrase create?

5. The title of the poem suggests that there is a strong connection between Orkney and the writer's life.
   a. Which of the three stanzas are about Orkney and which are about the writer's life?
   b. Write a sentence to sum up each stanza.

6. What do you think are the key themes of 'Orkney/This life'? Select some of the ideas below or others of your choice:

Orkney	love	life	death	community	travel	the natural world

Developing your ideas

1. Look at the quotations below and the first annotation:

    A 'each face coming away with a hint / of the other's face pressed in it.'

    This suggests how close the people on the island are and how closely the sea, the sky and the people of Orkney are connected.

    B 'as if / we are each other's prevailing;'

    C 'a clatter of white whoops and rises ... '

    D 'we enter friends' houses / to leave what we came with,'

    E 'an empty arch against the sky / where birds fly through instead of prayers,'

    a. Copy and annotate quotations B to E, explaining what each suggests about Orkney and the writer's life. You may feel some quotations have more than one interpretation.

    b. Briefly explain the possible effects of each image on the reader.

Developing your response

1. Think about the title of this collection: 'Somewhere, anywhere'.

    a. How do you think this poem fits in with the theme of the collection?

    b. What other poems in the collection does it remind you of? Briefly explain your choices.

2. Look at this example of an examination-style question:

    Explain how Greig conveys his relationship with Orkney in the poem. Use examples from the poem to support your answer.

    Write one section on Orkney, its natural setting and the writer's own life that could be included in your answer.

ResultsPlus
Self/Peer assessment

1. Look at the paragraphs you wrote in Activity 4 and at the mark schemes on pages 166 and 171. Which band would your answer fall into?

2. What could you change or add to improve your answer? Use the mark schemes to identify the two things most likely to improve your mark.

3. Redraft your answer, making these changes.

4. Look again at the mark schemes. Check that your work has moved into a higher band.

Orkney: a large group of islands off the north-east tip of Scotland

prevailing: the wind direction that is the strongest and most frequent

Hoy Sound: a narrow stretch of sea

My learning objectives

- to explore and develop my response to 'The Stone Hare' by Gillian Clarke
- to explain how Clarke uses language and form to explore the relationship between a beautiful object and the earth.

Comparing Poems

To prepare for your English Literature exam:

- explore specific comparisons and links between Clarke's 'The Stone Hare' and other poems in this collection, for example how the writer reflects on the passing of time in 'Sea Timeless Song', or the ways in which the writers present their ideas in 'Assynt Mountains', or 'Composed upon Westminster Bridge'

- practise comparing in detail and evaluating the ways in which two writers express their ideas and achieve effects.

The Stone Hare
by Gillian Clarke

First thoughts
Activity 1

1. Why has it taken 'three hundred million years' for the stone hare to come into existence?

Looking more closely
Activity 2

1. Re-read the first three lines of the poem.
   a. Which words describe the sculpture in its present form?
   b. Which words describe the sculpture three hundred million years ago?
   c. Why was it not yet stone, but only a 'premonition of stone', do you think?

2. Look at this quotation:

   > 'a moonlit reef
   > where corals reach for the light through clear
   > waters of warm Palaeozoic seas.'

   Why do you think Clarke is describing this scene of ocean life from 300 million years ago?

3. Look at lines 6–11. What does the poem tell the reader about how limestone is formed and how the hare was created? You could write your answer in a flowchart:

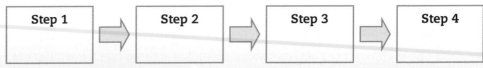

Step 1	Step 2	Step 3	Step 4

4. Look closely at line 6:

   'In its limbs lies the story of the earth,'

   Why does Clarke see the creation of the hare as the same thing as 'the story of the earth'?

5. Why do you think that Clarke describes the hare's eye as 'a planet'? Write down as many possible explanations as you can.

Developing your ideas

Activity 3

1. Look at the last word of each line. Some lines are connected with *rhyme* (lines 6 and 7, for example) and some are connected with *assonance* (lines 2 and 3, for example).

   a. Make a note of the poem's *rhyme scheme*.

   b. What is the effect of the full rhyme in the last two lines of the poem?

2. Look at the final image in the poem:

   'the stems of sea lilies slowly turned into stone.'

   Why does Clarke focus on this particular image of sea life at the end?

3. The hare is often seen as a symbol of spring and new life. Why do you think Clarke chose a hare as the focus for this poem?

4. A *sonnet* is a fourteen-line poem often expressing the writer's love or admiration. Why do you think Clarke chose the sonnet form for this poem?

Glossary

premonition: an impression or foretelling of a future event

Palaeozoic: literally, 'ancient life'; an era of time between around 550 and 250 million years ago

trajectories: the paths that moving objects follow as they travel through space

feather stars/crinoids: marine animals

calcite: a mineral

Developing your response

Activity 4

1. There are two references to moonlight in the poem (lines 3 and 13). Try to make a connection between the two references. What effect do the images create?

2. Look at this example of an examination-style question:

   Explain how Clarke explores ideas of change and continuity in 'The Stone Hare'. Use examples from the poem to support your answer.

   Write one section on the poet's use of *form* and imagery that could be included in your answer.

ResultsPlus
Self/Peer assessment

1. Read this paragraph written in response to the task above.

2. Annotate your paragraphs using similar notes to those on the right. If you've forgotten to include anything in your paragraphs, add it in.

3. Using the mark schemes on pages 166 and 171, decide which band your paragraphs would fall into.

— A clear point

Evidence to support it —

In 'The Stone Hare', Clarke makes a connection between the sculpture of the hare and the history of the planet itself: 'In its limbs lies the story of the earth'. The poem makes us think about, not the hare itself, but the material from which it is made: the 'living ocean' which, over millions of years, has been transformed into stone. So, in the final couplet of the *sonnet*, Clarke connects the 'muscle and bone' of the hare which the sculpture represents, and the life from which the stone was made. Again Clarke emphasises her focus on the stone, not the hare: the final couplet ends on the emphatic rhyme of 'stone': the end product of millions of years of history.

— An explanation of the effect of the quotation

Explores the writer's intention

Close focus on form —

Comparing the 'Somewhere, anywhere' poems

My learning objective

• to make specific comparisons between two poems supported with evidence and to evaluate the writers' techniques.

When you compare two poems, it can be helpful to think about three different areas:

• Language: the words, images or techniques (such as simile or metaphor) used
• Structure: the shape, rhyme and rhythm of the poem
• Viewpoint: the writer's attitude to the subject of the poem

Read the poems 'Cape Town Morning' and 'London Snow', then complete the activities below.

ResultsPlus
Examiner tip

The comparison answer is worth 15 marks (out of 50 for the whole unit). The whole exam lasts 1 hour and 45 minutes so make sure you spend an appropriate amount of time answering the comparison question.

Making comparisons and links between poems   Activity 1

1. Look again at 'Cape Town Morning' and then answer the following questions:
   a. Is the writer's attitude to this place positive or negative?
   b. Does the writer focus on the place or the people who live there?
   c. Is the poem simply descriptive or is the writer making a point?
2. Look again at 'London Snow' and then answer the same questions.
3. Write one sentence about each poem, summing up what the poem is about and the writer's attitude to this place.

Evaluating ways of expressing meaning and achieving effects   Activity 2

1. a. All the words below are taken from the poem 'Cape Town Morning'. Choose one word that sums up the writer's viewpoint.

| rust | summer | treasure | knives | fresh | sour | sediment | jaws |

   b. All the words below are taken from the poem 'London Snow'. Choose one word that sums up the writer's viewpoint.

| hushing | deadening | marvelled | stillness | wonder | war | beauty | broken |

   c. Compare the words you have chosen to sum up each poet's viewpoint. What do you notice?

2. a. Compare the shape and structure of the two poems by writing a sentence or two for each of the bullets below:
   • compare the length of the two poems
   • compare the use of stanzas
   • compare the length of the lines in each poem
   • compare the use or lack of rhyme.

   b. For each poem, choose **one** effect from the list of possible effects on the reader below and on page 107 that most closely matches your personal response. Then, for each poem, write one or two sentences explaining the features that create the effect you have chosen.
   • Suggests a series of scenes: snapshots of life in the city.
   • Creates a sense of how fractured and separate the people of this city and their lives are.
   • Suggests the whole city is connected and unified.

- Reflects what the poem is about.
- Suggests that everyone and everything in the city is affected.

Selecting appropriate examples
Activity 3

1. Copy and complete the grid below to help you compare the two poems:

	Language	Structure	Viewpoint
Cape Town Morning	Decay and deprivation Quotation:	A series of snapshots: a fractured society Quotation:	Quotation:
London Snow	Wonder and beauty – but spoilt by people Quotation:	Quotation:	Quotation:

2. **a.** Look at this quotation from 'Cape Town Morning':
   > yesterday's blooms, sour buckets /
   > filled and spilling.

   b. Now look at your completed grid. Which of your points do you think this quotation supports? Add the quotation to your grid.

   c. Choose five more quotations from the poems: one to support each of the three areas in each of the poems.

Putting it into practice
Activity 4

1. Look at the paragraphs below written in response to the examination-style question:

Explain how the writer of 'London Snow' presents different thoughts and feelings about a city from those given in 'Cape Town Morning'.

— A clear point   Evidence to support it —

'London Snow' describes a time when snow transformed the city.

'Silently sifting and veiling road, roof and railing; Hiding difference, making unevenness even' —

It is as if the snow has covered the city's differences and flaws, unifying its landscape and its people as they come out to enjoy and wonder at its beauty. The writer reflects this in the relentless rhyme and rhythm of the poem, making it seem unstoppable in its one long stanza.

However, in 'Cape Town Morning' we are presented with four very different images of city life.

'trucks digest the city's sediment
Men gloved and silent
In the municipal jaws'

This negative image suggests a town filled with rubbish, and monsters roaming the streets devouring not only the rubbish but the men themselves in its 'jaws'. Like 'London Snow', the writer reflects her viewpoint through the structure of the poem: four disconnected snapshots in four disconnected stanzas suggest a broken and decaying society.

— An explanation of the   Words and phrases   Exploration of the —   Close focus on language, —
effect of the quotation   to show comparison   writer's intention   structure or tone

2. Now try writing four paragraphs giving your response to a different examination-style question:

Explain how the writers of 'London' and 'Upon Westminster Bridge' offer different pictures of life in the city.

Use the same structure as in the paragraphs above.

3. Annotate your paragraphs using the same annotations as above. If you've forgotten to include anything in your paragraphs, add it in.

4. Using the mark schemes on pages 166 and 171, decide which band your paragraphs would fall into.

Build better answers

Here are some extracts from student answers to Higher Tier English Literature examination questions. Read the answers together with the examiner comments to help you understand what you need to do to build better answers.

> (a) Explore how the writer presents her thoughts and feelings about Cape Town in 'Cape Town morning'.
>
> Use **evidence** from the poem to support your answer.
>
> **(15 marks)**

Student 1 – Extract typical of a grade C answer

The student shows a grasp of the context of the poem and the writer's intentions.

The writer of this poem is saying that Cape Town is a city with big problems. She does this by presenting some pictures of the less attractive side of the city. The reference to 'street children' makes us see that there are some very poor children who do not have homes and who live a life full of fear, as it mentions a 'treasure of small knives' which they keep to protect themselves. Even the picture of the 'flower sellers' is not a beautiful one as it talks about 'sour buckets' and 'yesterday's blooms'.

This would need to be developed more fully for a higher grade response, but the point is securely made.

Examiner summary

This part of the answer is typical of grade C performance. The student has shown understanding of the way in which the writer presents her ideas in the poem. The student comments on appropriate features of the writer's language, although for a higher grade the explanation of these examples would need to be developed more fully. The student's comments are focused and based on a secure reading of the poem.

Student 2 – Extract typical of a grade A answer

This is a convincing explanation of the writer's use of language, and is well supported.

The city of Cape Town is often thought of as beautiful, with many rich people living in gated mansions. Ingrid de Kok shows us another side, squalid and unglamorous. Even the approach of summer is shown through the sound of the wind rattling on 'old rust'. The 'street children' are described through powerful imagery. Fear and death are all around. 'Shaven mummies in sacks' recalls the Egyptian dead, and 'eyelids weighted by dreams of coins' shows children so poor they lack even the coins to place on the eyes of the dead. Knives, to protect themselves, are their only 'treasure'. The picture of the morning street-cleaners is similarly stark: the dustcarts are personified as monsters that live on the city's filth.

The student has picked up well on the idea of the dust carts as mechanical monsters, through the writer's choice of vocabulary.

Examiner summary

This part of the answer is typical of grade A performance. There is ample evidence that the student fully grasps de Kok's purposes. There are several apt quotations, and these are commented on in a way that indicates an appreciation of the writer's language and an ability to focus closely on particular references, in this case from mythology.

(b) (i) Compare how the writers explore different thoughts and feelings about towns in 'Our Town with the Whole of India!' and 'Cape Town morning'.

Use **evidence** from the poems to support your answer.

You may include material you used to answer (a).

(15 marks)

Student 1 – Extract typical of a grade C answer

> The student has made a straightforward contrast between the poems, providing a suitable start to the answer.

The writer of 'Cape Town morning' shows scenes of poverty and ugliness. However, Daljit Nagra writes in 'Our Town...' about the people and scenes of a town with colourful celebrations of Indian culture in England.

The writing contains unusual words and colourful sights bringing a new way of life to the English town, replacing Western objects and fashions with things from India. The title's exclamation mark shows the writer's positive feelings about the exciting smells and sights, especially the description of the café which has 'brass woks frying flamingo-pink syrup-tunnelled jalebis'. The language has lots of Indian references. This contrasts with the quiet of the Cape Town morning, with sleeping children and men who are working 'gloved and silent'.

> Focusing on the use of punctuation is justified – exclamation marks are indeed inserted to show emotion.

Examiner summary

This part of the answer is typical of grade C performance. It is focused and makes a number of appropriate points, basing the comments securely on the text. This extract focuses mainly on 'Our Town...', but it does show the student's ability to make comparisons. There is control of language and subject matter, indicating that the answer as a whole is likely to offer a reasonable interpretation of the two poems.

Student 2 – Extract typical of a grade A answer

> This is an extremely well made point about de Kok's writing, showing very good interpretation.

Daljit Nagra creates an array of sights, smells and sounds, with richly varied language. Ingrid de Kok shows detachment and economy of language, contrasting strongly with the sense of belonging in 'Our town...!' Cape Town has an unpleasant side which the writer wishes to highlight, but Nagra embraces the multicultural diversity even when incongruous or ugly: 'bloodied men sling out skinned legs...'. The subdued silence of Cape Town's morning contrasts with the packed streets of Nagra's bustling, colourful town. The first stanza is particularly striking in its commentary on the religious buildings ('temples, mandirs and mosques'), festivals ('Eidh' and 'Diwali') and myths, where Rama's and Sita's story is subtly interwoven with the Western legend of Odysseus and Penelope.

> This demonstrates an excellent grasp of the allusions and juxtapositions of East and West.

Examiner summary

This part of the answer is typical of grade A performance. This student writes successfully on the poems, making comparative points that demonstrate an extremely good interpretation. The focus on the first stanza, with the religious and mythological references, is impressive and shows that the student has thought hard about the cultural references. The candidate's writing is fluent and controlled, with good vocabulary to support the points.

TAKING A STAND

My learning objectives

- to explore and develop my response to 'On the Life of Man' by Sir Walter Raleigh
- to explain how Raleigh uses language features, including extended metaphor to communicate his view of life.

Comparing Poems

To prepare for your English Literature exam:

- explore specific comparisons and links between Raleigh's 'On the Life of Man' and other poems in this collection, for example the ways in which the writers explore their view of life in 'Pessimism for Beginners' or 'The world is a beautiful place', or the ways in which the writer expresses his ideas in 'A Consumer's Report'
- practise comparing in detail and evaluating the ways in which two poets express their ideas and achieve effects.

On the Life of Man *by Sir Walter Raleigh*

First thoughts
Activity 1

Sir Walter Raleigh was born in 1552. He was at one time a favourite of Queen Elizabeth I and was knighted in 1585. However, he married one of Elizabeth's ladies-in-waiting without the Queen's permission and was imprisoned in the Tower of London. He was imprisoned again for plotting against Elizabeth's successor, James I, and was eventually beheaded in 1618.

1. **a.** How would you describe the view that Raleigh expresses of life in this poem?

   b. At what point in his life do you think Raleigh might have written it?

Looking more closely
Activity 2

1. Identify where Raleigh has used *rhyme* – including the use of *partial rhyme* in the first two lines.

2. Write down all the words in the poem which could be associated with the theatre. What do you think Raleigh might be suggesting about life?

3. Look at the ideas below which Raleigh writes about in the poem:

   a. times of happiness

   b. the duration of the play

   c. an unborn child

   d. death

   e. the dressing room

   f. the ending of the play

   g. heading towards old age

   h. music played between acts

   i. the audience

   j. God watching and judging everyone.

   Pick out the words and phrases from the poem where he writes about each one.

4. Look again at your answers to question 3.

   a. Raleigh connects all these ideas in pairs: for example, he compares times of happiness to the music played between the acts of the play. Link up the other comparisons into pairs.

   b. Pick three of these comparisons. Briefly explain each one, exploring what Raleigh is suggesting about the nature of life. For example:

   > In the lines 'What is our life? a play of passion, / Our mirth the music of division' Raleigh seems to be suggesting that laughter is just a brief, happy interruption to the tragic events which make up the main action of our lives.

Developing your ideas **Activity 3**

1. **a.** Using your own ideas, make a list of ten words and phrases which you associate with the theatre and plays.

   b. Look carefully at your list. Why do you think Raleigh chose this *extended metaphor* to present his attitude towards life?

2. Look at the words below in the poem:

   'dressed' (line 4)

   'short' (line 4)

   'sharp' (line 5)

   'act' (line 6)

   'march' (line 9)

   Briefly explain the effect you think Raleigh intended each one to have.

Glossary

passion: strong feeling, emotion

mirth: laughter, happiness

music of division: the music played between the acts of a play

tiring houses: dressing rooms

judicious: wise

amiss: wrong, faulty

jest: joke

Developing your response **Activity 4**

1. Raleigh describes 'On the Life of Man' as a 'short Comedy'. To a modern reader, comedy is associated with humour; in Raleigh's time comedy was associated with plays providing amusement and a happy ending. Do you think Raleigh presents life in either of these ways in the poem?

2. Look at this example of an examination-style question:

   **Explain how Raleigh reflects on an attitude to life in his poem.
   Use examples from the poem to support your answer.**

   Write one section on extended metaphor that could be included in your answer.

ResultsPlus
Self/Peer assessment

1. Read this paragraph written in response to the task above.

2. Annotate your paragraphs using similar notes to those given on the right. If you've forgotten to include anything in your paragraphs, add it in.

3. Using the mark schemes on pages 166 and 171, decide which band your paragraphs would fall into.

┌─ A clear point   Evidence to support it ─┐

Raleigh compares our lives with a performance in the theatre: 'Heaven the Judicious sharp spectator is, / That sits and marks still who doth act amiss'. Raleigh is comparing God to the theatre audience, watching the actors and judging their performance. The word 'sharp' suggests not only how keenly God is watching us but also, perhaps, that He may not be very forgiving of our mistakes. Raleigh also uses a pun on the word 'act', a reference to both acting in a play and the way we behave in our lives. The extended metaphor could suggest that our lives are just a pretence – a part we play – and that our real lives begin when we have left the stage.

└─ An explanation of the   Explores the   Close focus on ─┘
   effect of the quotation   writer's intention   word choice

My learning objectives

- to explore and develop my response to 'I Shall Paint My Nails Red' by Carole Satyamurti
- to explain how Satymurti uses form and imagery to convey a sense of a specific mood.

I Shall Paint My Nails Red

by Carole Satyamurti

Comparing Poems

To prepare for your English Literature exam:

- explore specific comparisons and links between Satyamurti's 'I Shall Paint My Nails Red' and other poems in this collection, for example how the writer explores his feelings in 'No Problem', or the ways in which the writers present their ideas in 'Do not go gentle into that good night' or 'The Penelopes of my homeland'
- practise comparing in detail and evaluating the ways in which two poets express their ideas and achieve effects.

First thoughts

Activity 1

1. What are your first impressions of the narrator in the poem? Think of at least three words to describe her.

2. Look at the first word in each line of the poem. What is the effect of this repetition?

3. The poem has ten lines. What might be a connection between the structure of the poem and its subject?

Looking more closely

Activity 2

1. **a.** Look carefully at the first line of the poem. There could be a link here with the colour red and how it is used in public, perhaps for alerting the public and for emergencies. Look at the remaining lines of the poem. What other links can you identify with the colour red?

   b. In what other ways could it be considered a 'public service' for women to paint their nails and make themselves look good?

2. In line 4, the writer says she will 'look like a survivor' if she paints her nails red.

   a. What does the phrase 'look like' suggest?

   b. What does this tell you about the person speaking?

3. Look at the daughter's and lover's reactions in lines 6 and 7. What does this suggest about:

   a. the daughter?

   b. the lover?

   c. the narrator?

4. **a.** Look at the title of the poem. What does the phrase 'I shall' suggest about the poet's intention to paint her nails red?

   b. Now look at line 10, the final line of the poem. What effect does this line have on the 'stand' which the writer is taking?

   c. Line 10 is the shortest line in the poem. Briefly explain why the writer may have decided to make this a short line and place it at the end of the poem.

Developing your ideas

Activity 3

1. Look at each line in the poem.

   a. Think of a word to describe the impression you get of the narrator from each of the ten lines in the poem. You could use some of the words below, or come up with your own choices:

   practical   proud   tough   romantic   unhappy   busy

   b. Look carefully at each line of the poem and at the words you chose to describe the narrator. Which word or phrase in each line most strongly suggested the word you chose to describe her? Explain each of your choices.

Developing your response

Activity 4

1. In what way is the narrator in this poem 'taking a stand'?

2. Look at this example of an examination-style question:

   Explore how Satyamurti expresses her attitude to life in 'I Shall Paint My Nails Red'.
   Use examples from the poem to support your answer.

   Write one section on the poet's use of imagery, vocabulary and structure that could be included in your answer.

ResultsPlus
Self/Peer assessment

These sentences are all taken from different students' writing in response to the task above.

1. Use some of these sentences, and the mark schemes on pages 166 and 171, to create a paragraph that you think would achieve a high band mark.

2 **a.** Look again at the paragraphs you wrote in Activity 4. Use the mark schemes to identify the two things most likely to improve your mark.

   b. Redraft your answer, making those changes. Check that your new answer has moved up to the next band.

> This could suggest that she does not feel restricted by the opinions of her family but is free to express herself – or it could suggest an unhappy woman finally rebelling against her normally quiet life.

> 'Because it will remind me I'm a woman.' This suggests that she has forgotten who and even what she is; as though life has taken away all her identity and self-esteem.

> The narrator in the poem is answering a question in so many different ways that she is justifying her decision to paint her nails red – perhaps to herself.

> Each line of the poem takes the form of a minor sentence and begins with the same word: 'because'.

> Although the narrator seems defiant in deciding to paint her nails red, she sounds insecure and uncertain throughout the poem.

> The narrator seems pleased that she will shock or even irritate the people she loves: 'Because my daughter will say ugh. / Because my lover will be surprised.'

My learning objectives

- to explore and develop my response to 'The Penelopes of my homeland' by Choman Hardi
- to explain how Hardi uses allusion and language to show how the widows of Anfal coped with their situation.

Comparing Poems

To prepare for your English Literature exam:

- explore specific comparisons and links between Hardi's 'The Penelopes of my homeland' and other poems in this collection, for example how the writer explores human experience in 'Living Space', or the ways in which the writers present their ideas in 'I Shall Paint My Nails Red' or 'Remember'
- practise comparing in detail and evaluating the ways in which two poets express their ideas and achieve effects.

The Penelopes of my homeland
by Choman Hardi

First thoughts

Activity 1

1. Throughout the poem, Hardi uses *allusion* to the story of Penelope to explore the experience of the Anfal women. What connection is Hardi making between Penelope and the women?

Looking more closely

Activity 2

1. **a.** Look at the first *stanza* of the poem. Hardi writes about the women weaving 'their own and their children's shrouds'. What different ideas does this phrase suggest?

   b. How does *enjambement* in the first stanza help to emphasise the 'years and years' that the women have waited?

2. **a.** How is the idea of death explored further in the second stanza?

   b. What effect does the *alliteration* in line 7 have on the point Hardi is making?

3. Look at the third stanza. What is Hardi's attitude to palm-readers and to God?

4. Look at line 16:

   'Years and years of raising more Penelopes and Odysseuses'

   What is Hardi suggesting here?

5. In the fifth stanza, Hardi writes about all the things that have not happened.

   a. When should these things have happened?

   b. Why did they not happen?

6. Look at the final line of the poem.

   a. How does this echo line 16?

   b. What does it suggest about Hardi's view of the future for these people?

7. The phrase 'Years and years' is repeated throughout the poem. What effect does this have?

Developing your ideas

1. Re-read the poem and note down where and how Hardi explores the feelings of the women she is writing about.

2. **a.** Make a list of the similarities and differences between the widows in the poem and Penelope.

    b. How does Hardi use the allusion to the legend of Penelope and Odysseus to enrich the point she is making?

3. Hardi refers to 'my homeland'. What is the effect of this on the reader?

Developing your response

1. How would you describe the mood of the poem? Select some of the words below or come up with your own choices:

    angry   bitter   sympathetic   pitying   neutral

2. Look at this example of an examination-style question:

    Explore how Hardi expresses her feelings in 'The Penelopes of my homeland'. Use examples from the poem to support your answer.

    Write one section on the poet's use of allusion and language that could be included in your answer.

ResultsPlus
Self/Peer assessment

1. Look at the paragraphs you wrote in Activity 4 and at the mark schemes on pages 166 and 171. Which band would your answer fall into?

2. What could you change or add to improve your answer? Use the mark schemes to identify the two things most likely to improve your mark.

3. Redraft your answer, making these changes.

4. Look again at the mark schemes. Check that your work has moved into a higher band.

Glossary

Penelope: the faithful wife of Odysseus, who waited 20 years for his return, promising to re-marry only when she had finished weaving a shroud for her father-in-law. She wove it by day and unpicked it by night. She became a symbol of loyalty and fidelity

Anfal: the al-Anfal campaign was a campaign against the Kurdish population of Iraq, led by Saddam Hussein between 1986 and 1989. An estimated 182,000 Kurds disappeared. There were an estimated 50,000 women left widowed by the disaster

shroud: the cloth in which a body is buried

Odysseus: hero from Greek legend who fought in the Trojan wars and had many adventures on his long return journey to Greece

A Consumer's Report
by Peter Porter

First thoughts

1. Look at the title of the poem.

   a. In what *form* has Porter written about his subject matter?

   b. Why has he used this approach?

Looking more closely

1. The narrator in the poem says he has completed 'the form you sent me'. Imagine there had been a form. What questions does the narrator seem to be answering in the poem? Record your answers in a table like the one below.

Lines	The question asked
4	Where did you get this product?
5–6	How did it make you feel?

2. For each answer the narrator in the poem gives, briefly explain what it suggests about his attitude to life. Think about different possible interpretations. For example:

   > In line 4, the narrator says that he was given life as a gift. This could suggest that he thinks life is precious and special – or that he did not ask for it and it was not the gift he wanted!

3. The poem is written as an **extended metaphor**, comparing life to a product. Look at the quotations below. What aspects of life do you think each one is referring to?

   • 'the instructions'

   • 'a lot of different labels'

   • 'the price'

4. Imagine you were considering buying this product.

   a. List some of the advantages and some of the disadvantages of the product mentioned in the poem.

   b. On balance, does the product seem worth buying?

Developing your ideas

1. Look at the first three lines of the poem.

   a. What is the purpose of this opening?

   b. Why has Porter separated these lines in one short *stanza*?

2 a. How would you describe the tone of the poem and the narrator's attitude to life? Select three words from those below (or others of your choice):

sarcastic   bitter   optimistic   dissatisfied

aggressive   balanced   cautious

b. Find a quotation to support each of your choices.

c. For each quotation, briefly explain how it supports your ideas.

Developing your response

Activity 4

1. In the final line of the poem, Porter writes about:

'the competitive product you said you'd send.'

What do you think this competitive product could be?

2. What does this final line – and poem as a whole – suggest about human nature? Look at these students responses to the poem. Which of these answers do you agree with most? Briefly explain your answer.

> **Student A**
> Porter seems to be suggesting that, though life is not perfect, we still 'buy it'.

> **Student B**
> In the final lines of the poem, Porter suggests that we are never happy with the life we've been given and feel that 'the grass is always greener'.

> **Student C**
> The narrator in the poem says that, although it has many good points, life is a disappointment. Perhaps we do take it for granted, as the narrator suggests.

3. Look at this example of an examination-style question:

Explore how Porter comments on life in 'A Consumer's Report'.
Use examples from the poem to support your answer.

Write one section on the poet's use of language and extended metaphor that could be included in your answer.

ResultsPlus
Self/Peer assessment

1. Look at the paragraphs you wrote in Activity 4 and at the mark schemes on pages 166 and 171. Which band would your answer fall into?

2. What could you change or add to improve your answer? Use the mark schemes to identify the two things most likely to improve your mark.

3. Redraft your answer, making these changes.

4. Look again at the mark schemes. Check that your work has moved into a higher band.

Comparing Poems

To prepare for your English Literature exam:

- explore specific comparisons and links between Porter's 'A Consumer's Report' and other poems in this collection, for example the ways in which the writers explore their view on life in 'The world is a beautiful place' or 'Pessimism for Beginners', or the ways in which the writer presents his ideas in 'On the Life of Man'

- practise comparing in detail and evaluating the ways in which two poets express their ideas and achieve effects.

My learning objectives

- to explore and develop my response to 'Pessimism for Beginners' by Sophie Hannah
- to explore how Hannah uses exaggeration and ridicule to humorous effect in looking at our everyday attitude to life.

Glossary

pessimism: taking a negative view of events

venal: dishonest, corrupt

stalwart: firm and unwavering

quirk: a peculiarity of manner or action

Hitler: German Nazi dictator

herpes: viral disease which causes cold sores

cursory: hasty or superficial

endorsing: giving approval to

Pessimism for Beginners
by Sophie Hannah

First thoughts

Activity 1

1. The title of the poem suggests that it will help the reader become pessimistic. Sum up in one sentence the advice given in the poem.

Looking more closely

Activity 2

1. **a.** List the ten most negative words in the poem or highlight them on a copy of the poem.

   b. List the ten most positive words in the poem or highlight them.

   c. Look at where the majority of words in each list appear in the poem. What does the pattern suggest about the structure of the poem?

2. Look at the last two lines of the poem. What advice is Hannah trying to give the reader?

3. **a.** Look at the phrases below. Each one reflects an attitude to life. Which do you think match the message of the poem?

   a. *If it can go wrong, it will.*

   d. *If you have low expectations in life you'll never be disappointed.*

   b. *Where there's a will there's a way.*

   e. *Every cloud has a silver lining.*

   c. *The glass is half full.*

   f. *It never rains but it pours.*

   b. Briefly explain how each phrase that you have selected matches the message of the poem. Use quotations from the poem to support your ideas.

4. Although the theme of the poem is about pessimism, how does Hannah make it humorous? (Think about the use of **hyperbole**.) Briefly explain your answer with reference to the poem.

Developing your ideas

Activity 3

1. Write one or two sentences summing up the argument in the poem. Do you agree with Hannah's ideas? Explain your point of view.

2. Look at these quotations taken from the poem.

   a. 'your eyes should be pecked by an eagle.'

   b. 'bash in your head with a stone!'

   c. 'spatter their basin with vomit.'

   d. 'Hitler and herpes and you.'

   e. 'pickle your heart in pure joy.'

   f. 'gouge out your eyes!'

   g. 'a stunning and perfect surprise.'

   h. 'a small portion of boundless delight.'

   For each one, briefly explain why they are effective. For example,

   > a. This is effective because, although it creates an agonising image of torture, it is so unlikely to occur that it becomes absurd and therefore amusing.

3. In the poem Hannah uses *rhyme* and *alliteration*.

   a. Pick out one or two examples of each of these techniques.

   b. How do they contribute to the tone of the poem and the poet's point of view?

Developing your response

Activity 4

1. Think about how Hannah's use of humour changes the way the reader responds to the poem. What would be the impact of the poem if it was written without humour?

2. Look at this example of an examination-style question:

   Explore how Hannah presents her point of view in 'Pessimism for Beginners'. Use examples from the poem to support your answer.

   Write one section on the poet's use of exaggeration, humour and imagery that could be included in your answer.

Comparing Poems

To prepare for your English Literature exam:

- explore specific comparisons and links between Hannah's 'Pessimism for Beginners' and other poems in this collection, for example the ways in which the writers explore their view of life in 'On the Life of Man' or 'A Consumer's Report', or the ways in which the writer presents his ideas in 'Those bastards in their mansions'

- practise comparing in detail and evaluating the ways in which two poets express their ideas and achieve effects.

ResultsPlus
Self/Peer assessment

1. Read this paragraph written in response to the task above.

2. Annotate your paragraphs using similar notes to those given on the right. If you've forgotten to include anything in your paragraphs, add it in.

3. Using the mark schemes on pages 166 and 171, decide which band your paragraphs would fall into.

— A clear point   Evidence to support it —

Hannah begins by assuring us that our worst fears are probably correct – that we are right to think our parents, friends, siblings or lovers are avoiding us because: 'Everything that you are and you do / Makes them spatter their basin with vomit.' Hannah plays on our paranoia and insecurities, using them to establish her argument before going on to convince us that we should believe the worst in order to avoid disappointment. The repetition of 'you' adds to the all-encompassing effect of the word 'everything', and together with the extreme reaction of vomiting, emphasises that this is not simply dislike but total revulsion. Through the use of exaggeration and humour, it seems clear that Hannah's advice in the poem is not entirely serious and that, perhaps, she is mocking this attitude to life.

— An explanation of the effect of the quotation   Explores the writer's intention   Close focus on word choice —

My learning objectives

- to explore and develop my response to 'Solitude' by Ella Wheeler Wilcox
- to understand how Wilcox explores reasons for solitude in life through form, language and rhyme.

Comparing Poems

To prepare for your English Literature exam:

- explore specific comparisons and links between Wilcox's 'Solitude' and other poems in this collection, for example the ways in which the writers present their thoughts and feelings in 'The archbishop chairs the first session' or 'Remember,' or how the writer expresses his attitude in 'One World Down the Drain'
- practise comparing in detail and evaluating the ways in which two poets express their ideas and achieve effects.

Solitude
by Ella Wheeler Wilcox

First thoughts

Activity 1

1. Write down the different emotions in the poem which are connected with:
   a. being in solitude
   b. being in company.

2 **a.** What is the writer's attitude to solitude?
   b. Is the poet advising readers about how they should live their lives or is she just expressing an opinion about life? Briefly explain your ideas.

Looking more closely

Activity 2

1. Look at the opening words of the first two lines of each *stanza*. What effect do they create?

2. There are contrasting pairs of words throughout the poem. Choose three of these pairs and briefly explain Wilcox's view of how positive or negative feelings can change our lives. For example:

   In lines 1 and 2, Wilcox contrasts 'laugh' and 'weep'. She is suggesting that people who laugh will be surrounded with friends while those who weep will be shunned and live solitary, lonely lives.

3. Read the first two lines of the poem aloud, emphasising the underlined syllables:

   'Laugh, and the world laughs with you;
      Weep, and you weep alone;'

   a. How many 'beats' can you hear in each line?
   b. Read the rest of the first stanza aloud. How many beats can you hear in each line?
   c. What pattern does the *rhythm* of this stanza follow?
   d. Do the other two stanzas follow the same pattern?
   e. What is the effect of this rhythm? Does it remind you of any other poems you have read or heard?

4 **a.** Which lines *rhyme* in the poem?
   b. Can you spot a rhyming pattern?
   c. Rhyme can be used to connect or emphasise the ideas on two different lines. Can you find any connection between the lines that rhyme?

Developing your ideas

1. **a.** Find three examples of *alliteration* and three examples of *internal rhyme* in the poem.

   b. How do these examples reinforce the message that the poet is trying to communicate?

2. Look closely at the last four lines of the poem.

   a. Think about the phrases 'the halls of pleasure' and the 'narrow aisles of pain'. What visual contrast do they suggest?

   b. How do they support the overall message of the poem?

   c. Is it an effective end to the poem?

Developing your response

1. How does this poem fit in with the theme of this collection: Taking a stand? In what way is Wilcox 'taking a stand'?

2. Look at this example of an examination-style question:

   Explain how Wilcox explores the reasons for solitude in this poem. Use examples from the poem to support your answer.

   Write one section on the poet's use of negative and positive images that could be included in your answer.

Glossary

solitude: being alone

mirth: laughter, happiness

woe: sadness

nectared: sweetened by the sugary liquid produced by plants

gall: bitterness

train: a line or procession of people

file: a line of people one behind another

aisles: a gangway between rows of seats

ResultsPlus
Self/Peer assessment

1. Look at the paragraphs you wrote in Activity 4 and at the mark schemes on pages 166 and 171. Which band would your answer fall into?

2. What could you change or add to improve your answer? Use the mark schemes to identify the two things most likely to improve your mark.

3. Redraft your answer, making these changes.

4. Look again at the mark schemes. Check that your work has moved into a higher band.

My learning objectives

My learning objectives

- to explore and develop my response to 'No Problem' by Benjamin Zephaniah
- to explore how Zephaniah uses language to communicate that we should challenge preconceptions.

Comparing Poems

To prepare for your English Literature exam:

- explore specific comparisons and links between Zephaniah's 'No Problem' and other poems in this collection, for example how the writers explore their thoughts and feelings in 'I Shall Paint My Nails Red' or 'Zero Hour', or ways in which the writer presents his ideas in 'Do not go gentle into that good night'

- practise comparing in detail and evaluating the ways in which two poets express their ideas and achieve effects.

No Problem
by Benjamin Zephaniah

First thoughts

Activity 1

1. **a.** Pick out all the things which people say or think about the narrator.

   b. What do people *not* see or notice about the narrator in the poem?

2. **a.** What are your first impressions of the narrator in the poem?

   b. How would you describe other people's attitudes to the narrator in the poem?

3. The poem is written in *dialect*. What initial effect does this create for the reader?

Looking more closely

Activity 2

1. Look at the first four lines of the poem.

   a. What is the problem which the narrator in the poem is having?

   b. Briefly explain what the narrator means by:

   'I am not de problem'

2. **a.** What chain of events is described in lines 6–8?

   b. How does Zephaniah use language and wordplay to connect these events?

3. In line 11, the narrator says he:

   'can teach yu of Timbuktu'

   Why has Zephaniah chosen to name this place? Refer to the glossary opposite to help you.

4. **a.** In line 16, the narrator tells us he is 'versatile'. What do you think he means by this?

   b. How does this contrast with the 'pigeon hole' he talks about in line 15?

5. The poem is written in Caribbean dialect.

   a. Pick out all the words and phrases in dialect and make a note of their meaning. Use the glossary to help you.

   b. Why do you think Zephaniah chose to write the poem in this dialect?

Developing your ideas

Activity 3

1. **a.** This sentence is repeated throughout the poem:

   'I am not de problem'

   What is the effect of this repetition?

   b. Why do you think Zephaniah decided to call the poem 'No Problem'?

2. The narrator says he has:

   'no chips on me shoulders,'

   a. What do you think he means?

   b. Do you agree with the narrator or is there any evidence in the poem to suggest otherwise?

   c. Why do you think Zephaniah uses the word 'chips', not 'chip'?

3. In line 22 the narrator says:

   'Mother country get it right,'

   a. Is this a statement that the mother country is getting it right or an *imperative* suggesting that the mother country should try harder to get it right?

   b. Why does Zephaniah use the phrase 'mother country' here, do you think?

Developing your response

Activity 4

1. Look at the final line of the poem. Why is the narrator making this point, do you think?

2. Look at this example of an examination-style question:

   Explain how Zephaniah puts forward his point of view in 'No Problem'.
   Use examples from the poem to support your answer.

   Write one section on the poet's use of language and *form* that could be included in your answer.

Glossary

de: the

bear de brunt of: to suffer more than others from

dey: they

branded: a mark burnt into the skin to show ownership; labelled

Timbuktu: a city in Mali, West Africa; often used to mean a faraway place

pigeon hole: compartment for putting things, or people, into a particular category

chips on me shoulders: deep resentments

Mother country: the country where a person was born

fe: for

ResultsPlus
Self/Peer assessment

1. Read this paragraph written in response to the task above.

2. Annotate your paragraphs using similar notes to those given on the right. If you've forgotten to include anything in your paragraphs, add it in.

3. Using the mark schemes on pages 166 and 171, decide which band your paragraphs would be marked as.

— A clear point   Evidence to support it —

The narrator in 'No Problem' is a victim of racism and bullied because of it. He is portrayed as intelligent: 'I am born academic / But dey got me on de run / Now I am branded athletic'. This suggests that his academic progress is suffering because of the bullying he undergoes. The phrase 'on de run' suggests he has no choice but to try and escape from the racism. Yet this only exaggerates the problem as his running causes him to be 'branded athletic', a stereotypical assumption about black people. Zephaniah is suggesting that racism will grow and become more entrenched unless it is challenged.

— An explanation of the   Explores the   Close focus on —
effect of the quotation   writer's intention   word choice

Those bastards in their mansions
by Simon Armitage

First thoughts
Activity 1

1. In this poem, Armitage writes in the voice of a narrator, or *persona*.

   a. What are your first impressions of this persona?

   b. Briefly summarise the narrator's feelings about the rich people in their mansions.

Looking more closely
Activity 2

1. How does the language used in the title and first line of the poem make the narrator's feelings clear?

2. At what time and place in history do you think the poem could be set? Explain your ideas with reference to the poem.

3. **a.** Pick out all the uses of **full rhyme** and **assonance** in the poem. Note: not all the rhyming words will be at the end of a line.

   b. The first full stop in the poem is at the end of line 9. What kind of tone does Armitage's use of **rhyme** and punctuation give to the voice of this narrator?

4. **a.** Identify how the narrator describes the rich people in the first *stanza*. What impression does the narrator give of them?

   b. Has the narrator in the poem actually done all the things he describes or is he just talking about how he expects the rich to behave? Use evidence from the poem to support your answer.

5. In the second stanza, the narrator talks about helping ordinary people.

   a. What are the three kinds of help he describes?

   b. Why do the people need this kind of help?

6. If he did all these things, how would the narrator in the poem expect to be punished?

Developing your ideas
Activity 3

In classical mythology, Prometheus stole fire from the gods to give heat and light to man. His punishment was to be chained to a rock where his liver would be pecked out every day by an eagle – only for it to grow back again, ready for the eagle the next day.

1. What connections can you find between the story of Prometheus and the narrator in the poem? Think about:

   - what is stolen
   - who steals it
   - who it is stolen from
   - the differences between Prometheus and the narrator.

2. Having imagined this punishment, the narrator says:

'Me, I stick to the shadows, carry a gun.'

a. Why do you think he says he does this?

b. Does the narrator's *allusion* to a story from classical mythology change the way you think about him?

Glossary

stocking feet: wearing socks, not shoes

britches: trousers

ditch: remove

cuffs and shackles: metal chains around wrists and ankles used to restrain a prisoner

Developing your response

Activity 4

1. Look at these three students' responses to the poem:

Student A

I think it's all in the narrator's head. He hears a rich person 'shriek' about something and imagines they are shrieking about poor people coming to steal from them.

Student B

He makes the rich people's punishment sound ruthless and frightening and he makes the narrator sound scary with his gun in the shadows. I think it's about the division between the rich and the poor – neither of them understand each other and both are scared of each other.

Student C

I don't think the poem's set in the past. Because the narrator talks about rich people's old-fashioned ideas, I think it's about the aristocracy in their palaces and castles being outdated and out of touch with real people.

Which of these ideas do you agree with most? Write two or three sentences explaining your answer.

2. Look at this example of an examination-style question:

Explain how Armitage presents the narrator's views about the wealthy in 'Those bastards in their mansions'.
Use examples from the poem to support your answer.

Write one section on the poet's use of imagery and sound effects that could be included in your answer.

ResultsPlus
Self/Peer assessment

1. Look at the paragraphs you wrote in Activity 4 and at the mark schemes on pages 166 and 171. Which band would your answer fall into?

2. What could you change or add to improve your answer? Use the mark schemes to identify the two things most likely to improve your mark.

3. Redraft your answer, making these changes.

4. Look again at the mark schemes. Check that your work has moved into a higher band.

My learning objectives

- to explore and develop my response to 'Living Space' by Imtiaz Dharker
- to explain how Dharker uses imagery to explore the fragile and unpredictable nature of life.

Living Space
by Imtiaz Dharker

First thoughts

Activity 1

1. Think about the term 'Living Space'. What does this phrase make you think of? What effect does your living space have on your life?

Looking more closely

Activity 2

1. **a.** Look at the word 'lines' in line 2 of the poem. List six other words in the poem that could describe a line.

   b. List eight words or phrases that relate to a building.

   c. What is the link between these two lists of words and phrases?

2. In line 10, Dharker suggests that the structure is almost 'miraculous'. In what way, do you think, this building is like a miracle?

3. In the second *stanza,* Dharker reveals that it is someone's 'living space' she has described. Why does she wait until the second stanza to do this?

4. In the third stanza, Dharker focuses on one particular object in the living space.

   a. What is it?

   b. Why do you think Dharker has chosen to focus on this object? In what way is it a *metaphor* for the structure described in the first stanza?

Developing your ideas

Activity 3

1. There is more than one possible meaning of the poem's title: 'Living Space':
   - a space in which people live; a house
   - life; the space between birth and death.

   a. How does the second possible meaning add to your understanding of the poem?

b. Briefly explain the different ways in which the whole poem is an *extended metaphor* for life.

Think about:

- the house where 'Beams / balance crookedly'
- the eggs with their 'fragile curves'.

2 **a.** Identify at least five words in the poem which suggest risk and danger.

b. What do these words suggest about Dharker's view of life?

3. Look at these words from the third stanza:

'light'   'fragile'   'universe'   'faith'   'eggs'

a. What links can you identify between these words?

b. What point is Dharker trying to make?

Developing your response

Activity 4

1. **a.** Dharker uses *enjambement* at several points in the poem. Identify these lines.

b. How does the use of enjambement reflect the imagery and ideas in the poem?

2. Look at this example of an examination-style question:

**Explain how Dharker explores her view of life in 'Living Space'.
Use examples from the poem to support your answer.**

Write one section on the poet's use of imagery and extended metaphor that could be included in your answer.

Comparing Poems

To prepare for your English Literature exam:

- explore specific comparisons and links between Dharker's 'Living Space' and other poems in this collection, for example how the writer explores human experience in 'The Penelopes of my homeland', the ways in which the writer reflects on the fragility of life in 'One World Down the Drain', or the ways in which the writer expresses his attitude to life in 'A Consumer's Report'
- practise comparing in detail and evaluating the ways in which two poets express their ideas and achieve effects.

ResultsPlus
Self/Peer assessment

These sentences are all taken from different students' writing in response to the task above.

1. Use some of these sentences, and the mark schemes on pages 166 and 171, to create a paragraph that you think would achieve a high band mark.

2 **a.** Look again at the paragraphs you wrote in Activity 4. Use the mark schemes to identify the two things most likely to improve your mark.

b. Redraft your answer, making those changes. Check that your new answer has moved up to the next band.

Dharker says that the eggs' white shells are like the shells with which we protect our lives: 'the bright, thin walls of faith'.

This reminds us of the precarious beams and supports in the first stanza, suggesting that the lives of everyone in this universe are as fragile and vulnerable as the eggs.

In the third stanza, Dharker connects our lives with the fragility of a basket of eggs: 'fragile curves of white / hung out over the dark edge / of a slanted universe'.

Dharker is perhaps suggesting that none of us is secure in this life and all we have is faith which is 'thin' and therefore fragile. This could be a religious faith, or our faith in physical possessions like our seemingly solid houses.

Dharker describes a living space, a home where nothing is safe or secure: 'Beams / balance crookedly on supports'.

Dharker is aiming to make us more aware of, and create our sympathy for, the conditions in which some people live.

My learning objectives

- to explore and develop my response to 'The archbishop chairs the first session' by Ingrid de Kok
- to explain how de Kok uses form and language to explore the significance and impact of the Truth and Reconciliation Commission in South Africa.

Comparing Poems

To prepare for your English Literature exam:

- explore specific comparisons and links between de Kok's 'The archbishop chairs the first session' and other poems in this collection, for example the ways in which the writer conveys her thoughts and feelings in 'Solitude', how the writer explores the impact of recent events in 'One World Down the Drain', or the ways in which the writer expresses her ideas in 'Living Space'

- practise comparing in detail and evaluating the ways in which two poets express their ideas and achieve effects.

First thoughts

Activity 1

1. What is the main image created in the poem and what effect does it have on the reader?

2. Select one of the words below (or another of your choice) to describe the overall tone of the poem:

   shocking   curious   angry   confused

Looking more closely

Activity 2

1. Why do you think the Archbishop begins to weep? What clues are you given in the poem?

2. **a.** How many sentences are there in the poem all together?

   b. Identify any examples of *enjambement* in the poem.

   c. Briefly comment on how enjambement and sentence lengths help to create pace and mood in the poem.

   d. Why has de Kok chosen to end more than half of the sentences in the poem in the same way?

3. Look at the description of the Archbishop in the poem. We are told of his:

   - 'grey head'   • 'misted glasses'   • 'sobbing shoulders'

   How does this choice of language influence the reader's response to the Archbishop?

4. In line 14, de Kok says:

   'It doesn't matter what you thought / of the archbishop'

   What do you think she means?

Developing your ideas

1. Compare the first *stanza* and the fourth stanza of the poem.
   a. What does each stanza describe?
   b. Why has the poet chosen to start and finish the poem in this way, do you think?

2. Compare the vocabulary in the third stanza with the other three stanzas.
   a. What do you notice?
   b. What is the effect of this vocabulary choice?

3. The last stanza of the poem consists of one line: a four-word sentence.
   a. What is the effect of this final stanza?
   b. What could it suggest about the sessions of the Truth and Reconciliation Commission which followed this first session?

Developing your response

1. In lines 23 and 24, de Kok suggests:

   'It doesn't matter... even if you think this poem /simplifies, lionizes / romanticizes, mystifies.'

   a. In what way could it be said that the poem does all or any of these things?
   b. Why does it not matter if it did?
   c. What is it that the poem suggests <u>does</u> matter?

2. Look at this example of an examination-style question:

   Explore how de Kok creates a sense of emotion and drama in 'The archbishop chairs the first session'.
   Use examples from the poem to support your answer.

   Write one section on the poet's use of *form* and language that could be included in your answer.

ResultsPlus
Self/Peer assessment

1. Look at the paragraphs you wrote in Activity 4 and at the mark schemes on pages 166 and 171. Which band would your answer fall into?
2. What could you change or add to improve your answer? Use the mark schemes to identify the two things most likely to improve your mark.
3. Redraft your answer, making these changes.
4. Look again at the mark schemes. Check that your work has moved into a higher band.

Glossary

The Truth and Reconciliation Commission: a group formed in 1996 to examine the violations of human rights that took place under Apartheid (the system of racial segregation in South Africa, 1948 to 1992). Archbishop Desmond Tutu was the chairman.

testimony: evidence given by witnesses to a court

protocols: rules agreed

recess: a temporary halt to an activity

vestment: a ceremonial garment, especially one worn by priests and bishops

anthropologists: people who study human beings and their societies

discourse: a formal speech or conversation

doctorates: the highest level of degree from a university

lionizes: treats someone as being of great importance

My learning objectives

- to explore and develop my response to 'The world is a beautiful place' by Lawrence Ferlinghetti
- to explain how Ferlinghetti uses form and tone to convey his views on human nature and life.

Comparing Poems

To prepare for your English Literature exam:

- explore specific comparisons and links between Ferlinghetti's 'The world is a beautiful place' and other poems in this collection, for example how the writers convey their view of life in 'On the Life of Man' or 'A Consumer's Report', or the ways in which the writer expresses his ideas in 'Zero Hour'

- practise comparing in detail and evaluating the ways in which two poets express their ideas and achieve effects.

The world is a beautiful place
by Lawrence Ferlinghetti

First thoughts
Activity 1

1. What is Ferlinghetti's view of life expressed in this poem? Briefly explain your answer.

2. Select one of the words below (or another of your choice) to describe the overall tone of the poem:

   optimistic   pessimistic   constantly changing   mocking

3. Which words show that the poet is American rather than British?

Looking more closely
Activity 2

1. In the first three *stanzas*, Ferlinghetti repeats the phrase:

   'if you don't mind...'

   a. How does he use this phrase to introduce his ideas?

   b. What effect does it have on the *tone* of the poem?

2. a. Write a summary of each stanza (stanza one: lines 1–11; stanza two: lines 12–19; stanza three: lines 20–39; stanza four: lines 40–63).

   b. What aspects of life and human nature is Ferlinghetti drawing our attention to in each stanza?

   c. Choose a short quotation which sums up the mood or tone of each stanza.

   d. Now choose a word or two to describe the mood of each stanza.

3. Look at each of the phrases below in the poem:
   - 'a touch of hell' (line 6)
   - 'dead minds' (line 23)
   - 'Name Brand society' (line 29)

   What do you think Ferlinghetti means by each of these? Briefly explain your answer.

4. Look at lines 31–32.

   a. What is the difference between 'men of distinction' and 'men of extinction'?

   b. How does Ferlinghetti's choice of language in these lines encourage you to make this comparison?

5. a. Look at all the imagery used in the final stanza. How would you describe almost all the activities listed?

   b. How does Ferlinghetti connect all these images into one long sentence?

   c. What effect does this have?

6. a. Why do you think the final stanza, and the poem, ends on the image of the mortician?

   b. Look at line 60. How does the language choice and structure of this line change the mood of the stanza?

   c. Why does Ferlinghetti describe the mortician as 'smiling'?

   d. Notice that stanza four is the longest in the poem. How does this, and the final image of the mortician, contribute to the overall effect of the poem?

Developing your ideas

Activity 3

1. Look at the *form* of the poem. Why do you think Ferlinghetti chose this zig zag arrangement of lines?

2. Which words or phrases are particularly emphasised by this form? Pick out five words or phrases and write a sentence or two explaining how each is emphasised by the poem's form and the effect this has. Write your ideas in a table like the one below:

Point	Evidence	Explanation
On lines 14–15, Ferlinghetti uses the form of the poem to emphasise that the world is not always a beautiful place.	'if you don't mind some people dying all the time'	This line break creates a dramatic and emphatic pause before Ferlinghetti adds this shocking afterthought to the statement on the previous line.

Developing your response

Activity 4

1. In what ways could it be said that Ferlinghetti is 'taking a stand' in this poem?

2. Look at this example of an examination-style question:

   Explore how Ferlinghetti conveys his message in 'The world is a beautiful place'. Use examples from the poem to support your answer.

   Write one section on the poet's use of form and *tone* that could be included in your answer.

Glossary

improprieties: inappropriate behaviour

segregations: the divisions of people into groups, often according to their race

congressional investigations: investigations conducted by politicians in the US

goosing: pinching someone's bottom

mortician: undertaker

ResultsPlus
Self/Peer assessment

1. Read this paragraph written in response to the task above.

2. Annotate your paragraphs using similar notes to those given on the right. If you've forgotten to include anything in your paragraphs, add it in.

3. Using the mark schemes on pages 166 and 171, decide which band your paragraphs would fall into.

— A clear point   Evidence to support it —

Throughout the poem, Ferlinghetti tells us the world is a beautiful place then draws our attention to the most negative images: 'if you don't mind some people dying / all the time / or maybe only starving'.

This suggests that Ferlinghetti believes the world is far from a beautiful place unless we can selfishly ignore the suffering of others. Placing 'all the time' on its own line and to the right of the page adds even more emphasis to the unavoidable pain of life while the word 'only' suggests sarcastically that starvation is an improvement on death. Ferlinghetti seems to believe that enjoying life is possible but only if we can turn a blind eye to the misery all around us.

— An explanation of the effect of the quotation   Explores the writer's intention   Close focus on form and word choice —

My learning objectives

- to explore and develop my response to 'Zero Hour' by Matthew Sweeney
- to explore how Sweeney shows us a possible image of the future through the use of tone and language.

Comparing Poems

To prepare for your English Literature exam:

- explore specific comparisons and links between Sweeney's 'Zero Hour' and other poems in this collection, for example how the writer conveys his view of the future in 'One World Down the Drain', or the ways in which the writers present their ideas in 'Those bastards in their mansions' or 'The world is a beautiful place'
- practise comparing in detail and evaluating the ways in which two poets express their ideas and achieve effects.

Zero Hour
by Matthew Sweeney

First thoughts

Activity 1

1. 'Zero Hour' describes a vision of the future. Briefly sum up the poet's vision.

2. What may have caused the situation described in the poem? Look for clues in the poem.

Looking more closely

Activity 2

1. Write a short summary of each *stanza* in the poem, briefly explaining what's happening and the narrator's thoughts.

2. On lines 18–19 we're told:

   'The first riots / are raging as I write,'

   Note down anything the poem tells you about the narrator.

3. **a.** The poem begins with a prediction about tomorrow. What impact does this have?

   b. Re-read lines 2–8. Write down the details which the poet uses to set the scene and briefly comment on what each detail suggests.

4. **a.** Why is having a bicycle so dangerous?

   b. What effect does the image of the doctor on a horse with a rifle have on the reader?

5. **a.** Pick out five lines or phrases from the poem which suggest how the poem's narrator is feeling.

   b. Briefly explain what each quotation suggests about how the narrator is feeling.

6. Look at these quotations taken from the final stanza of the poem.

   a. 'The first riots / are raging'

   b. 'this sudden countdown to zero hour,'

   c. 'paraphernalia of our comfort'

   d. 'stamped obsolete,'

   e. 'our memories / fighting to keep us sane and upright?'

   Briefly explain what each quotation suggests about the situation being described, how the situation might develop, or how people are feeling.

7. What will happen at zero hour, do you think?

Developing your ideas

Activity 3

1. **a.** What does the poem *not* tell you about the narrator, but as a reader you want to know? For example: who he/she is and where he/she is.

   b. What effect does this create?

2. In the final stanza, the narrator asks two *rhetorical questions*. What do they convey about the mood of the narrator and what effect do they have on the overall *tone* of the poem?

3. What is Matthew Sweeney 'taking a stand' against in 'Zero Hour'?

4. Briefly explain how the structure or *form* of the poem helps Sweeney to convey his ideas.

Developing your response

Activity 4

1. What words and phrases would you use to describe the tone of the poem? Briefly explain your choices, with reference to the poem.

2. Look at this example of an examination-style question:

   Explain how Sweeney conveys his vision of a possible future in 'Zero Hour'. Use examples from the poem to support your answer.

   Write one section on the poet's use of language, tone and imagery that could be included in your answer.

1. Look at the paragraphs you wrote in Activity 4 and at the mark schemes on pages 166 and 171. Which band would your answer fall into?

2. What could you change or add to improve your answer? Use the mark schemes to identify the two things most likely to improve your mark.

3. Redraft your answer, making these changes.

4. Look again at the mark schemes. Check that your work has moved into a higher band.

Glossary

paraphernalia: various bits of equipment, items used for a particular activity

obsolete: not used or required anymore

One World Down the Drain
by Simon Rae

My learning objectives

- to explore and develop my response to 'One World Down the Drain' by Simon Rae
- to explain how Rae uses humour, rhythm and rhyme to communicate his message that we must take an active stand against global warming.

Glossary

ciao: (Italian) an informal greeting at meeting or parting

Kiribati: a group of islands in the Pacific Ocean

atolls: small coral islands

First thoughts

Activity 1

1. Read the information on One World Week which prefaces the poem. Why do you think the poet has included this?

2. The poem is a warning about what could happen in the future. Why has Rae chosen to call the poem 'One World Down the Drain'?

Looking more closely

Activity 2

1. **a.** What is the poet's opinion on global warming?

   b. Select one of the following words (or one of your own choice) to describe the *tone* in which the poet gives his opinion:

   worried   angry   amused   sarcastic   bored   mocking

   c. Identify two or three quotations from the poem where this tone is particularly noticeable.

2. Find five different ways in which the poet says global warming will affect the world. What is the effect of these images on the message of the poem?

3. Sometimes the poet does not seem concerned by the consequences of global warming – and he makes excuses for this. For example, on line 9 he says, 'we don't care'. Find other examples of this attitude.

4. In line 11, the poet writes about:

   'Our acid greenhouse party'

   What ideas does this phrase suggest to you? Think about the word associations you can make and the poet's choice of language.

5. **a.** Look at the information on One World Week and then at line 21 where the poet suggests another conference should be held to discuss the effects of carbon dioxide. Is the poet being serious or *ironic*?

   b. Find other possible examples of irony. For each example, briefly explain the point you think the poet is making.

6. Look at the last line of the poem. What is the poet suggesting about our politicians?

Developing your ideas

Activity 3

1. **a.** Identify all the examples of *rhyme* (including *internal rhyme*) in the poem.

   b. What effect does the poet's use of rhyme have on the sound and tone of the poem?

2. **a.** What is the effect of line 23 when read alone and then when read with line 24?

   c. Why has the poet chosen such an unusual place to break the lines, do you think?

   d. How does this choice contribute to the tone of the poem?

Developing your response

1. Why do you think Simon Rae decided to write this poem? What response did he want to create in the reader? Look at these three students' ideas:

Student A
The poem's quite funny. It makes you laugh at a really serious subject.

Student B
It's shocking. We shouldn't laugh about the end of the world when we can all break our bad habits and do something about it.

Student C
The poem is criticising our politicians who do not seem to care about global warming and the future of our planet. They are only bothered about whether people vote for them now.

a. Whose ideas do you agree with most strongly?

b. Briefly explain your own ideas.

2. Look at this example of an examination-style question:

**Explain how Rae conveys his views in 'One World Down the Drain'.
Use examples from the poem to support your answer.**

Write one section on the poet's use of rhyme, rhythm and humour that could be included in your answer.

Comparing Poems

To prepare for your English Literature exam:

- explore specific comparisons and links between Rae's 'One World Down the Drain' and other poems in this collection, for example how the writer conveys his view of the future in 'Zero Hour', or the ways in which the writers express their ideas in 'Pessimism for Beginners' or 'Do not go gentle into that good night'

- practise comparing in detail and evaluating the ways in which two poets express their ideas and achieve effects.

ResultsPlus
Self/Peer assessment

1. Read this paragraph written in response to the task above.

2. Annotate your paragraphs using similar notes to those given on the right. If you've forgotten to include anything in your paragraphs, add it in.

3. Using the mark schemes on pages 166 and 171, decide which band your paragraphs would fall into.

A clear point ———— *Evidence to support it*

The poem tells us what will become of the beautiful, historic city of Venice: 'It won't be there in fifty years – Great City. Pity. Ciao.' Rae uses humour to shock us into facing the future which we are creating for ourselves. The short sentences, the rhyme, and the informality of the Italian 'ciao' suggest an ironically dismissive lack of concern for such a significant loss. Rae is using humour and irony to emphasise indirectly how worried we should be about global warming.

An explanation of the effect of the quotation | *Explores the writer's intention* | *Close focus on form and word choice*

My learning objectives

- to explore and develop my response to 'Do not go gentle into that good night' by Dylan Thomas
- to explore how Thomas communicates his thoughts on old age and death through his use of language and form.

Comparing Poems

To prepare for your English Literature exam:

- explore specific comparisons and links between Thomas' 'Do not go gentle into that good night' and other poems in this collection, for example how the writer explores her attitude to death in 'Remember', or the ways in which the writers present their ideas in 'Those bastards in their mansions'
- practise comparing in detail and evaluating the ways in which two poets express their ideas and achieve effects.

Do not go gentle into that good night by Dylan Thomas

First thoughts

Activity 1

1. The poem was written for, and is directly addressed to, the poet's father. What does it suggest about:
   a. the poet   **c.** their relationship
   b. his father   **d.** the poet's view of people in general?

2. What is Thomas 'taking a stand' against in the poem?

Looking more closely

Activity 2

1. The poem is a *villanelle* which is a form of poetry with strict rules about :
   - the number of lines
   - the *rhyme scheme*
   - the use of repetition.
   a. Using the poem, work out the rules for a villanelle.
   b. What is the effect of the repetition in the poem?

2. Look at the second line of the poem. Thomas suggests that:
   'Old age should burn and rave at close of day;'
   What do you think is meant by:
   a. 'close of day'   **b.** 'burn'   **c.** 'rave'?

3. Identify all the words and phrases in the poem which:
   a. suggest death
   b. suggest the fight against death
   c. What do you notice?

4. **a.** Look at stanzas 2, 3, 4 and 5. Thomas writes about four different types of men and their reactions to death. Match the types of men to the correct reaction.

Types of men	Reactions to death
a. Good men	**1.** Nothing they say can affect nature and prevent them dying
b. Grave men	**2.** Think they could do a lot more in life, however small their achievements
c. Wise men	**3.** They have lived their life intensely, even crazily, and now realise that they do not want their life to end
d. Wild men	**4.** Realise that they could have been less serious and enjoyed life more

   b. Why does Thomas write about these four different types of men?

Developing your ideas

1. **a.** Thomas describes his father 'on the sad height'. Where is his father?

   b. Thomas asks his father for 'fierce tears' to 'Curse, bless' him. What does this suggest about their relationship?

2. The final two lines of the poem are the lines which have been repeated throughout. What effect does this have?

3. How would you describe the *tone* of the poem? Select one of the words below (or choose your own):

   | rage | anguish | despair | anger |

   | calm | sadness | resignation |

Glossary

meteors: matter from space that burns brightly as it falls into the Earth's air and looks like a line of light

Developing your response

1. The poem suggests that we should fight and rage against death – which is compared to the darkness of night. Why, then, does Thomas describe it as *good* night, do you think?

2. Look at this example of an examination-style question:

   Explain how Thomas conveys his attitude to life and death in the poem 'Do not go gentle into that good night'?
   Use examples from the poem to support your answer.

   Write one section on the poet's use of language and *form* that could be included in your answer.

ResultsPlus
Self/Peer assessment

These sentences are all taken from different students' writing in response to the task above.

1. Use some of these sentences, and the mark schemes on pages 166 and 171, to create a paragraph which you think would achieve a high band mark.

2. **a.** Look again at the paragraphs you wrote in Activity 4. Use the mark schemes to identify the two things most likely to improve your mark.

   b. Redraft your answer, making those changes. Check that your new answer has moved up to the next band.

Thomas wants his father's attitude to death to be that of men who are 'wise', 'good', 'wild' and 'grave' and 'do not go gentle' to their deaths.

Thomas asks his father to 'curse, bless' him with his 'fierce tears'. This *oxymoronic* contrast suggests an uncertain, unpredictable relationship between father and son.

The strict form of the poem exaggerates the narrator's anger at his father. 'Rage, rage against the dying of the light.'

It is only in the final stanza that Thomas reveals that he is addressing his father who is on the 'sad height', on the verge of death.

It is as if Thomas is trying to contain his feelings within the rhyme and rhythm of the poem but it spills out in his desperate repetition of the plea for his father to 'rage' against death.

The final repetition in the final two lines of the poem forms a final plea, taking on a new significance now we know who they are spoken to.

My learning objectives

- to explore and develop my response to 'Remember' by Christina Rossetti
- to explain how Rossetti uses form and repetition to explore attitudes towards coping with death and loss.

Comparing Poems

To prepare for your English Literature exam:

- explore specific comparisons and links between Rossetti's 'Remember' and other poems in this collection, for example how the writer explores his attitude to death in 'Do not go gentle into that good night', or the ways in which the writer expresses his thoughts and feelings in 'On the Life of Man'
- practise comparing in detail and evaluating the ways in which two poets express their ideas and achieve effects.

Remember
by Christina Rossetti

First thoughts

Activity 1

1. What does the poem tell you about:
   a. the narrator in the poem
   b. who she is speaking to
   c. their relationship?
   Use evidence from the poem to support each of your ideas.

2. On the second line of the poem, the narrator talks about:
   'the silent land'.
   a. What do you think she is referring to?
   b. What effect does this image create?

Looking more closely

Activity 2

1. **a.** The word 'remember' is repeated throughout the poem. What effect does this create?
   b. What other examples of repetition can you find in the poem? What is their effect?

2. Line 4 of the poem describes the narrator turning away and turning back. Why does Rossetti use this image here?

3. In line 6, the narrator talks about the future. What effect is this line intended to have on the reader?

4. **a.** The poem is a **sonnet**: a fourteen-line poem which is sometimes divided into two sections: the first eight lines, called the **octet**, and the last six lines, called the **sestet**. What changes in attitude can you identify between the two sections?
   b. Which word does the narrator use to signal these changes? What is the effect of this?

5. Look at the lines below. Briefly explore the ideas and feelings they suggest.

   - 'Gone far away'
   - 'It will be late to counsel then or pray'
   - 'darkness and corruption'
   - 'Better by far you should forget'

   For example:

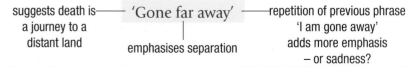

suggests death is a journey to a distant land — 'Gone far away' — repetition of previous phrase 'I am gone away' adds more emphasis – or sadness?
emphasises separation

Developing your ideas Activity 3

1. The poem frequently refers to death.

   a. Pick out all the direct references to death and then all the indirect references.

   b. What do you notice? Why do you think this is?

2. The poem is written in the *first person*, and directly addressed to a second person. What effect does this have?

Glossary

counsel: advise

corruption: decay or dishonesty

vestige: trace or remnant

Developing your response Activity 4

1. In what ways is the narrator in the poem 'taking a stand'?

2. **a.** What do you think this poem is about?

   death   love   memory   faithfulness   grief

   b. Select two or three of the words above (or others of your choice), then briefly sum up the narrator's attitude to each one.

3. Look at this example of an examination-style question:

   Explain how Rossetti explores attitudes to loss and grief in 'Remember'. Use examples from the poem to support your answer.

   Write one section on the poet's use of *form* and language that could be included in your answer.

ResultsPlus
Self/Peer assessment

1. Look at the paragraphs you wrote in Activity 4 and at the mark schemes on pages 166 and 171. Which band would your answer fall into?

2. What could you change or add to improve your answer? Use the mark schemes to identify the two things most likely to improve your mark.

3. Redraft your answer, making these changes.

4. Look again at the mark schemes. Check that your work has moved into a higher band.

Comparing the 'Taking a stand' poems

When you compare two poems, it can be helpful to think about three different areas:

• Language: the words, images or techniques (such as simile or metaphor) used
• Structure: the shape, rhyme and rhythm of the poem
• Viewpoint: the writer's attitude to the subject of the poem

Read the poems 'I Shall Paint My Nails Red' and 'No Problem', then complete the activities below.

Making comparisons and links between poems Activity 1

1. Look again at 'I Shall Paint My Nails Red' and then answer the following questions:
   a. Is the writer focusing on their own attitudes and actions or on other people's?
   b. What point is the writer making? Is their attitude positive or negative?
2. Look again at 'No Problem' and then answer the same questions.
3. Write one sentence about each poem, summing up what the poem is about and the writer's attitude.

Evaluating ways of expressing meaning and achieving effects Activity 2

1. a. All the words below are taken from the poem 'I Shall Paint My Nails Red'. Choose one word that sums up the writer's viewpoint.

proud	survivor	admire	ugh	surprised	reversible

   b. All the words below are taken from the poem 'No Problem'. Choose one word that sums up the writer's viewpoint.

taunts	racist	problem	smile	pigeon hole	Mother country

   c. Compare the words you have chosen to sum up each poet's viewpoint. What do you notice?

2. a. Compare the shape and structure of the two poems by writing a sentence or two for each of the bullet points below:
   • compare the length of the two poems and the use of stanzas
   • compare the length of the lines in each poem
   • compare the use or lack of rhyme
   • compare the use of repetition.

   b. For each poem, choose **one** effect from the list of possible effects on the reader below that most closely matches your personal response. Then, for each poem, write one or two sentences explaining the features that create the effect you have chosen.
   • Suggests a fast-paced, angry tone.
   • Suggests a series of thoughts as the writer tries to justify their actions.
   • Suggests an informal, conversational tone.

Selecting appropriate examples

Activity 3

1. Copy and complete the grid below to help you compare the two poems:

	Language	Structure	Viewpoint
I Shall Paint My Nails Red	Quotation:	A series of justifications connected through repetition Quotation:	Quotation:
No Problem	Contrast of others' negative attitudes and the writer's positive qualities Quotation:	Quotation:	Quotation:

2. **a.** Look at this quotation from 'I Shall Paint My Nails Red':

   > Because I will look like a survivor

   b. Now look at your completed grid. Which of your points do you think this quotation supports? Add the quotation to your grid.

   c. Choose five more quotations from the poems: one to support each of the three areas in each of the poems.

Putting it into practice

Activity 4

1. Look at the paragraphs below written in response to the examination-style question:

   Explain how the writer of 'No Problem' presents different thoughts and feelings about identity from those in 'I Shall Paint My Nails Red'.

   —— A clear point ——   Evidence to support it ——

   'I Shall Paint My Nails Red' shows how identity can be created through appearance.
   'Because it will remind me I'm a woman. Because I will look like a survivor.'
   It suggests that the writer feels she can assert her femininity simply by wearing nail varnish. However, her appearance may be an illusion as she only 'looks' like a survivor. This and the use of repetition suggests that the writer is trying to convince herself that the nail varnish will create her identity— but is not quite convinced.
   'No Problem', however, is not about the writer's perception of his own identity but the perceptions of others and the problems these create.
   'I am not de problem... / Yu put me in a pigeon hole / But I am versatile'
   The writer is, he says, the very opposite of how others see him – but this is not the writer's problem. The problem is created by the attitudes of others. The writer repeats the phrase 'I am not de problem' throughout the poem to emphasise this point. Whereas the repetition in 'I Shall Paint My Nails Red' undermines the writer's stand with some doubt, the repetition of 'I am not de problem' leaves us in no doubt that racism is a problem caused by racists.

   —— An explanation of the   —— Exploration of the   Words and phrases   Close focus on language, ——
   effect of the quotation   writer's intention   to show comparison   structure or tone

2. Now try writing four paragraphs giving your response to a different examination-style question:

   Explain how the writers of 'Do not go gentle into that good night' and 'Remember' present different ideas about the approach of death.

   Use the same structure as in the paragraphs above.

3. Annotate your paragraph using the same annotations as above. If you've forgotten to include anything in your paragraphs, add it in.

4. Using the mark schemes on pages 166 and 171, decide which band your paragraphs would fall into.

Here are some extracts from student answers to Higher Tier English Literature examination questions. Read the answers together with the examiner comments to help you understand what you need to do to build better answers.

(a) Explore how the writer presents her ideas about her identity in 'I Shall Paint My Nails Red'.

Use **evidence** from the poem to support your answer.

(15 marks)

Student 1 – Extract typical of a grade C answer

The student notes that part of the reason is simply for her own pleasure.

The writer, Carole Satyamurti, writes her identity in just ten lines, one for each finger whose nails she has painted red. She is looking at her life as a woman, lover and mother, and she thinks painting her nails red will please herself, 'I can admire them...' and it will also shock her lover and daughter, 'ugh', 'will be surprised'. The woman is being defiant, because red is such a bright colour, often used for warning. Perhaps she is saying that she should not be taken for granted. However, at the end of the poem, she makes it clear that this is only temporary, because it does not take long to remove the nail varnish.

There is a worthwhile attempt at commentary on the ideas behind the poem – the cautious use of 'perhaps' is justified, as this is not a necessary interpretation, but the quotations about the daughter and lover could support this view.

Examiner summary

This part of the answer is typical of grade C performance. The student has shown a secure grasp of how the writer looks at herself from different perspectives, and feels that her defiant act will affect her in her different roles. The quotations are relevant and help to explain the writer's motives and thoughts.

Student 2 – Extract typical of a grade A answer

This is a well-focused comment, since the idea that she may need to be reminded that she is a woman does tell us that she is feeling a loss of her female identity.

The poem is neatly constructed in a single ten-line stanza with ten answers to the question: 'Why will you paint your nails red?' The reasons are varied, relating closely to her perception of herself. The emphasis on surprising her lover and daughter suggests that she feels too predictable: she is amused at the idea of disgusting her daughter, (who 'will say ugh'), by doing something unexpected. There is humour, but also some frustration about her life, especially in 'it will remind me I'm a woman', as though her everyday life has drained away her femininity. The final stress on this easily 'reversible' act, 'a ten-minute moratorium', tells us that this is a small but significant action.

The student notes that the writer's 'reasons' show a mixture of feelings, with a degree of self-mockery in the admission that this is only a small gesture which can quickly be undone.

Examiner summary

This part of the answer is typical of grade A performance. This student looks closely at the narrator's multiple identities, and notes that the narrator is interested in how those closest to her will react. There is an intelligent grasp of the way in which the woman appears to feel that the act of defiance itself is less important than being seen to do something, but she can easily undo it.

(b) (i) Compare how the writers of 'I Shall Paint My Nails Red' and **one** poem of your choice from the Taking a Stand collection reflect on feelings of defiance or opposition.

Use **evidence** from the poems to support your answer.

You may include material you used to answer (a).

(15 marks)

Student 1 – Extract typical of a grade Ⓒ answer

This point about Zephaniah's language demonstrates a secure grasp of his writing.

> I am comparing 'I Shall Paint My Nails Red' with 'No Problem', because they are about someone not wishing to be stereotyped. Zephaniah says 'yu put me in a pigeon hole'. He feels that white people think all black people are the same. Carole Satyamurti aims her defiant gesture at those closest to her, whereas in 'No Problem' the writer addresses all those prejudiced against him. He writes 'if yu give I a chance'. By the use of dialect, the poet stresses he wants to be different from what people expect. In both poems, the person speaking is saying that they do not like being taken for granted, and that people should think about what they are really like.

The point made is a very fair one, but needs to be supported by evidence from the poem.

Examiner summary

This part of the answer is typical of grade C performance. The student has chosen a second poem which allows for relevant comparative comments. In particular, the answer focuses on how both narrators may be seen as anxious to question stereotyping, showing that they can behave in ways which would not be expected from someone in their situation. The comment on dialect is securely based on a reasonable interpretation.

Student 2 – Extract typical of a grade Ⓐ answer

This is an effective use of technical language, as the student is aware that the landowners are not really going to send wild birds to chase him, and is using extreme images for exaggerated effect.

> The gently ironic tone of Carole Satyamurti, poking fun at herself and family rather than 'taking a stand' dramatically, contrasts strikingly with Simon Armitage's powerful anger against the rich, conveyed in the ferocity of the title, with its use of the swear word 'bastards'. His opposition to those living in 'palaces and castles' shows a deep resentment of the class system. He has been made to feel inferior and thinks these people blame him for everything that goes wrong: 'you'd think I'd poisoned the dogs'. He imagines himself being attacked by not only beagles, but even eagles, the rhyme emphasising the grim hyperbole. While Satyamurti wishes only to shock her daughter and lover, Armitage threatens retaliation or self-defence by carrying a gun, the ominous last word of the poem.

This is a well-justified final comment which shows that the speaker is prepared to take his opposition to extreme lengths: he comes across as a revolutionary, or a terrorist, who is prepared to kill.

Examiner summary

This part of the answer is typical of grade A performance. This student has chosen a strikingly contrasting second poem, and has justified this by intelligent, thoughtful links and comparative points. The student's language shows an excellent ability to offer an interpretation based firmly on the text. The reference to the title of the collection is neatly brought in: a 'stand' may be on minor matters or on something more serious.

Unseen poetry

- to understand how to approach an unseen poem and to explore its key ideas and themes.

Making sense of the poem

This lesson will help you to practise some of the techniques you can use to begin to understand the unseen poem that you will face in your exam. These techniques include looking at the title and the first line for clues as to what the poem is about, and trying to identify the **lexical field** to set up related words.

First thoughts

Activity 1

1. You are going to practise tackling an unseen poem using a poem called 'Nettles'.

    a. When you are given an unseen poem, first look at the title. A poem's title can help you identify the ideas or themes the poet wants the reader to think about. List **five** words or phrases that you associate with nettles.

    b. What do you think might happen in a poem entitled 'Nettles'? Try to think of **three** possible ideas.

Looking more closely

Activity 2

1. Read the poem 'Nettles' on page 14 of your Anthology. Look at the first line of the poem and work out what the poem is likely to be about.

    'My son aged three fell in the nettle bed.'

    a. What does this line tell you about the relationship explored in the poem?

    b. How do you think the poet wants you to feel as you read this opening line?

    c. How has the poet created this feeling? Choose your answer from the methods below, or come up with your own:

    | by giving factual information | through his choice of language | through the simplicity of this first line | through all of the methods suggested here |

2. Now, look at these words taken from the rest of the poem:

    | regiment | recruits | wounds |

    a. What is the connection between these three words?

    b. Pick out **three** more words or phrases from the poem which could be added to this group.

3. A lexical field is a set of related words. For example, the words

    | mother | father | son | daughter | cousin |

    could all be part of the lexical field of 'family'. Identifying words in the main lexical field can give you clues about the theme of the poem.

    What does the lexical field which you explored in question 2 tell you about the meaning or theme of the poem 'Nettles'?

Developing your ideas

Thinking about the emotions explored in an unseen poem can help you develop your response.

1. Pick out all the words and phrases from the poem which express emotions. Organise them under two headings:

The emotions of the child	The emotions of the parent
Sobs and tears	Fury

2. How does the father feel about the nettle bed? Find **two or three** quotations from the poem to support your ideas.

3. Look again at the last line of the poem.

   a. Why have the events described in the poem led the father to say this, do you think?

   b. What kinds of wounds might he be referring to? Try to think of at least **three** different kinds of wounds which the son might experience as he grows older.

Developing your response

Identifying a key quotation from an unseen poem can help you sum up the main theme and understand what the poem is about.

1. **a.** Choose **one** line which you feel sums up the theme of 'Nettles'.

   b. Write **one** sentence explaining what you think is the theme of the poem. Use evidence from the poem to support your answer.

2. **a.** Read the poem aloud to a partner. Select **one** of the words below, or another of your choice, to describe the writer's voice in the poem.

   sad   angry   regretful   resentful   disappointed

   b. Write down **one or two** quotations from the poem to support your answer.

3. Look at this example of an examination-style question:

   Explain how Scannell explores the subject of a father's relationship with his son.

   Write a paragraph supported by evidence from the poem that could be included in your answer.

ResultsPlus
Self/Peer assessment

1. Read this response to the above task.
2. Annotate your paragraphs using similar notes to those given on the right. Add in anything you've forgotten.
3. Using the mark schemes on pages 163 and 168, decide which band your paragraphs would fall into.
4. Look again at the techniques mentioned at the beginning of the lesson. How confident are you in using these techniques to approach an unseen poem? If you feel less confident with any of the techniques, discuss them with a partner. Look again at the poem and your answers to the questions on these pages to help you.

Explanation of the quotation's effect   A clear point   Evidence to support it

Throughout the poem, Scannell uses language from the lexical field of war. He describes the nettles as: 'That regiment of spite'. By describing the nettles as spiteful the father suggests that the nettles attacked his son on purpose, wanting to hurt him. The military image created by the word 'regiment' reinforces this idea, suggesting an organised force like an army, intent on causing pain and destruction. The close contrast between the army and the army's victim – a defenceless three-year-old child – prompts the reader's sympathy for the boy and his helpless father.

Explores the writer's intention   Close focus on word choice

My learning objective

• to explore how non-standard language choices create tone and contribute to the poet's presentation of theme, ideas and setting in an unseen poem.

Non-standard forms

This lesson will help you to practise some more techniques that will help you tackle the unseen poem. These include identifying words that set the tone of the poem, identifying and exploring the effect of **non-standard** language, and exploring **lexical fields**.

First thoughts

Activity 1

1. Read the poem 'Green Beret' by Ho Thien on the next page.

2. **a.** Look at the first line of the poem. What does this tell you?

   b. Briefly summarise the events described in the poem.

Looking more closely

Activity 2

1. **a.** Write down any words or phrases from the poem which are written in informal, non-standard English such as slang or *dialect* – the word 'kid' in line 11, for example.

   b. Look at where non-standard English is used in the poem. What do you notice?

2. Look at the lines below, taken from the poem.

   "Right kid tell us where they are,

   tell us where or your father – dead."

   "You've got one minute kid', said Green Beret,

   'tell us where or we kill father"

   a. How does the poet make what Green Beret says sound brutal? Think about the words used, words that are missed out and the use of the *imperative* 'tell'.

   b. Why do you think the poet has chosen to write what Green Beret says as direct speech?

3. Now look at line 19 of the poem:

   "OK boy ten seconds to tell us where they are"

   Why does the poet use the word 'boy' here instead of 'kid' which he used in lines 11 and 15?

4. Look at line 22 of the poem.

   "Kill the old guy' roared Green Beret'

   What difference would it have made to the poem if the poet had used 'man' instead of the non-standard English 'guy' in this line?

5. None of the characters in the poem are named. What effect does this create, do you think?

6. Write a paragraph or two exploring how the writer has created the character of Green Beret. Don't forget to include details of the poet's use of non-standard English and the effects the poet achieves.

Green Beret

He was twelve years old,
and I do not know his name.
The mercenaries took him and his father,
whose name I do not know,
one morning upon the High Plateau.   5
Green Beret looked down on the frail boy
with the eyes of a hurt animal and thought,
a good fright will make him talk.
He commanded, and the father was taken away
behind the forest's green wall.   10
'Right kid tell us where they are,
tell us where or your father – dead.'
With eyes now bright and filled with terror
the slight boy said nothing.
'You've got one minute kid', said Green Beret,   15
'tell us where or we kill father'
and thrust his wrist-watch against a face all eyes,
the second-hand turning, jerking on its way.
'OK boy ten seconds to tell us where they are'
In the last instant the silver hand shattered the   20
    sky and the forest of trees.
'Kill the old guy' roared Green Beret
and shots hammered out
behind the forest's green wall
and sky and trees and soldiers stood   25
in silence, and the boy cried out.
Green Beret stood
in silence, as the boy crouched down
and shook with tears,
as children do when their father dies.   30
'Christ', said one mercenary to Green Beret,
'he didn't know a damn thing
we killed the old guy for nothing'
so they all went away.
Green Beret and his mercenaries.   35

And the boy knew everything.
He knew everything about them, the caves,
the trails, the hidden places and the names,
and in the moment that he cried out,
in that same instant,   40
protected by frail tears
far stronger than any wall of steel,
they passed everywhere
like tigers
across the High Plateau.   45

Ho Thien

145

Unseen poetry

Developing your ideas | Activity 3

1. a. How would you describe the tone of the poem? Select **one** of the following words, or a different word of your own choice:

> brutal   violent   disturbing   moving   triumphant

b. Pick out **five** words or phrases in the poem which you feel help to create the tone.

c. Write a sentence or two about **each** word or phrase you have chosen, explaining how it helps to create the tone of the poem. For example:

> The boy's eyes are 'filled with terror' when they take his father away, reminding us how young and vulnerable he is. This makes the attitude of Green Beret, and the tone of the poem, all the more disturbing.

2. Look at line 36 of the poem:

'And the boy knew everything.'

a. How does this line change the tone of the poem?

b. How does this line change the way the reader feels about:
- the boy?
- his father?
- Green Beret?

Developing your response | Activity 4

1. Look at some of the key vocabulary from the poem below.

> mercenaries   father   Green Beret   frail   boy   hurt animal   fright
> commanded   forest   kid   dead   terror   kill   trees   shots
> hammered   sky   trees   silence   cried out   crouched   shook   tears
> children   dies   caves   trails   steel   tigers

a. Write down **three** lexical fields which this vocabulary suggests to you. Remember that a lexical field is a set of related words.

b. Choose at least **three** examples of the key vocabulary from each lexical field to support your answer. You could write your answers in a table like the one below.

Lexical field	Examples		
1. Fear	hurt animal		
2.			
3.			

2. How does each of the lexical fields you identified in question 1 contribute to the creation of characters, setting and tone of the poem?

3. Think about the use of characters and their voices in poems you have read.

   a. What do they help to create or reflect? Select your answer from at least one of the following:

- the tone or atmosphere of a poem
- the ideas in a poem
- the poet's attitude or point of view
- the theme of the poem.

   b. Choose examples from the Poetry Anthology to support your ideas.

4. Look at this example of an examination-style question:

Explain how Thien conveys his thoughts and feelings about war in 'Green Beret'.

Write two paragraphs supported by evidence from the poem that could be included in your answer.

ResultsPlus
Self/Peer assessment

These sentences are all taken from different students' writing in response to the task above.

1. Use some of these sentences, and the mark schemes on pages 163 and 168, to create a paragraph which you think would achieve your target band or higher.

2. Look again at the paragraphs you wrote in Activity 4. How could you improve them to ensure you achieve your target band?

3. Look again at the techniques mentioned at the beginning of the lesson. How confident are you in using these techniques to approach an unseen poem? If you feel less confident with any of the techniques, discuss them with a partner. Look again at the poem and your answers to the questions on these pages to help you.

> The Green Beret misses out words as though he is making his threat clear to someone who is not an English speaker. It also has the effect of creating a dramatic pause before the even more dramatic threat which follows.

> This older man and his life have become nothing more than a tool which the soldiers are using to get information.

> The phrase 'old guy' reminds us of his age and vulnerability and suggests how little value the soldiers place on his life.

> 'Right kid tell us where they are, tell us where or your father – dead.'

> The word 'kid' not only emphasises the youth of the victim he is interrogating but suggests a kind of familiarity or even disrespect which the end of the poem shows to be completely misplaced.

> The poet uses non-standard English in the Green Beret's dialogue.

> The non-standard word 'guy' dehumanises the Green Beret's victim. Like all the other characters in the poem, he is not named so we focus not on who but what these people are.

> "Kill the old guy' roared Green Beret and shots hammered out behind the forest's green wall'

- to explore how imagery helps a poet to present themes and ideas in an unseen poem.

Writing about imagery

This lesson will help you to practise looking at imagery and its effects, exploring the use of personification and identifying powerful words that influence the tone of the poem. These are all useful techniques when tackling an unseen poem.

First thoughts

Activity 1

1. Imagery is the use of language to create pictures in the readers' minds. Create a spider diagram of all the techniques you can think of that writers use to achieve this.

2. **a.** Read 'City Jungle' on page 38 of the Poetry Anthology.

   b. When exploring an unseen poem, look for imagery that is particularly effective at showing the poet's ideas. Choose one of the images from line 5 onwards of 'City Jungle' which you feel is particularly effective.

Looking more closely

Activity 2

Identifying and exploring the imagery in an unseen poem can help you develop your response to it.

1. **a.** Look again at 'City Jungle'. Identify **two** further images from line 5 onwards in the poem.

   b. Why has the poet used each of the images you have selected, do you think? Briefly explain your ideas.

2. **a.** What do the three images you have explored so far have in common?

   b. How do these images influence your view of the city described in the poem?

   c. What technique has the poet used to create most of the imagery in the poem?

3. Look at these three images from the poem. Each one has been annotated with some of the different ideas they might suggest. Which of these ideas do you agree with and which do not really fit with your reading of the whole poem?

like a reptile, crawling, low, sneaky

'lizard cars cruise by'

sleek and shiny

a menacing, intimidating smile

'their radiators grin'

happy – the cars really like the city

not enough food, hungry?

'thin headlights stare'

mean, intimidating

Developing your ideas

When tackling an unseen poem and trying to work out what an image suggests, you need to think about:

* the poet's choice of language
* the image it creates in your mind
* the way it makes you feel.

1. a. Identify any words or phrases in the poem that suggest a feeling of menace.

  b. Which of these are the most effective, do you think? Briefly explain your ideas.

2. The poet uses a range of powerful verbs, such as 'grin', 'stare', 'cough', 'snarls', 'flinch' and 'lashes'.

  a. What do these **verbs** suggest to you?

  b. How do they help to convey how the writer feels about the city?

3. Look at the following line.

> 'Newspapers shuffle by,
> hands in their pockets.'

  What ideas does this image suggest to you? Write a sentence or two exploring your ideas.

Developing your response

1. Think about the effect of imagery in poetry and how it can influence:

* the tone or atmosphere
* the ideas
* the poet's attitude or point of view
* the theme of the poem.

Choose examples from the Poetry Anthology to support your ideas.

2. Look at this example of an examination-style question:

How does Corbett use imagery to present his ideas and attitudes to city life in 'City Jungle'? Use evidence from the poem to support your answer.

Write two or three paragraphs supported by evidence from the poem that could be included in your answer.

ResultsPlus
Self/Peer assessment

1. Look again at the paragraphs you wrote in answer to the question above, and at the mark schemes on pages 163 and 168. Which band would your answer fall into?

2. What could you change or add to improve your answer? Use the mark schemes to identify the two things most likely to improve your mark.

3. Redraft your answer, making those changes.

4. Check that your new answer has moved up to the next band.

5. Look again at the techniques mentioned at the beginning of the lesson. How confident are you in using these techniques to approach an unseen poem? If you feel less confident with any of the techniques, discuss them with a partner. Look again at the poem and your answers to the questions on these pages to help you.

Unseen poetry

My learning objective

- to explore how a poet uses alliteration and onomatopoeia to create tone and atmosphere in an unseen poem.

The use of sound to create tone and atmosphere

This lesson will help you to practise exploring how imagery contributes to the tone of a poem and how sounds (**onomatopoeia** and **alliteration**) are used to create atmosphere. These techniques will help you to tackle the unseen poem in the exam.

First thoughts

Activity 1

When you first read an unseen poem, it can be helpful to try to sum up the poem in a single sentence. Picking out one key quotation can also help you clarify your thoughts.

1. Read '04/01/07' by Ian McMillan on page 18 of the Poetry Anthology. Write one sentence explaining what happened to the poet on this date.

2. **a.** Choose **one line** from the poem which you feel sums up the poet's feelings on this date. Explain your choice.

   b. Choose **one word** from the poem which you feel sums up the poet's feelings on this date. Explain your choice.

Looking more closely

Activity 2

When you are asked to write about the poet's thoughts and feelings in an unseen poem, it is important to explore the tone or atmosphere which the writer has created.

1. Look at this image taken from the first line of the poem:

   'The telephone shatters the night's dark glass.'

   a. Explain the picture this creates in your mind.

   b. What tone does this image create at the beginning of the poem? You can use a word from the green box on the next page, or another of your own choice.

2. Look at line 3 of the poem.

   'the moment it takes a life to pass
    From waking to sleeping'

   a. What do you think the poet is suggesting?

   b. What does this suggest about the writer's thoughts and feelings about the death of his mother?

3. The *sound* of the words in a poem often contributes to its tone and atmosphere. Find these examples of onomatopoeia in the poem:

shatters	clinks	drones	slap	smashed

   a. Which of these words suggests or mirrors how the poet himself is feeling?

   b. Which of these words suggests that everyday life continues despite this terrible news?

   c. Can you think of connections that could be made between these words? What is the effect of the connections?

Developing your ideas

Activity 3

1. Copy and complete the sentences below, using words from the green box. These sentences explain how onomatopoeia helps to create a particular tone in the poem.

   a. The click of the light switch creates a tone of _____ .

   b. The clink of milk bottles creates a tone of _____ .

   c. It could be argued that the droning plane creates a similar tone of _____ .

   d. However, it could be argued that it adds a tone of _____ .

   e. This is a strong contrast to the tone of _____ created by the images of smashed and shattered glass.

reflection	cynicism	shock	mundanity
anguish	quiet contemplation	sadness	sadness
everyday ordinariness	upset	aggression	impending disaster

   Add a sentence to each of the above sentences, explaining your ideas.

Developing your response

Activity 4

1. Think about the effect of sound in poetry in general. Explain how it can help create or reflect:

   - the tone or atmosphere of a poem
   - the poet's attitude or point of view
   - the ideas in a poem
   - the theme of the poem.

   Choose examples from the Poetry Anthology to support your ideas.

2. Look at this example of an examination-style question:

   How does the tone and atmosphere of '04/01/07' convey McMillan's thoughts and feelings about the death of his mother?

   Write two paragraphs supported by evidence from the poem that could be included in your answer.

ResultsPlus
Self/Peer assessment

1. Read this paragraph written in response to the above task.

2. Annotate your paragraphs using similar notes to those given on the right. If you've forgotten to include anything in your paragraphs, add it in.

3. Using the mark schemes on pages 163 and 168, decide which band your paragraphs would fall into.

4. Look again at the techniques mentioned at the beginning of the lesson. How confident are you in using these techniques to approach an unseen poem? If you feel less confident with any of the techniques, discuss them with a partner. Look again at the poem and your answers to the questions on these pages to help you.

— A clear point   Evidence to support it —

The description of sound really helps create atmosphere in "04/01/07". The opening line of the poem:

"The telephone shatters the night's dark glass"

introduces the phone call which brings the devastating news of his mother's death. The image of sleep as fragile glass shattered by the sound of the telephone reflects the emotional effect the news has on McMillan creating a tone of shock and anguish. The familiarity of the sound combined with the intriguing imagery creates an atmosphere of emotional and physical disturbance and upset.

— An explanation of the effect of the quotation   Explores the writer's intention   Close focus on word choice and punctuation —

- to explore how a poet uses rhyme, rhythm, repetition, structure and form to present themes and ideas in an unseen poem.

Rhyme, rhythm, repetition, structure and form

This lesson will help you to practise some more techniques that might come in handy when responding to the unseen poem in the exam. These include identifying **lexical fields** and the main theme, exploring the effect of **rhythm**, **rhyme** and varying line length, and exploring the use of **stanzas** and repetition.

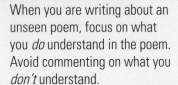

ResultsPlus

Examiner tip

When you are writing about an unseen poem, focus on what you *do* understand in the poem. Avoid commenting on what you *don't* understand.

First thoughts

Activity 1

When reading an unseen poem in your exam, you may find names or words that you do not understand. Don't panic! Focus on parts that you do understand and try to identify lexical fields that will give you an idea of the overall theme and message of the poem.

1. **a.** Read 'The Penelopes of my homeland' on page 57 of the Poetry Anthology. (If you don't understand the allusion to Penelope and Odysseus, look at the lexical fields to gain a general understanding of the poem.)
   b. Write a summary of the poem's main idea in one sentence.

Looking more closely

Activity 2

When reading an unseen poem, remember that the pace and rhythm often reflect its subject matter.

1. Read the first stanza of the poem aloud to a partner.

   Look at the pattern of stressed and unstressed *syllables* in the first line:

   'Years and years of silent labour'

   Does this pattern continue:
   - in the rest of this stanza?
   - in the rest of the poem?

2. How does the irregular rhythm of the poem help the poet to appear to be sharing her thoughts with the reader?

3. Look at these two sentences, spoken by a teacher to a student.

   You sit there chattering on and on while the rest of the class are waiting and waiting and waiting patiently for you to be quiet.

   Be quiet!

   a. Why do you think the teacher chose to make the first sentence so long?
   b. Why do you think he or she chose to make the second sentence so short?
   c. Some of the lines in the poem are very long. Others are very short. Identify one of each.
   d. What is the effect of the different length of these lines on the reader?

4. Identify **three** examples of repetition in the poem. How do these contribute to the pace and tone of the poem?

5. **a.** Can you identify any use of rhyme in the poem?
   b. How does this affect the pace and tone of the poem?

Developing your ideas

1. When reading and exploring an unseen poem, think about the key features of rhyme, rhythm, repetition, structure and form. Features in this poem include:

- no regular rhythm
- repetition
- no rhyme
- division into irregular stanzas.
- lines begin with a lower case letter
- longer lines
- shorter lines

Which of the key features above contributes to which of these effects?

a. Reflects the time for which the widows waited?

b. Emphasises the widow's futile denial of their husbands' deaths?

c. Suggests the poet is thinking aloud, sharing her thoughts with the reader?

d. Adds dramatic emphasis to a particular idea?

Developing your response

1. Think about the effect of the rhyme, rhythm, repetition, structure and form in poetry in general. Explain how it can create or reflect:

- the tone or atmosphere
- the ideas
- the poet's attitude or point of view
- the theme of a poem.

Choose examples from the Poetry Anthology to support your ideas.

2. Look at this example of an examination-style question:

Explain how Hardi conveys her thoughts and ideas about the widows of Anfal in 'The Penelopes of my homeland'.

Write two or three paragraphs supported by evidence from the poem that could be included in your answer.

ResultsPlus
Self/Peer assessment

These sentences are all taken from different students' writing in response to the task above.

1. Use some of these sentences, and the mark schemes on pages 163 and 168, to create a paragraph which you think would achieve your target band or higher.

2. Look again at the paragraphs you wrote in Activity 4. How could you improve them to ensure you achieve your target band?

3. Look again at the techniques mentioned at the beginning of the lesson. How confident are you in using these techniques to approach an unseen poem? If you feel less confident with any of the techniques, discuss them with a partner. Look again at the poem and your answers to the questions on these pages to help you.

> 'Years and years of widowhood they lived without realising, without ever thinking that their dream was dead the day it was dreamt'

> The uncertain, irregular rhythm of these lines reflects the tone of uncertainty in these widows' lives as they wait for their husbands who will never return.

> The broken rhythm of these lines creates uncertainty, even discomfort in the reader, building our sympathy for the widows of Anfal.

> The repetition of 'years' and 'without' emphasises the time that has passed, their loss, and their refusal to face it.

> The poem explores the feelings of women who cannot accept that their husbands have died and will not return to them.

> 'The Penelopes of my homeland / wove their own and their children's shrouds'

My learning objective

- to explore how use of personal pronouns, enjambement and the ordering of lines into stanzas helps to create voice in an unseen poem.

Form, structure and voice

This lesson will help you to practise the following techniques which you may need when responding to the unseen poem in your exam.

- Looking at the level of formality of a poem and what contributes to this.
- Considering the effects of *enjambement*, line length, *rhythm*, and pattern of *stanzas*.
- Exploring the use of the *sonnet* form.
- Looking at the effect of imagery and the use of *personal pronouns*.

First thoughts   Activity 1

1. Read 'The Stone Hare' on page 54 of the Poetry Anthology.

2. Make some notes about the poem, thinking about:
   - language and imagery
   - tone and atmosphere
   - structure and *form*.

   For example:

   > Language and imagery.
   > - related to ocean, e.g. 'reef', 'coral'
   > - final rhyming couple 'bone/stone' to summarise process by which stone is formed

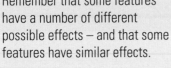

ResultsPlus

Examiner tip

Remember that some features have a number of different possible effects – and that some features have similar effects.

Looking more closely   Activity 2

1. Look closely again at 'The Stone Hare'.

   a. Would you describe the language and form of the poem as formal or informal?

   b. Which of the following features contribute to this, do you think?
   - the poet's choice of language
   - the use of the sonnet form
   - the lack of personal pronouns (I, you, we).
   - the irregular rhythm
   - the use of enjambement

2. Thinking about the effect that these features might have on your response to a poem, match the features below to their possible effects.

Features of form, structure and voice	Possible effects
• personal pronouns	creates a tone of fear and disorder
• irregular rhythm	suggests that we are hearing the poet's spontaneous thoughts
• regular rhythm	suggests control and certainty
• long lines	reflects the passing of a very long time
• short lines	suggests uncertainty
• enjambement	creates a close relationship between the poet and the reader, as though we are being spoken to directly
• *end-stopped lines*	suggests the clear, controlled voice of the speaker in the poem
• regular stanza pattern	
• irregular stanza pattern	creates a dramatic moment in the poem
	gives emphasis to a particular idea or event
	suggests careful, thoughtful reflection on the poem's subject matter
	makes the reader feel involved in the poem

3. Choose **three** features of form, structure and voice from the list on page 154. For **each** feature, find an example in one of the poems in the Anthology and explain why you think it is effective. Use a quotation in each of your answers.

Developing your ideas   Activity 3

1. **a.** How would you describe the voice and atmosphere of 'The Stone Hare'? You could choose from the list below, or come up with your own ideas.

   aggressive   disturbing   mysterious   shocking   sad   mundane   admiring   reflective

   b. Which of the features you have explored so far make the most significant contribution to creating the tone of the poem? Write a paragraph explaining your ideas and supporting them with evidence from the poem. For example:

   > The voice of 'The Stone Hare' is mysterious and admiring. One of the factors which contributes strongly to this tone is the use of enjambement: 'the slow birth/of limestone from the long trajectories/of starfish'. This really emphasises the millions of years over which this almost magical transformation has occurred.

Developing your response   Activity 4

1. Read 'Valentine' by Carol Ann Duffy on page 2 of the Poetry Anthology.

2. When you approach an unseen poem, the first thing to focus on is its main theme. In this poem, the main theme is about the reality of being in love. Then you need to explore the techniques that the poet uses to express this theme.

   a. Identify the following techniques and features in 'Valentine':

   - *metaphor*
   - *simile*
   - repetition
   - personal pronouns
   - emotive vocabulary
   - words that form a *lexical field*.

   b. Explain how the poet uses each of these to focus the reader on the theme.

3. Now look at the first line, the last line and the form of the poem (including stanza pattern, *rhyme* and rhythm). Write a comment about how these help to present the poet's ideas.

4. Look at this example of an examination-style question:

   Explore how the different techniques used in 'Valentine' encourage the reader to consider the reality of being in love.

   Write three or four paragraphs supported by evidence from the poem that could be included in your answer.

ResultsPlus
Self/Peer assessment

1. Look again at the paragraphs you wrote in Activity 4, and at the mark schemes on pages 163 and 168. Which band would your answer fall into?

2. What could you change or add to improve your answer? Use the mark schemes to identify the two things most likely to improve your mark.

3. Redraft your answer, making those changes.

4. Check that your new answer has moved up to the next band.

5. Look again at the techniques mentioned at the beginning of the lesson. How confident are you in using these techniques to approach an unseen poem? If you feel less confident with any of the techniques, discuss them with a partner.

Unseen **poetry**

My learning objective

- to learn how to write a successful response to the unseen poetry examination question.

Tackling the unseen poetry question

This lesson gives you the opportunity to:

- read an unseen poem (that is not in your Anthology)
- look at an exam question (either at Foundation or Higher Tier)
- practise how to plan your answer carefully
- use the skills you have developed to respond to the question.

First thoughts

Activity 1

1. Read *either* the Foundation Tier unseen poem 'Dress Sense' by David Kitchen *or* the Higher Tier unseen poem 'From the motorway' by Anne Stevenson, opposite.

2. Based on this first reading, write one sentence which summarises what you think are the main ideas in the poem.

Looking more closely

Activity 2

Read the poem again and the relevant exam question below.

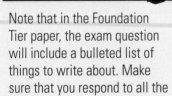

ResultsPlus
Examiner tip

Note that in the Foundation Tier paper, the exam question will include a bulleted list of things to write about. Make sure that you respond to all the bullet points in your answer.

Foundation Tier

Explain how David Kitchen explores the subject of a father's relationship with his daughter in 'Dress Sense'.

Write about:

- what is happening in the poem
- how the poet uses voice
- how the poet has organised the poem to present ideas.

Support your answer with examples from the poem.

Higher Tier

Explore how Anne Stevenson presents her ideas about the motorway in 'From the motorway'. Support your answer with examples from the poem.

Whether you're answering the Foundation or the Higher question, complete the questions below to help develop your understanding and ideas.

1. Read the question carefully. Underline the key words.

2. Look at the title of the poem. What does it mean to you? What does it suggest to you about the subject of the poem and the poet's attitude to it?

3. Look at the opening and the end. What is the poem likely to be about?

4. Read the poem carefully and underline words in the main *lexical field*. What indications do these words give about the theme and tone of the poem?

5. What is the main storyline and where is it set? Is the setting important?

Dress Sense

You're not going out in that, are you?
I've never seen anything
More ridiculous in my whole life.
You look like you've been dragged
Through a hedge backwards
And lost half your dress along the way.

What's wrong with it?
You're asking me what's wrong with that?
Everything: that's what.
It's loud, it's common,
It reveals far too much of your …
Your … well your 'what you shouldn't be
revealing'.

No, I'm not going to explain;
You know very well what I mean, young lady
But you choose to ignore
Every single piece of reasonable helpful advice
That you are offered.

It's not just the neckline I'm talking about
- And you can hardly describe it as a neckline,
More like a navel-line
If you bother to observe the way it plunges.
Have you taken a look at the back?
(What little there is of it.)
Have you?

Boys are only going to think
One thing
When they see you in that outfit.
Where on earth did you get it?
And don't tell me that my money paid for it
Whatever you do.

You found it where?

Well, it probably looked different on her
And, anyway, you shouldn't be going through
Your mother's old clothes.

David Kitchen

From the motorway

Everywhere up and down the island
Britain is mending her desert;
marvellous we exclaim as we fly on it,
tying the country in a parcel,
London to Edinburgh, Birmingham to Cardiff,
No time to examine the contents,

thank you, but consider the bliss of
sitting absolutely numbed to your
nulled mind, music when you want it,
while identical miles thunder under you,
the same spot coming and going
seventy, eighty times a minute,

till you're there, wherever there
is, ready to be someone in
Liverpool, Leeds, Manchester,
they're all the same to the road,
which loves itself, which nonetheless
here and there hands you training

necklaces of fumes in which to be
one squeezed breather among
rich and ragged, sprinter and staggerer,
a status parade for Major Roadworks
toiling in his red-trimmed triangle,
then a regiment of wounded orange witches
N----- 3

defending a shamelessly naked
(rarely a stitch of work on her)
captive free lane,
while the inchlings inch on
without bite or sup, at most
a hard shoulder to creep on,

while there, on all sides,
lie your unwrapped destinations,
lanes trickling off into childhood
or anonymity, apple-scented villages
asleep in their promise of being
nowhere anyone would like to get to.

Anne Stevenson

Now, depending on whether you are tackling the Foundation or the Higher question, answer some more specific questions.

Foundation Tier

6. Consider the level of formality of the poem. Why do you think the poet has chosen to write the poem in this way?

7. What do you learn about the characters and their relationship in the poem? How has the writer suggested this through his choice of language and form?

8. Look for examples of humour. How is the poet trying to get the reader to identify with the situation?

9. Look at the *stanza* pattern, *rhythm*, *rhyme* scheme, length of lines and use of *enjambement*/end-stopped lines. What tone is suggested by these? What is the writer saying and what is his attitude toward his topic?

Higher Tier

6. Identify any imagery: *metaphors*, *similes* or *personification*. Consider the connotations of these. How do these match your initial ideas about the main ideas and the theme of the poem? Also look for instances of *onomatopoeia* and *alliteration* and explore why the poet uses them.

7. What picture is emerging about the writer's feelings on the subject being explored?

8. Identify any *personal pronouns* (e.g. he/she/it, we, this, that). What do these suggest about the level of formality of the language?

9. Look at the *stanza* pattern, *rhythm*, *rhyme* scheme, length of lines and use of *enjambement* or *end-stopped lines*. What tone is suggested by these? What is the writer saying and what is her attitude towards the topic? Is there a logical pattern of argument?

Developing your response

Activity 3

1. Now plan your response to the exam question on your poem. To do this, complete the following tasks:

    a. Look at your answers to the questions in Activity 2.

    b. Choose four key points which you will use in your response.

    c. Choose four quotations which support your four key points.

    d. Note down any comments which you can make on those quotations, thinking about the writer's choice of language, structure or form.

    e. Decide on the order in which you will put these points in your essay and create a plan.

    You could record your plan using a spider diagram like the one opposite.

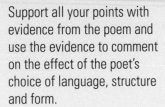

ResultsPlus

Examiner tip

Support all your points with evidence from the poem and use the evidence to comment on the effect of the poet's choice of language, structure and form.

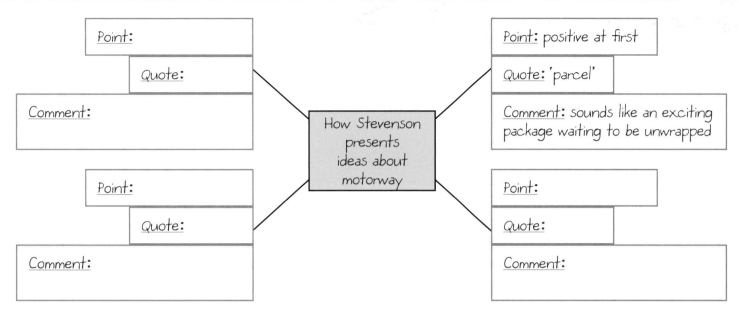

Or a table like this:

How David Kitchen presents the father's relationship with his daughter		
Points	Quotes	Comments
I. Opens with question	'You're not going out in that, are you?'	Rhetorical question – obviously not happy. Sounds aggressive.

2. Use your plan to write your response to the exam question on your poem.

ResultsPlus
Peer/Self assessment

1. Look again at your answer to the exam question on your chosen poem, and at the mark schemes on pages 163 and 168 for 'Dress Sense' by David Kitchen, or 'From the motorway' by Anne Stevenson. What band would you award your answer?

2. What could you change or add to improve your answer? Use the mark scheme to identify the two things most likely to improve your mark.

3. Redraft your answer, making those changes.

4. Look again at the mark scheme. Have you improved your mark?

Here are some extracts from student answers to Higher Tier English Literature examination questions. Read the answers together with the examiner comments to help you understand what you need to do to build better answers.

Read the following poem.

Blackberry Picking

Late August, given heavy rain and sun

For a full week, the blackberries would ripen.

At first, just one, a glossy purple clot

Among others, red, green, hard as a knot.

You ate that first one and its flesh was sweet

Like thickened wine: summer's blood was in it

Leaving stains upon the tongue and lust for

Picking. Then red ones inked up and that hunger

Sent us out with milk cans, pea tins, jam-pots

Where briars scratched and wet grass bleached our boots.

Round hayfields, cornfields and potato-drills

We trekked and picked until the cans were full

Until the tinkling bottom had been covered

With green ones, and on top big dark blobs burned

Like a plate of eyes. Our hands were peppered

With thorn pricks, our palms sticky as Bluebeard's.

We hoarded the fresh berries in the byre.

But when the bath was filled we found a fur,

A rat-grey fungus, glutting on our cache.

The juice was stinking too. Once off the bush

The fruit fermented, the sweet flesh would turn sour.

I always felt like crying. It wasn't fair

That all the lovely canfuls smelt of rot.

Each year I hoped they'd keep, knew they would not.

Seamus Heaney

Explore how Seamus Heaney presents his experiences of blackberry-picking.

Use **evidence** from the poem to support your answer.

(20 marks)

Student 1 – Extract typical of a grade Ⓒ answer

This is a very suitable piece of evidence on which to focus, since the phrase selected is a powerful one which, in a sense, sets the scene for what is to follow.

In this poem, Heaney's language gives the reader strong impressions of the blackberries, by using words to do with the senses, like taste, touch and sight. Examples include: 'a glossy purple knot' which describes the texture of the fruit as well as its colour and shape. He also makes a big contrast between the fresh fruit and the way it quickly goes off, with words like 'rat-grey fungus' and 'rot'. Although he is an adult, looking back, Heaney does use some simple, childish language. Children are always saying 'It wasn't fair' even when it is not anybody's fault.

The student shows an awareness of the different 'voices' in the text: here, Heaney does indeed seem to be more obviously reverting to his childish reactions.

Examiner summary

This part of the answer is typical of grade C performance. The student has certainly understood the main focus of the poem, and has commented in a suitable way on some language effects. The student makes reasonable points, especially about the contrast between the fresh fruit and how it changes after being picked. The comment about the difference between adult and childish language is supported by the quotations.

Student 2 – Extract typical of a grade Ⓐ answer

This is a mature and sophisticated analysis of the language, bringing out very strongly its implications and associations.

Like many of Seamus Heaney's poems, 'Blackberry Picking' shows him looking back to his country childhood, imagining a vivid summer's scene. Although he describes in detail the children's visits, he focuses first on the fruit itself, using rich, sensuous vocabulary to visualise and even 'taste' the fruit. The simile 'its flesh was sweet like thickened wine' effectively makes the reader think of drinking a sweet, concentrated liquid, but it is not a simile that we would expect a child to use. This shows how Heaney blends straightforward memories with adult interpretation. He fills the lines with hard-sounding one-syllable nouns ('milkcans, pea tins, jam-pots'), using rhyme or half-rhyme ('clot', 'knot') to add to the effect. This creates an intense experience, as the reader is thrown into the scene and shares the young Heaney's excitement and disappointment.

This shows the student is willing to offer a personal interpretation and explain the effect the poem has on the reader.

Examiner summary

This part of the answer is typical of grade A performance. This student writes powerfully and with a real grasp of how Heaney uses language to express his ideas. The point about the use of monosyllabic nouns shows strong awareness of the link between sound and meaning. There is much purposeful and focused attention to detail, and the poet's use of the language of the senses is analysed convincingly.

GCSE English Literature

You will answer two questions on poetry as part of the **Unit 2: Understanding Poetry** exam. The exam will last 1 hour and 45 minutes, and is worth 25% of your total GCSE. The exam is divided into two sections:

Section A: Unseen Poetry – You will be presented with an unseen poem. Read through this poem and answer the question set. Section A is worth 20 marks.

Section B: Anthology Poems – You will answer one question in two parts. Section B is worth 30 marks in total, 15 marks for each part.

- In **part (a)** you will be asked a question about a named poem from the anthology collection that you have studied.

- In **part (b)** you will answer one question from a choice of two in which you will be expected to link/compare two poems.

Sample Foundation Tier exam paper: Section A

> Read the poem before writing your answer. You may find it useful to read it twice: once without writing anything and once using a pen or highlighter to mark points you find interesting.

> You will be asked to **explain**, so you must make your ideas clear to the reader, saying why you think as you do. Use the bullet points to help you structure your answer.

> The way a poem is organised includes how it is set out and the use of stanzas. Who is addressed? Is there a first person speaker ('I')? Is there one topic throughout or is there a 'twist' at the end?

> Think about words the writer uses to show how he feels.

> Giving **evidence** from the poem means using short quotations that support the points you are making.

SECTION A: UNSEEN POEM

Read the following poem:

Remembering Snow
I did not sleep last night.
The falling snow was beautiful and white.
I dressed, sneaked down the stairs
And opened wide the door.
I had not seen such snow before.
Our grubby little street had gone.
The world was brand-new, and everywhere
There was a pureness in the air.
I felt such peace.
Watching every flake
I felt more and more awake.
I thought I had learned all there was to know
About the trillion million different kinds
Of swirling frosty flakes of snow.
That was not so.
I did not know how vividly it lit
The world with such a peaceful glow.
Upstairs my mother slept.
I could not drag myself away from that sight
To call her down and have her share
The mute miracle of the snow.
It seemed to fall for me alone.
How beautiful our grubby little street had grown!

Brian Patten

*1 Explain how Brian Patten feels about the snow and its effect on the street where he lives.

Write about:
- what happens in the poem
- how the writer has organised the poem
- how the writer uses language to show his feelings.

Use **evidence** from the poem to support your answer.

(Total for Question 1 = 20 marks)

Sample Foundation Tier mark scheme: Section A

Band	Mark	AO2: Explain how language, structure and form contribute to writers' presentation of ideas, themes and settings
1	1-4	• Little understanding of the poem's content/ideas. • Little explanation of how the writer uses language, structure and form to present the poem's content/ideas. • Little relevant textual reference to support response. *Material has simple organisation and little communication of ideas. Basic accuracy in spelling, punctuation and grammar hinders meaning
2	5-8	• Limited understanding of the poem's content/ideas. • Limited explanation of how the writer uses language, structure and form to present the poem's content/ideas. • Limited relevant textual reference to support response. *Material has limited organisation and limited communication of ideas. Limited accuracy in spelling, punctuation and grammar may hinder meaning.
3	9-12	• Some understanding of the poem's content/ideas. • Some explanation of how the writer uses language, structure and form to present the poem's content/ideas. • Some relevant textual reference to support response. *Some control in organising and communicating ideas. Spelling, punctuation and grammar sometimes accurate with meaning hindered on occasion.
4	13-16	• Generally sound understanding of the poem's content/ideas. • Generally sound explanation of how the writer uses language, structure and form to present the poem's content/ideas. • Generally sound relevant textual reference to support response. *Generally sound organisation and communication of ideas. Spelling, punctuation and grammar is mostly accurate; any errors do not hinder meaning.
5	17-20	• Sound understanding of the poem's content/ideas. • Sound explanation of how the writer uses language, structure and form to present the poem's content/ideas. • Sound relevant textual reference to support response. *Sound organisation and communication of ideas. Spelling, punctuation and grammar is mostly accurate, with some errors.

Section A of the poetry paper is assessed against this objective. Think about **what the writers say** and **how they say it** – such as choice of words, images and sound effects – and **how they organise and arrange their ideas** – such as the use of stanzas, length of lines, who is spoken to, rhyme and rhythm, 'twists'.

It is important to write and spell clearly and accurately so that the examiner understands what you are trying to say.

Organising and communicating your ideas are key skills: having a clear opening and ending is important, as is the use of paragraphs. Think about how words like 'therefore' and 'however' can act as signposts.

For the higher bands, you must pick out words and phrases (make textual reference) from the actual poem that are important in communicating ideas or subject matter.

Sample Foundation Tier exam paper: Section B

Although you will only answer one question in Section B, you should read **all** of the examiner's tips on pages 164 and 165 because they apply to all collections.

SECTION B: ANTHOLOGY POEMS

There is one question on each collection of poems.
Answer ONE question from this section.

Collection A: Relationships

2 (a) Describe the writer's thoughts and feelings about remembered love in 'Song for Last Year's Wife'.

Use **evidence** from the poem to support your answer. (15)

Answer EITHER 2(b)(i) OR 2(b)(ii)

(b) (i) Explain how the writer of 'Kissing' presents different ideas about love from those given in 'Song for Last Year's Wife'.

Use **evidence** from the poems to support your answer.
You may include material you used to answer 2(a). (15)

(ii) Explain how the writer of **one** poem of your choice from the 'Relationships' collection presents different ideas about relationships from those given in 'Song for Last Year's Wife'.

Use **evidence** from the poems to support your answer.
You may include material you used to answer 2(a). (15)

(Total for Question 2 = 30 marks)

Collection B: Clashes and Collisions

3 (a) Describe the writer's attitudes to twentieth century war in 'August 6, 1945'.

Use **evidence** from the poem to support your answer. (15)

Answer EITHER 3(b)(i) OR 3(b)(ii)

(b) (i) Explain how the writer of 'The Drum' presents different ideas about war from those in 'August 6, 1945'.

Use **evidence** from the poems to support your answer.
You may include material you used to answer 3(a). (15)

(ii) Explain how the writer of **one** poem of your choice from the 'Clashes and Collisions' collection presents different ideas about conflict from those in 'August 6, 1945'.

Use **evidence** from the poems to support your answer.
You may include material you used to answer 3(a). (15)

(Total for Question 3 = 30 marks)

You must answer the question relating to the collection you have studied. You need to complete **both** parts of the question – (a), and **either** (b)(i) or (b)(ii).

In **part (a)** you will be asked a question about a named poem from the anthology collection that you have studied.

In **part (b)** you will answer **one** question from a choice of two in which you will be expected to compare two poems.

When asked to **describe** someone's thoughts or feelings, or the writer's attitude to something, give a clear account of what you learn about these from reading the poem.

Make sure you include short quotations to support the points you are making. Remember to use P-E-E to help with this. Always comment on the evidence you include.

Collection C: Somewhere, Anywhere

4   (a) Describe the writer's thoughts and feelings about Cape Town
         in 'Cape Town morning'.

         Use **evidence** from the poem to support your answer.   (15)

Answer EITHER 4(b)(i) OR 4(b)(ii)

     (b) (i) Explain how the writer of 'London Snow' presents ··········
              different thoughts and feelings about a city from
              those in 'Cape Town morning'.

              Use **evidence** from the poems to support your answer.
              You may include material you used to answer 4(a). ···:   (15)

         (ii) Explain how the writer of **one** poem of your choice from the
              'Somewhere, Anywhere' collection presents different thoughts
              and feelings about a place from those in 'Cape Town morning'.

              Use **evidence** from the poems to support your answer.
              You may include material you used to answer 4(a).   (15)

                                   (Total for Question 4 = 30 marks)

> If you are asked to **explain**, you must make your ideas clear to the reader, saying **why** you think as you do.

> You should only include points on the first poem that are relevant for making links and comparisons with the second one.

Collection D: Taking a Stand

5   (a) Describe the writer's thoughts and feelings about her
         identity in 'I Shall Paint My Nails Red'.

         Use **evidence** from the poem to support your answer.   (15)

Answer EITHER 5(b)(i) OR 5(b)(ii)

     (b) (i) Explain how the writer of 'No Problem' presents different ··········
              thoughts and feelings about identity from those in
              'I Shall Paint My Nails Red'.

              Use **evidence** from the poems to support your answer.
              You may include material you used to answer 5(a).   (15)

         (ii) Explain how the writer of **one** poem of your choice from ··········
              the 'Taking a Stand' collection presents different strong
              feelings from those in 'I Shall Paint My Nails Red'.

              Use **evidence** from the poems to support your answer.
              You may include material you used to answer 5(a).   (15)

                                   (Total for Question 5 = 30 marks) ········

> In **part (b)(i)** you will be given two named poems to compare.

> In **part (b)(ii)** you will be given one named poem and will need to choose a second to compare it with. Make sure you have interesting points to make about the poem you choose.

> There are a total of 30 marks available for this question – 15 marks for part (a) and 15 marks for part (b). You should spend around the same amount of time and effort on each part of the question.

Section B part (a) of the poetry paper is assessed against this objective. Think about **what the writers say and how they say it** – such as choice of words, images and sound effects – and **how they organise and arrange their ideas**, such as the use of stanzas, length of lines, who is spoken to, rhyme and rhythm, any 'twists'.

Sample Foundation Tier mark scheme: Section B

Part (a) questions

Band	Mark	AO2: Explain how language, structure and form contribute to writers' presentation of ideas, themes and settings
1	1-3	• Little explanation of how the writer conveys his thoughts and feelings. • Little relevant connection made between the presentation of thoughts and feelings and the language used. • Little relevant textual reference to support response.
2	4-6	• Limited explanation of how the writer conveys his thoughts and feelings to create effect. • Limited relevant connection made between thoughts and feelings and the language used. • Limited relevant textual reference to support response.
3	7-9	• Some explanation of how the writer conveys his thoughts and feelings to create effect. • Some relevant connection made between thoughts and feelings and the presentation of ideas. • Occasional relevant textual reference to support response.
4	10-12	• Generally sound explanation of how the writer conveys his thoughts and feelings to create effect. • Generally sound relevant connection made between his thoughts and feelings and the presentation of ideas. • Mostly clear, relevant textual reference to support response.
5	13-15	• Sound explanation of how the writer uses thoughts and feelings to create effect. • Sound, relevant connection made between his thoughts and feelings and the presentation of ideas. • Clear, relevant textual reference to support response.

Relevant answers keep to the point, so don't just write down everything that you know about a poem. Always make sure you work out exactly what you should include and what you should leave out. For example, if the question asks you what someone is **thinking**, don't write about what he or she is **doing**.

Part (b) questions

Band	Mark	AO3: make comparisons and explain links between texts
1	1-3	• Basic (or no) comparisons/links. • Basic (or no) evaluation of the different ways of expressing meaning. • Selection of examples is basic.
2	4-6	• Limited (or no) comparisons/links. • Limited (or no) evaluation of the different ways of expressing meaning. • Selection of examples is limited.
3	7-9	• Some comparisons and links. • Some evaluation of the different ways of expressing meaning and achieving effects. • Selection of examples is valid but undeveloped.
4	10-12	• Generally sound comparisons and links. • Some clear evaluation of the different ways of expressing meaning and achieving effects. • Selection of examples is mostly appropriate; shows some support of the points being made.
5	13-15	• Sound comparisons and links. • Some clear evaluation of the different ways of expressing meaning and achieving effects. • Selection of examples is appropriate; shows some support of the points being made.

Section B part (b) of the poetry paper is assessed against this objective. Making **comparisons** and **links** is the key to part (b) questions. Think about what is **similar** and what is **different** about the poems. Use **evidence** to support your points.

To achieve higher marks, you must give your own **evaluation** of the similarities and differences in how the two poems say things. This means that you have to make a judgement about what you feel works well in each poem and why.

Sample Higher Tier exam paper: Section A

SECTION A: UNSEEN POEM

Read the following poem:

Blackberry Picking
Late August, given heavy rain and sun
For a full week, the blackberries would ripen.
At first, just one, a glossy purple clot
Among others, red, green, hard as a knot.
You ate that first one and its flesh was sweet
Like thickened wine: summer's blood was in it
Leaving stains upon the tongue and lust for
Picking. Then red ones inked up and that hunger
Sent us out with milk cans, pea tins, jam-pots
Where briars scratched and wet grass bleached our boots.
Round hayfields, cornfields and potato-drills
We trekked and picked until the cans were full
Until the tinkling bottom had been covered
With green ones, and on top big dark blobs burned
Like a plate of eyes. Our hands were peppered
With thorn pricks, our palms sticky as Bluebeard's.

We hoarded the fresh berries in the byre.
But when the bath was filled we found a fur,
A rat-grey fungus, glutting on our cache.
The juice was stinking too. Once off the bush
The fruit fermented, the sweet flesh would turn sour.
I always felt like crying. It wasn't fair
That all the lovely canfuls smelt of rot.
Each year I hoped they'd keep, knew they would not.

Seamus Heaney

*1   Explore how Seamus Heaney **presents his experiences of blackberry-picking**.

Use **evidence** from the poem to support your answer.

(Total for Question 1 = 20 marks)

Read the poem before writing your answer. You may find it useful to read it twice: once without writing anything and once using a pen or high lighter to mark points you find interesting.

Remember to comment on examples of language that you think are particularly interesting, unusual or striking. This line might be a good example to choose, if you feel you understand what the writer is saying.

Always focus on the key words of the question: here, you need to look closely at what Heaney says about his experience of picking blackberries, and how he uses language, form and structure to present his feelings.

You need short quotations to support the points you are making. Remember to use P-E-E to help with this.

Sample Higher Tier mark scheme: Section A

Section A of the poetry paper is assessed against this objective. Think about **what the writers say** and **how they say it** – such as choice of words, images and sound effects – and **how they organise and arrange their ideas** – such as the use of stanzas, length of lines, who is spoken to, rhyme and rhythm, 'twists'.

Band	Mark	AO2: Explain how language, structure and form contribute to writers' presentation of ideas, themes and settings
1	1-4	• Generally sound understanding of the poem's content/ideas. • Generally sound explanation of how the writer uses language, structure and form to present the poem's content/ideas. • Generally sound relevant textual reference to support response. *Generally sound organisation and communication of ideas. Spelling, punctuation and grammar is mostly accurate; any errors do not hinder meaning.
2	5-8	• Sound understanding of the poem's content/ideas. • Sound explanation of how the writer uses language, structure and form to present the poem's content/ideas. • Sound relevant textual reference to support response. *Sound organisation and communication of ideas. Spelling, punctuation and grammar is mostly accurate, with some errors.
3	9-12	• Thorough understanding of the poem's content/ideas. • Thorough explanation of how the writer uses language, structure and form to present the poem's content/ideas. • Sustained relevant textual reference to support response. *Appropriate organisation and sustained communication of ideas. Spelling, punctuation and grammar is almost always accurate, with occasional errors.
4	13-16	• Assured understanding of the poem's content/ideas. • Assured explanation of how the writer uses language, structure and form to present the poem's content/ideas. • Pertinent relevant textual reference to support response. *Purposeful organisation and assured communication of ideas. Spelling, punctuation and grammar is almost always accurate, with minimal errors.
5	17-20	• Perceptive understanding of the poem's content/ideas. • Perceptive explanation of how the writer uses language, structure and form to present the poem's content/ideas. • Convincing relevant textual reference to support response. *Convincing organisation and sophisticated communication of ideas. Spelling, punctuation and grammar is consistently accurate.

To achieve the higher bands, your writing must be free from errors. If it is not, set yourself (with help from your teacher) the challenge of cutting out errors from your writing.

Have a clear sense of the level you need to aim at for the highest grades: the Band 5 descriptors are a good starting point. The word **perceptive** is used in the first two bullet points. Perceptive writing shows that you have got to the heart of the poem's meaning and can demonstrate your overall judgement and interpretation.

Another key word in the Band 5 descriptors is **convincing**. You need to be able to convince the examiners of your understanding of the poem through:
- strong analysis
- quality evidence (quotations)
- good writing.

Sample Higher Tier exam paper: Section B

Although you will only answer one question in Section B, you should read **all** of the examiner's tips on pages 169 and 170 because they apply to all collections.

SECTION B: ANTHOLOGY POEMS

There is one question on each collection of poems.
Answer ONE question from this section.

Collection A: Relationships

2   (a)   Explore how the writer conveys his attitudes towards remembered love in 'Song for Last Year's Wife'.

Use **evidence** from the poem to support your answer. (15)

Answer EITHER 2(b)(i) OR 2(b)(ii)

(b)   (i)   Compare how the writers explore different ideas about love in 'Kissing' and 'Song for Last Year's Wife'.

Use **evidence** from the poems to support your answer.
You may include material you used to answer 2(a). (15)

OR

(ii)   Compare how the writers of 'Song for Last Year's Wife' and **one** poem of your choice from the 'Relationships' collection reflect on loving relationships.

Use **evidence** from the poems to support your answer.
You may include material you used to answer 2(a). (15)

(Total for Question 2 = 30 marks)

Collection B: Clashes and Collisions

3   (a)   Explore how the writer presents her ideas about twentieth century war in 'August 6, 1945'.

Use **evidence** from the poem to support your answer. (15)

Answer EITHER 3(b)(i) OR 3(b)(ii)

EITHER

(b)   (i)   Compare the different ways the writers explore the theme of war in 'The Drum' and 'August 6, 1945'.

Use **evidence** from the poems to support your answer.
You may include material you used to answer 3(a). (15)

OR

(ii)   Compare how the writers of 'August 6, 1945' and **one** poem of your choice from the 'Clashes and Collisions' collection reflect on attitudes to war.

Use **evidence** from the poems to support your answer.
You may include material you used to answer 3(a). (15)

(Total for Question 3 = 30 marks)

You must answer the question relating to the collection you have studied. You need to complete **both** parts of the question – (a), and **either** (b)(i) or (b)(ii).

In **part (a)** you will be asked a question about a named poem from the anthology collection that you have studied.

In **part (b)** you will answer **one** question from a choice of two in which you will be expected to compare two poems.

Explore is a key word. When you explore a subject, you need to try to cover it in depth and look at it from different angles. You may wish to consider different possible interpretations.

Giving **evidence** from the poem means referring closely to what it actually says. You need to include short quotations to support the points you are making. Remember to use P-E-E to help with this.

Collection C: Somewhere, Anywhere

4   (a) Explore how the writer presents her thoughts and feelings about Cape Town in 'Cape Town morning'.

Use **evidence** from the poem to support your answer.   (15)

Answer EITHER 4(b)(i) OR 4(b)(ii)

EITHER

(b) (i) Compare how the writers explore different thoughts and feelings about towns in 'Our Town with the Whole of India' and 'Cape Town morning'.

Use **evidence** from the poems to support your answer. You may include material you used to answer 4(a).   (15)

OR

(ii) Compare how the writers of 'Cape Town morning' and **one** poem of your choice from the 'Somewhere, Anywhere' collection reflect on a place.

Use **evidence** from the poems to support your answer. You may include material you used to answer 4(a).   (15)

(Total for Question 4 = 30 marks)

Collection D: Taking a Stand

5   (a) Explore how the writer presents her ideas about her identity in 'I Shall Paint My Nails Red'.

Use **evidence** from the poem to support your answer.   (15)

Answer EITHER 5(b)(i) OR 5(b)(ii)

EITHER

(b) (i) Compare how the writers present different ideas of identity in 'No Problem' and 'I Shall Paint My Nails Red'.

Use **evidence** from the poems to support your answer. You may include material you used to answer 5(a).   (15)

OR

(ii) Compare how the writers of 'I Shall Paint My Nails Red' and **one** poem of your choice from the 'Taking a Stand' collection reflect on feelings of defiance or opposition.

Use **evidence** from the poems to support your answer. You may include material you used to answer 5(a).   (15)

(Total for Question 5 = 30 marks)

In the **part (b)** questions, the quality of your writing about **links and comparisons** is crucial; you should consider how the two poems handle the same theme and the way language is used. Look closely also at the form and structure of each poem, and how any differences affect the writer's ideas and presentation.

You should only include points on the first poem that are relevant for making links and comparisons with the second one.

In **part (b)(i)** you will be given two named poems to compare.

In **part (b)(ii)** you will be given one named poem and will need to choose a second to compare. Think carefully about which poem to choose to make sure you have interesting points to make.

There are a total of 30 marks available for this question – 15 marks for part (a) and 15 marks for part (b). You should spend around the same amount of time and effort on each part of the question.

Sample Higher Tier mark scheme: Section B

Part (a) questions

Band	Mark	AO2: Explain how language, structure and form contribute to writers' presentation of ideas, themes and settings
1	1-3	• Generally sound explanation of how the writer conveys his attitudes. • Generally sound, relevant connection made between the presentation of attitudes and the language used. • Mostly clear, relevant textual reference to support response.
2	4-6	• Sound explanation of how the writer conveys his attitudes to create effect. • Sound, relevant connection made between attitudes and the presentation of ideas. • Clear, relevant textual reference to support response.
3	7-9	• Thorough explanation of how the writer conveys his attitudes to create effect. • Sustained, relevant connection made between attitudes and the presentation of ideas. • Sustained, relevant textual reference to support response.
4	10-12	• Assured explanation of how the writer conveys attitudes to create effect. • Relevant connection made between attitudes and the presentation of ideas. • Pertinent textual reference to support response.
5	13-15	• Perceptive explanation of how the writer uses attitudes to create effect. • Discriminating, relevant connection made between attitudes and the presentation of ideas. • Convincing, relevant textual reference to support response.

Part (b) questions

Band	Mark	AO3: make comparisons and explain links between texts
1	1-3	• Generally sound comparisons and links. • Some clear evaluation of the different ways of expressing meaning and achieving effects. • Selection of examples is mostly appropriate; shows some support of the points being made.
2	4-6	• Sound comparisons and links. • Some clear evaluation of the different ways of expressing meaning and achieving effects. • Selection of examples is appropriate; shows some support of the points being made.
3	7-9	• Specific and detailed comparisons and links. • Developed evaluation of the different ways of expressing meaning and achieving effects. • Selection of examples is detailed, appropriate and supports the points being made.
4	10-12	• Assured comparisons and links. • Pertinent evaluation of the different ways of expressing meaning and achieving effects. • Selection of examples is assured, appropriate and supports the points being made.
5	13-15	• Discriminating comparisons and links showing insight. • Perceptive evaluation of the different ways of expressing meaning and achieving effects. • Selection of examples is discriminating; fully supports the points being made.

Section B part (a) of the poetry paper is assessed against this objective. Think about **what the writers say** and **how they say it** – such as choice of words, images and sound effects – and **how they organise and arrange their ideas**, such as the use of stanzas, length of lines, who is spoken to, rhyme and rhythm, any 'twists'.

To achieve the best marks, you will need to think carefully about the attitude the writer takes towards the subject (for example, are they very serious or do they use irony or humour), and then relate this closely to the way the construction and language of the poem put across the ideas.

Choose your quotations and textual references carefully so that you can make comments that show insight and a strong personal engagement with and interpretation of the poem.

Section B part (b) of the poetry paper is assessed against this objective. Making **comparisons** and **links** is the key to part (b) questions. Think about what is **similar** and what is **different** about the poems. Use **evidence** to support your points.

To achieve marks in the highest band, it is not just comparing the poems that is important, but doing so with **discrimination** – find a fresh way of thinking, which shows perceptive understanding of the poems.

For ideas and examples of how to do this, look at the extracts from typical grade A answers on the Build better answers pages.

GCSE English

You will complete one task on poetry as part of the **Unit 3: Creative English**, **English** controlled assessment. The poetry task is worth 24 marks and counts for 10% of your total GCSE.

The task for the controlled assessment will be a question about a literary heritage poem and two poems from the anthology collection you have studied. You can produce either a written response of up to 1,000 words or a digital media/multi-modal response (such as a short film or PowerPoint presentation).

You must complete the task on your own in school.

You will be able to use brief notes on the poems that you have prepared in advance, but will have to complete the task in **two hours**.

Do remember that if you choose a video or multi-modal response, it must be completed in no more than two hours. It must focus on the question you are set, so that your ideas about the three poems come across really well.

Guidance for students: Poetry (Reading) Task

What do I have to do?
You will complete one reading task on poetry, from one of the four themed collections in the Edexcel Poetry Anthology.
You must complete this task on your own.

How much time do I have?
Following preparation, you will have up to two hours to complete the task.

How do I prepare for the task?
- Your teacher will choose one of the four themed collections from the Edexcel Poetry Anthology and you will study all fifteen poems.
- You or your teacher will choose one of the following three options for how to respond to the task (written, digital media or multi-modal). Further details are given below.
- You should then plan your response to the task.

What must the response to the task show?
The response must show that you can:
- read the poems with insight and engagement
- interpret the writers' ideas and perspectives.

How should I present the response?
EITHER
A written response of up to 1,000 words.
OR
A digital-media response that demonstrates that you have read and understood the poems, which could include a podcast, creation of a website, edit of digital video material presented by you or a short digital video production.
OR
A multi-modal response that combines any of the above options.

Sample controlled assessment task

The Poetry (Reading) Task for the student

The Poetry (Reading) Task for the student
Choose **one** collection and complete the task from the choice below.

Collection A: Relationships
Task: Explore the ways poets present their feelings about relationships.
You should refer to the poem below and two poems from the
Relationships collection. (24)

Collection B: Clashes and Collisions
Task: Explore the ways poets present their ideas about conflict.
You should refer to the poem below and two poems from the
Clashes and Collisions collection. (24)

Collection C: Somewhere, Anywhere
Task: Explore the ways poets convey a strong sense of location.
You should refer to the poem below and two poems from the
Somewhere, Anywhere collection. (24)

Collection D: Taking a Stand
Task: Explore the ways poets express attitude in a strong and
effective way. You should refer to the poem below and two
poems from the *Taking a Stand* collection. (24)

For each collection, one poem from outside the Anthology will be selected for study. The question asks you to choose **two** poems from the Anthology collection you are studying, to put with the one set poem; it is a good idea to prepare your notes carefully on these two poems.

Sample controlled assessment mark scheme

Band	Mark	Assessment Objective: AO2 (i/iii)
1	1-5	• Little explanation of how the writer uses literary techniques to create effect. • Basic understanding of how techniques contribute to the effects created. • Little relevant textual reference to support response.
2	6-10	• Some explanation of how the writer uses literary techniques to create effect. • Some understanding of how techniques contribute to the effects created. • Occasional relevant textual reference to support response.
3	11-15	• Sound explanation of how the writer uses literary techniques to create effect. • Sound understanding of how techniques contribute to the effects created. • Clear, relevant textual reference to support response.
4	16-20	• Thorough explanation of how the writer uses literary techniques to create effect. • Thorough understanding of how techniques contribute to the effects created. • Sustained, relevant textual reference to support response.
5	21-24	• Perceptive explanation of how the writer uses literary techniques to create effect. • Perceptive understanding of how techniques contribute to the effects created. • Convincing, relevant textual reference to support response.

It is important that you keep firmly in mind the range of techniques that writers can use, including such elements as tone, rhythm, imagery, sound effects and vocabulary. Spotting the writer's techniques will be credited as 'some explanation' at best. The important thing if you are aiming for Band 3 upwards is to say **how** the technique affects your reading.

Everything you say about the writer's techniques and the effects they create must be directly linked to short textual quotations. In the mark scheme for all bands there is a strong emphasis on relevance so remember to choose quotations that **support** what you are saying.

Perceptive understanding is a characteristic of performance at the highest level. Perceptive understanding will show how the writer's choices contribute to the meaning created.

Glossary

adverb – a word that describes a verb or adjective, e.g. *quickly, very*

alliteration – two or more words close together beginning with the same consonant, e.g. *slow silent slugs slithered*

allusion – a passing reference to an event, person, place or something in the arts, e.g. *The Penelopes of my homeland is an allusion to the story of Penelope and Odysseus*

assonance – the repetition of a vowel sound or stressed syllable, e.g. *you no longer look with love on me*

aural – relating to the sense of hearing

cliché – an over-used expression or phrase, e.g. *love is blind*

compound word – words made up of two separate words, e.g. *brother-in-law, dry-wither*

dialect – a form of language particular to specific region or group of people

end-stopped lines – lines of poetry with punctuation marks at the end

enjambement – (also known as run-on line) the running on of the meaning of one line of poetry to the next line without a punctuated pause

extended metaphor – a technique used where, over an extended period, a word, phrase, or image is used to represent something else to which it is not directly related, e.g. *the comparison of the mountains with old crones in* Assynt Mountains

first-person – if poems are written in the first person, the narrative voice talks about himself/herself

form – the pattern or structure of a poem, such as the sonnet form **(see sonnet)**

full rhyme – also known as *perfect rhyme*; this is when the later part of a word or phrase is identical in sound to another

hyperbole – exaggeration for dramatic effect, e.g. *They loathe Hitler and herpes and you* (Pessimism for Beginners)

imperative – an authoritative command, e.g. *get it right*

internal rhyme – rhyme that occurs in a single line of verse, e.g. *There are none to decline your nectared wine*

ironic – words, themes or images used in the opposite way to that expected for effect, often humorous, e.g. *It wants hard shoulders, Happy Eaters* (A Major Road for Romney Marsh)

juxtaposing – placing two things side-by-side, usually to compare or show contrast, e.g. *Guy Fawkes' Diwali* (Our Town with the Whole of India!)

lexical field – a set of related words. For example 'father', 'mother', 'sister' and 'brother' are part of the lexical field of family

metaphor – a link and comparison drawn between two different things by calling one by the other's name, e.g. *the woman was a witch*

non-standard – a form that is not accepted as standard English

noun – names a person, place, thing, quality or action

octet – a stanza of eight lines, often used as the first stanza of a sonnet

onomatopoeia – words or phrases which include the sounds associated with what they describe, e.g. *the whining wind*

parentheses – brackets (...)

partial rhyme – when two words almost rhyme, also known as half-rhyme, e.g. *shackles... ankles* (Those bastards in their mansions)

persona – a role or character which the poet takes on to narrate the poem, e.g. *Browning takes on the persona of the Duke of Ferrara in* My Last Duchess

personal pronouns – words which can replace nouns, e.g. *I, you, he, she, it*

personification – attribute a personal nature or human characteristics to something not human, e.g. *This City now doth, like a garment, wear / The beauty of the morning* (Composed upon Westminster Bridge)

proper nouns – the name of a particular person, place or title, usually beginning with a capital letter

rhetorical questions – questions asked for effect and which do not expect an answer, e.g. *What are we doing here?* (Exposure)

rhyme – a word with the same sound as another

rhyme scheme – the pattern of rhyme in a poem, the first rhyme represented by 'a', the second by 'b', and so on

rhythm – a flow of words and phrases determined by use of stressed and unstressed syllables

sestet – a stanza of six lines, often following an octet in a sonnet

sibilance – the repetition of the 's' or sh' sound, e.g. *Sea timeless* (Sea Timeless Song)

simile – a comparison of one thing with another thing of a different kind using 'like' or 'as', e.g. *The upper air like sapphire glowed* (In Romney Marsh)

sonnet – a short poem with 14 lines, usually with a strong rhyming pattern and written in iambic pentameter, e.g. Pity me not because the light of day, 04/01/07

stanza – a section of a poem, also known as a verse

syllables – the individual sounds within a word, e.g. *'language' has two syllables*

symbolise – to represent something with a symbol, e.g. *the hare is a symbol of springtime and new life*

verb – a word expressing an action or state of being

villanelle – a poem of nineteen lines in which only two rhymes are used, e.g. Do not go gentle into that good night

Published by Pearson Education Limited, a company incorporated in
England and Wales, having its registered office at Edinburgh Gate,
Harlow, Essex, CM20 2JE. Registered company number: 872828

www.pearsonschoolsandfecolleges.co.uk

Edexcel is a registered trademark of Edexcel Limited

Text © Pearson Education Limited 2011

First published 2011

15 14 13 12 11

10 9 8 7 6 5 4 3 2 1

British Library Cataloguing in Publication Data

A catalogue record for this book is available from the British Library.

ISBN 978 1 846909 37 5

Edited by Jenny Roberts

Designed and typeset by Juice Creative Limited

Original illustrations © Pearson Education Limited

Illustrated by Bob Doucet

Picture research by Katharine Oakes

Printed in the UK by Scotprint

Acknowledgements

The authors and publisher would like to thank the following individuals and organisations for
permission to reproduce photographs:

akg-images Ltd: Ludolf Backhuysen / Musées Royaux des Beaux-Arts. 10-11; **Alamy Images:** Jeff
Morgan 13 126, Albaimages 98-99, Compix 137, pierre d'alancaisez 120, Garry Gay 82, 83, 148, 149,
Skip Gleichman 46, John Glover 20-21, Michael Griffin 34, david hancock 102-103, apply pictures,
Simon Høgsberg 58, Roger Hutchings 112-113, Johner Images 74-75, JoeFox 44-45, LondonPhotos
86, Gareth McCormack 100-101, MM_photo 134, Melksham Landscape Photography 88,
paul ridsdale pictures 90, 91, Gregory Preest 96-97, Ingram Publishing 124, Nataliia Sdobnikova
110-111, Stocksearch 132, Peter Titmuss 84; **© Photo SCALA, Florence:** Photo Scala, Florence -
courtesy of the Ministero Beni e Att. Culturali 22; **Corbis:** 48-49, A. Inden 51, Pawel Libera 108-109,
Christian Simonpietri / Sygma 145; **Getty Images:** ML Harris / Iconica 131, Karin Smeds / Gorilla
Creative Images 28-29, Irene Lamprakou 54, Colen Campbell / The Bridgeman Art Library 122-123,
Mark Wilson 62; **iStockphoto:** Zuzana Buranová 65, Reinhold Foeger 76-77, gprentice 24-25, David
Joyner 92, Volkan Kurt 116, David H. Lewis 19, Marek Mnich 6-7, Aldo Murillo 16-17, Chris Schmidt
8, Alistair Scott 60-61, Hellen Sergeyeva 12-13, SteveStone 52, Dan Tero 118-119; **Pearson Education
Ltd:** National Archives and Records Administration 66-67, John Pallister 78, The Illustrated London
News Picture Library. Ingram Publishing. Alamy 94, Photodisc. Steve Cole 40-41, KPT Power Photos
42-43, Photodisc. StockTrek 128-129; **Photolibrary.com:** 14, 27, 80-81, 30-31, 56; **Reuters:** Ognen
Teofilovski 68-69

Cover images: Front: **Alamy Images:** Colin Crisford tl; **Getty Images:** Jason Hosking tr;
iStockphoto: Simon Alvinge bl, Huseyin Tuncer br

All other images © Pearson Education

Every effort has been made to trace the copyright holders and we apologise in advance for any
unintentional omissions. We would be pleased to insert the appropriate acknowledgement in any
subsequent edition of this publication.

Poetry A1 from *Valentine* by Carol Ann Duffy, published in "Mean Time", published by Anvil Press
Poetry, 1993, reproduced by permission of Anvil Press; Poetry A2 from *Rubbish at Adultery* by Sophie
Hannah, published in "Pessimism for Beginners", 2007, Carcanet Press Limited, reproduced with
permission; Poetry A5 from *Even Tho* by Grace Nichols, published in "Fat Black Women's Poetry",
1984. Copyright © Grace Nichols 1984, reproduced with permission of Curtis Brown Group Ltd;
Poetry A6 from *Kissing* by Fleur Adcock, published in "Poems 1960-2000", Bloodaxe Books, 2000.
Reproduced with permission; Poetry A7 from *One Flesh* by Elizabeth Jennings, published in "New
Collected Poems", Carcanet Press Limited. Reproduced by permission of David Higham Associates;
Poetry A8 from *Song for Last Years Wife* by Brian Patten, first published in "The Mersey Sound",
Penguin Classics, 2007, p.91. Copyright © Brian Patten. Reproduced by permission of the author
c/o Rogers, Coleridge & White Ltd., 20 Powis Mews, London W11 1JN; Poetry A10 from *Pity me not
because the light of day* by Edna St Vincent Millay, published in "Selected Poems", HarperCollins
1991. Copyright © 1923, 1951, by Edna St Vincent Millay and Norma Millay Ellis. Reprinted by
permission of Elizabeth Barnett, Literary Executor, The Millay Society; Poetry A11 from *The Habit*

of Light by Gillian Clarke, published in "Five Fields", 1998, Carcanet Press Limited, reproduced
by permission; Poetry A13 from *At the border, 1979* by Choman Hardi, published in "Life for Us",
Bloodaxe Books, 2004. Reproduced with permission; Poetry A14 from *Lines to my Grandfathers* by
Tony Harrison, published in "Selected Poems and Collected Poems", Penguin 1987/2007, by kind
permission of the author, Tony Harrison; Poetry A15 from 04/01/2007 by Ian McMillan, published in
"Talking myself home", 2008, copyright © Ian McMillan; Poetry B1 from Half-Caste by John Agard,
published in "Half-caste and other poems", 2005, copyright © 1996 by John Agard, reproduced
by kind permission of John Agard c/o Caroline Sheldon Literary Agency Limited; Poetry B2 from
Parade's End by Daljit Nagra, published in "Look Who's Coming to Dover!", 2007, reproduced by
permission of Faber and Faber Ltd; Poetry B3 from *Belfast Confetti*, Ciaran Carson, published in
"Collected Poems", 2008. Granted by kind permission of the author Ciaran Carson, The Gallery
Press, Loughcrew, Oldcastle, County Meath, Ireland; and Wake Forest University Press; Poetry B4
from *Our Sharpeville* by Ingrid de Kok, published in "No Sweetness Here", The Feminist Press, 1995,
reproduced by permission of Ingrid de Kok; Poetry B6 from *Catrin* by Gillian Clarke, published in
"Collected Poems", 2007, Carcanet Press Limited, reproduced with permission; Poetry B7 from *Your
Dad Did What?* by Sophie Hannah, published in "Leaving and Leaving You", 1999, Carcanet Press
Limited, reproduced with permission; Poetry B10 from *Hitcher* by Simon Armitage, published in
"Book Of Matches", 1993 (first edition), reproduced by permission of Faber and Faber Ltd; Poetry
B12 from *O What is that Sound* by W. H. Auden, published in "Collected Poems of W. H. Auden",
Faber & Faber. Copyright © 1976, 1991 by the Estate of W. H. Auden. Reproduced by permission of
The Wylie Agency (UK) Ltd and Random House, Inc.; Poetry B13 from *Conscientious Objector* by Edna
St. Vincent Millay, copyright © 1934, 1962, by Edna St. Vincent Millay. Reprinted by permission of
Elizabeth Barnett, Literary Executor, The Millay Society; Poetry B14 from *August 6, 1945* by Alison
Fell © Alison Fell 1987. First published in Kisses for Mayakovsky (Virago). Republished in Dreams
Like Heretics (Serpents Tail). Permission granted by Peake Associates, www.tonypeake.com; Poetry
B15 from *Invasion* by Choman Hardi, published in "Life for Us", Bloodaxe Books, 2004. Reproduced
with permission; Poetry C3 from *Postcard from a travel snob* by Sophie Hannah, published in "Hotels
Like Houses" p.47, Carcanet Press Limited, 1996, reproduced with permission; Poetry C4 from *Sea
Timeless Song* by Grace Nichols, published in "The Fat Black Woman's Poems" 1984. Copyright ©
Grace Nichols 1984, reproduced with permission of Curtis Brown Group Ltd; Poetry C5 from *My
Mother's kitchen* by Choman Hardi, published in "Life for Us", Bloodaxe Books, 2004. Reproduced
with permission; Poetry C6 from *Cape Town morning* by Ingrid de Kok, published in "Seasonal Fires",
Seven Stories Press, 2006, reproduced by permission of Ingrid de Kok; Poetry C7 from *Our Town with
the Whole of India!* By Daljit Nagra, published in "Look who's coming to Dover!", 2007, reproduced by
permission of Faber and Faber Ltd; Poetry C9 from *A Major Road for Romney Marsh* by U. A. Fanthorpe,
published in "New & Collected Poems", 2010, Enitharmon Press reproduced by permission of Dr
R.V. Bailey; Poetry C13 from *Assynt Mountains* by Mandy Haggith, published in "Letting Light In",
Essence Press, 2005, copyright © Mandy Haggith; Poetry C14 from *Orkney / This Life* by Andrew Greig,
published in "This Life, This Life: Selected Poems 1970-2006", Bloodaxe Books, 2006. Reproduced
with permission; Poetry C15 and U6 from *The Stone Hare* by Gillian Clarke, published in "Making
Beds for the Dead", 2004, Carcanet Press Limited, reproduced with permission; Poetry D2 from *I
Shall Paint My Nails Red* by Carole Satyamurti, published in "Stitching in the Dark: New and Selected
Poems", Bloodaxe Books 2005. Reproduced with permission; Poetry D3 and U5 from *The Penelopes
of my homeland* by Choman Hardi, published as "Life for Us", Bloodaxe Books, 2004. Reproduced
with permission; Poetry D4 from *A Consumer's Report* by Peter Porter, published in "Peter Porter
Collected Poems", granted by kind permission from Mrs C. Porter; Poetry D5 from *Pessimism for
Beginners* by Sophie Hannah, published in "Pessimism for Beginners", 2007, Carcanet Press Limited,
reproduced with permission; Poetry D7 from *No Problem* by Benjamin Zephaniah, published in
"Propa Propaganda" Bloodaxe Books, 1996. Reproduced with permission; Poetry D8 from *Those
bastards in their mansions* by Simon Armitage, published in "Book of Matches", 1993, reproduced
by permission of Faber and Faber Ltd; Poetry D9 from Living Space by Imtiaz Dharker, published
in "Poems 1955-2005", Bloodaxe Books, 2005. Reproduced with permission; Poetry D10 from *The
archbishop chairs the first session* by Ingrid de Kok, published in "Terrestrial Things", Kwela Books
Snailpress, reproduced by permission of Ingrid de Kok; Poetry D11 from *The World is a beautiful
place* by Lawrence Ferlinghetti, published in "Pictures of the Gone World", City Light Books; 2nd
Edition, 1986, copyright © 1955 by Lawrence Ferlinghetti. Reprinted by permission of City Lights
Books; Poetry D12 from *Zero Hour* by Matthew Sweeney, published in "Sanctuary" by Jonathan Cape.
Reprinted by permission of The Random House Group Ltd; Poetry D13 from *One world down the drain*
by Simon Rae, published in "Earth Shattering Eco Poems", Bloodaxe, 2004, copyright © Simon Rae;
Poetry D14 from *Do Not Go Gentle Into That Good night* by Dylan Thomas (J.M. Dent), from "Collected
Poems/The Poems of Dylan Thomas", Orion, copyright © 1952 Dylan Thomas. Reproduced by
permission of David Higham Associates and New Directions Publishing Corp; Poetry U7 from *Dress
Sense* by David Kitchen, copyright © David Kitchen; Poetry U7 from *From the Motorway* by Anne
Stevenson, published in "Propa Propaganda" Bloodaxe Books, 1996. Reproduced with permission;
Poetry AS1 from *Remembering Snow* by Brian Patten, published in "The Utter Nutters". Copyright
© 1994 Brian Patten. Reproduced by permission of the author c/o Rogers, Coleridge & White Ltd.,
20 Powis Mews, London W11 1JN; and Poetry AS2 from *Blackberry Picking*, by Seamus Heaney,
reproduced by permission of Faber and Faber Ltd and Farrar, Straus & Giroux.

In some instances we have been unable to trace the owners of copyright material, and we would
appreciate any information that would enable us to do so.

Disclaimer

This material has been published on behalf of Edexcel and offers high-quality support for the
delivery of Edexcel qualifications.

This does not mean that the material is essential to achieve any Edexcel qualification, nor does it
mean that it is the only suitable material available to support any Edexcel qualification. Edexcel
material will not be used verbatim in setting any Edexcel examination or assessment. Any
resource lists produced by Edexcel shall include this and other appropriate resources.

Copies of official specifications for all Edexcel qualifications may be found on the Edexcel
website: www.edexcel.com